Quantitative
Methods
for
Financial
Analysis

Quantitative Methods for Financial Analysis

Edited by
Stephen J. Brown
Mark P. Kritzman, CFA

Sponsored by
The Institute of
Chartered Financial Analysts

DOW JONES-IRWIN
Homewood, Illinois 60430

LC

ISBN 0-87094-978-0 (casebound)

ISBN 1-55623-022-2 (paperbound)

Library of Congress Catalog Card No. 86-72275

Printed in the United States of America

4 5 6 7 8 9 0 K 4 3 2 1 0 9 8 7

5-8-89

Financial and investment analysis is conducted within the context of increasingly sophisticated mathematical and statistical tools and techniques. The serious investment professional needs a sound understanding of these quantitative methods and concepts and an ability to apply them to the investment process.

The valuation of assets, rate of return mathematics, performance measurement, and concepts of risk all depend on the principles of quantitative analysis. More complicated quantitative methods measure how financial and economic variables interact with each other and provide a framework for understanding how various factors affect financial results.

The Institute of Chartered Financial Analysts has included quantitative analysis in its Candidate Study and Examination Program for many years. In 1971 the text *Quantitative Techniques for Financial Analysis* by Jerome J. Valentine, CFA, and Edmund A. Mennis, CFA, was sponsored by the CFA Research Foundation to fill an important gap in the professional literature on quantitative methods. A conference, "Improving the Investment Decision Process: Quantitative Assistance for the Practitioner—and for the Firm," was sponsored by the institute in 1984. Proceedings of the program were sent to all active CFAs as part of the institute's program of continuing education for members. In addition, it has been assigned in the Candidate Study and Examination Program.

This text, *Quantitative Methods for Financial Analysis*, edited by Stephen J. Brown and Mark P. Kritzman, CFA, is an extension of the institute's effort to keep the profession on the leading edge of this important topic area. Particular thanks is paid to those individuals who wrote and edited this text for the benefit of their fellow professionals. We applaud their contributions and dedicate it to all CFAs and CFA candidates—present and future.

Darwin M. Bayston, CFA
Vice President
Education and Research

v

Christopher B. Barry is Professor of Finance in the Edwin L. Cox School of Business at Southern Methodist University. Previously he was Chairman of the Department of Finance (1982–1986) and was the founding director of the school's Center for the Study of Financial Institutions and Markets. An Associate Editor of *Financial Management*, he teaches and conducts research in the fields of portfolio theory and capital markets. He holds a B.S. degree from Georgia Tech and a D.B.A. from Indiana University. He has previously served on the faculties of the University of Texas at Austin and the University of Florida. His research in finance has been published in the *Journal of Finance, Journal of Financial Economics, Journal of Financial and Quantitative Analysis, Journal of Portfolio Management*, and other journals.

Stephen J. Brown is Associate Professor of Finance at New York University. Previously he taught finance at the Yale School of Organization and Management. He worked for eight years at Bell Laboratories and consulted extensively for AT&T and the Bell System. In 1979 he spent four months as a District Manager assigned to the pension fund of AT&T. He attended Monash University in Australia and was awarded a Bachelor of Economics degree in 1971. He received an M.B.A. in 1974 from the University of Chicago and a Ph.D. from the same institution in 1976. Professor Brown has written two books and numerous articles in finance and economics-related areas, and is currently on the editorial boards of *Journal of Financial and Quantitative Analysis* and *Journal of Portfolio Management*.

Andrew H. Chen is a Distinguished Professor of Finance in the Edwin L. Cox School of Business at Southern Methodist University. He received an M.A. in economics and a Ph.D. in finance from the University of California, Berkeley. He previously taught at the State University of New York at Buffalo, the University of California, Berkeley, and the Ohio State University. He is Editor of *Research in Finance* published by JAI Press and is currently Associate Editor of the *Journal of Money, Credit, and Banking* and *The Financial Review*. He is a former Associate Editor of the *Journal of Financial and Quantitative Analysis, Management Science*, and the *Journal of Economics and Business*. His articles have been published in books and journals including *Journal of Financial Economics, Journal of Financial and Quantitative Analysis*, and *Journal of Futures Markets*.

Margaret A. Corwin is a Financial Consultant in the New York area for Ibbotson Associates, a firm with offices in Chicago and New Haven. Formerly she was the Financial Vice President for Abbot Contractors and prior to that was Senior Research Associate for the American Planning Association. Ms. Corwin holds a CPA from the University of Illinois and master's degrees from both the University of Chicago and Loyola University.

H. Russell Fogler is a Partner in the equity management firm of Aronson and Fogler, as well as a Professor of Management Science at the University of Florida. From 1975 to 1984 he was academic consultant to the Frank Russell Company on performance measurement, asset allocation, and optimization. He has authored several books and published over 25 articles in journals such as the *Journal of Finance, Journal of Portfolio Management, Journal of Financial and Quantitative Analysis, Management Science, Decision Sciences*, and the *Accounting Review*. He has been an Associate Editor of *Financial Management*, and he is currently on the editorial board of the *Journal of Portfolio Management*.

Susan Hudson-Wilson is Regional Director, Real Estate, in the Investment Division at UNUM Life Corporation, Portland, Maine. She is responsible for all of their real estate equity position in the northeast. She joined Union Mutual in 1983 as Director of Real Estate Research. In this capacity she developed the Real Estate Market Index and its portfolio implications and applications. Prior to joining Union Mutual she was a Senior Economist at Data Resources in Lexington, Massachusetts, from 1980 to 1983, where she constructed and managed various econometric forecasting models. Ms. Hudson-Wilson graduated from the University of Vermont in 1976 with a B.A. in economics. She received her M.A. in economics in 1982 from Boston University.

Roger G. Ibbotson is Professor in the Practice of Finance, Yale School of Management. He is also President of Ibbotson Associates, an investment consulting firm in Chicago and New Haven. Professor Ibbotson is coauthor (with Rex Sinquefield) of *Stocks, Bonds, Bills, and Inflation* and coauthor (with Gary Brinson) of *Investment Markets: Gaining the Performance Advantage*. He has also written numerous scholarly articles. He previously taught at the University of Chicago where he was Executive Director of the Center for Research in Security Prices. He received a B.S.

from Purdue University, an M.B.A. from Indiana University, and a Ph.D. from the University of Chicago.

Mark P. Kritzman, CFA, is a General Partner of New Amsterdam Partners, an investment advisory firm located in New York City. Before cofounding New Amsterdam Partners, Mr. Kritzman was a Vice President in the Investment Management Group at Bankers Trust Company. Mr. Kritzman also held investment-related positions at AT&T and The Equitable Life Assurance Society. He is a past President of the Investment Technology Association, a member of the Prize Committee of The Institute for Quantitative Research in Finance, and a member of the Candidate Curriculum Committee and the Council of Examiners of The Institute of Chartered Financial Analysts. Mr. Kritzman has published numerous articles on the application of financial theory to investment management. He holds a B.S. degree in economics from St. John's University and an M.B.A. from New York University.

This book is intended to motivate interest in the application of quantitative methods to financial analysis and, at the same time, to caution the financial analyst about the limitations of such methods. As editors, we have attempted to establish a broad structure for the book which would facilitate the realization of these goals. We have also tried to impose some uniformity of style in the presentation of the material. We wish to express our appreciation to the authors for their total contributions and especially for their indulgence in our editing. To the extent that this book succeeds in accomplishing its goals, the authors deserve much of the credit. To the extent that this book falls short of its goals, the editors acknowledge the fault to be theirs. We also wish to acknowledge the diligence the authors demonstrated in meeting our deadlines, which we admit were quite unreasonable.

We would like to thank colleagues at Yale, particularly Burton Malkiel and past and present students, especially Deborah Pederson who read through and gave extensive comments on early drafts of several chapters, our colleagues at Bankers Trust and New Amsterdam Partners who provided helpful advice and support, and Robert Whalen whose suggestions significantly improved the final manuscript.

In addition, we wish to express our gratitude to the staff at The Institute of Chartered Financial Analysts, especially Darwin Bayston, Tom Bowman, Cathryn Kittell, and Laurie Williams, who provided valuable comments and helped prepare the manuscript for the publisher, and to Pete Morley, for his support throughout the project. Finally, on a more personal note, we wish to thank Catherine and Sarah for their support throughout the many months it took to produce this book.

Stephen J. Brown
Mark P. Kritzman, CFA

CONTENTS

1. Introduction   **1**
Stephen J. Brown

2. Introduction to Quantitative Methods   **5**
Stephen J. Brown

Introduction, *5*
Mathematics of Valuation, *5*
Statistics and Data Analysis, *19*
Uncertainty and Valuation, *43*
Conclusion, *50*

3. Quantitative Methods in Equity Analysis   **51**
H. Russell Fogler

Introduction, *51*
Equity Valuation, *51*
Factor Analysis, *67*
Conclusion, *76*

4. Quantitative Methods in Fixed-Income Analysis   **79**
Roger G. Ibbotson and Margaret B. Corwin

Valuation of Fixed-Income Securities, *79*
Determinants of Bond Yields, *88*
Data Analysis, *93*
Factors that Affect Bond Markets, *103*
Conclusion, *105*

5. **Quantitative Methods in Real Estate Analysis**   **109**
   Susan Hudson-Wilson

   Introduction, *109*
   Property Valuation Issues, *110*
   Portfolio Analysis, *131*

6. **Quantitative Methods in Derivative Security Analysis**   **133**
   Christopher B. Barry and Andrew H. Chen

   Introduction, *133*
   Basic Properties of Option Values, *134*
   Simple Options Strategies, *136*
   Arbitrage and Option Valuation, *144*
   Option Pricing Models, *147*
   Empirical Analysis of Options, *164*
   Option Pricing Theory Applied to Other Assets, *167*
   Conclusion, *171*

7. **Quantitative Methods in Asset Allocation**   **173**
   Stephen J. Brown and Mark P. Kritzman, CFA

   Introduction, *173*
   Expected Return and Risk, *173*
   Estimation Issues, *178*
   The Optimal Portfolio, *182*
   Dynamic Hedging, *188*
   Conclusion, *193*

8. **Quantitative Methods in Performance Measurement**   **195**
   Mark P. Kritzman, CFA

   Introduction, *195*
   Rate of Return, *196*
   Time-Weighted and Dollar-Weighted Rates of Return, *197*
   Risk Adjustment, *205*
   Benchmark Error, *206*
   Ambiguity between Skill and Chance, *207*
   Performance Attribution, *209*
   Normal Portfolio, *210*

Nonparametric Performance Measurement, *212*
Incentive Fees, *213*
Gaming Performance Measurement, *217*
Conclusion, *219*

Index **221**

Quantitative
Methods
for
Financial
Analysis

CHAPTER ONE

Introduction

Stephen J. Brown

The recent and rapid growth of financial markets has corresponded to an increase in the application of quantitative methods in financial analysis. Quantitative methods have emerged from the domain of the academician and from institutional research departments to the desks of all serious financial analysts. To a large extent, interest in quantitative methods has been motivated by the introduction of the personal computer and the spreadsheet software and large data bases made accessible by the personal computer.

But are such methods useful? Appropriately exploited, quantitative methods allow the analyst to come to grips with the ever-increasing complexity and specialization of the financial markets. Quantitative illiteracy or careless application of these methods puts one at a serious disadvantage in a very competitive environment and can lead to disastrous results.

The purpose of this book is to review the use of quantitative methods in the context of the investment decision-making process. Our perspective is that the central role of the financial analyst is to determine the value of an investment, based upon all of the available information. Quantitative methods represent the analyst's toolbox:

- The mathematics of valuation can help determine the value of an investment, based upon what is known about the potential cash flow resulting from the investment.

- Statistics and data analysis can be used to simplify and refine the information relating to future cash flows.
- These techniques can also be used to allow the analyst to account for the uncertainty of future cash flows, the risk inherent in the investment process.

Our approach is to emphasize the application of quantitative methods in a wide variety of settings. Like all tools, however, they can be misused. Therefore, we try to focus attention on the limitations of quantitative methods and underscore the need to combine these tools with sound practical judgment.

This book does not offer a comprehensive treatment of financial mathematics and statistics, nor does it provide complete coverage of financial analysis. Rather, our intention is to cover that common ground where financial analysis is readily amenable to the application of quantitative principles and tools. And even within this context, we are limited to a small set of examples that we hope are representative of the broader set of opportunities for applying quantitative methods.

Chapter Two introduces the quantitative methods commonly used in financial analysis. We assume that the reader is to some extent familiar with the technical tools reviewed in that chapter. Most of the procedures we refer to are available as computer software applications. For this reason, we emphasize the intuitive basis of the material and the interpretation of the results. The mathematical development is at a minimum.

It is interesting to note that a great deal of the complexity of financial mathematics comes not from the mathematics but rather from the practical necessity to simplify very straightforward but tedious calculations. The advent of spreadsheet software has made many of these simplifications redundant, a development that has focused the attention of the analyst on a more basic problem, one the historical emphasis on financial mathematics has largely ignored. Where do the numbers come from? How reliable or meaningful are the numbers that go into the spreadsheet constructed with such care? For this reason, Chapter Two emphasizes statistics and data analysis.

The remaining chapters show how the procedures are actually applied in the context of a series of very different, specialized areas of analysis. Chapters Three and Four cover, respectively, equity and fixed-income analysis, areas where quantitative methods have long been important tools for the serious analyst. Chapter Five covers real estate analysis, which historically has relied more on qualitative methods of analysis but is, nonetheless, quite amenable to quantitative methods. Chapter Six covers the analysis of derivative securities; Chapter Seven covers asset allocation analysis; and Chapter Eight covers performance measurement.

These chapters not only demonstrate the practical application of a series of basic tools but also serve another function. The growth of financial markets has lead to an increase in specialization among analysts. Yet there is a striking degree of commonality in the quantitative methods used by the analysts across these specialized areas. For example, the concept of present value appears in each of the chapters, albeit in slightly different guises. It appears as the dividend discount model to the equity analyst, the bond valuation formula to the fixed-income analyst, and the capitalization rate to the real estate analyst. Present value is also a key concept in the arbitrage arguments that underlie the valuation of derivative securities; it appears in asset allocation analysis where funding of liabilities is important; and it is crucial to the measurement of performance. That seemingly disparate areas of financial analysis have a basic unity, depending on the same quantitative methods, is a fact that should be of considerable comfort to the financial analyst. It implies that the financial analyst who understands a few important quantitative principles should be able, in many instances, to recognize the appropriate method of quantitative analysis to solve new and unfamiliar problems. This ability should provide an important competitive edge!

CHAPTER TWO

Introduction to Quantitative Methods

Stephen J. Brown

INTRODUCTION

This chapter introduces quantitative methods and shows some of the ways in which they can be applied in the context of the investment decision-making process. Mathematics of Valuation covers the set of techniques that can be used to relate future cash flows to current value and to measure the return on alternative investments. The next section, Statistics and Data Analysis, introduces the statistical procedures that can be used to characterize and simplify the available information. Finally, Uncertainty and Valuation addresses procedures for measuring the impact of uncertainty on the valuation process. Subsequent chapters will show how these procedures are actually used in the analysis of equity, fixed income, real estate, and derivative securities and how they are applied in asset allocation and performance measurement.

MATHEMATICS OF VALUATION

Present Value

All investments can be characterized by the cash flows they generate. These cash flows represent cash received by the investor as a result of the decision to invest, including income received over the holding period of the investment as well as the cash received from the ultimate sale or disposal of the asset, after all taxes are paid. Valuation, then, is simply a problem of comparing alternative cash flows.

Present value answers the question "How much money must I set aside in a comparable investment of similar risk to *duplicate exactly* the cash flows of this investment?" The following example illustrates the concept of present value.

Example: You are solicited to participate in an Oklahoma oil venture that you are told will be worth $1.6 million one year from today, after the well is drilled. One thousand shares are to be offered at $1,000 a share, and the shareholders will share equally in the proceeds from the drilling.

The apparent simplicity of this example is deceptive. Assume that all tax implications are accounted for and that the commitment must be made today. Is the $1.6 million estimated value one year from now a reliable estimate? We will assume that it is, for now. If similar investments of a comparable risk earn 20 percent per year after taxes, what are 100 shares of this oil venture worth?

If the investor were to invest $133,333 in the alternative investment, he or she would expect to receive $160,000 at the end of the year:

$$\$133,333 \times (1 + .20) = \$160,000$$

Alternatively, $133,333 could be thought of as the maximum amount the investor could borrow against the $160,000 that represents the future value of the oil venture if investments of a similar risk require a 20 percent return:

$$\text{Maximum} = \frac{\$160,000}{1 + .20} = \$133,333$$

In this sense, the oil participation is worth $133,333. At $100,000 the oil participation is "undervalued" to the extent that the investor could borrow $133,333 and invest $100,000 in the oil venture, leaving the investor better off by $33,333. This amount represents the extent to which the oil venture is undervalued and is, in a sense, the arbitrage profit to the investor for financing the venture. The extent of this undervaluation is referred to as the *net present value* of the venture. In other words, the net present value is the present value of the cash received from the venture minus the initial investment.

Would it be worthwhile to receive the proceeds from the oil venture in two annual installments of $80,000 each, for a total of $160,000? The first installment, due a year from today, can be matched by $66,667 now invested at 20 percent interest. If money invested for two years requires a return of 20 percent per year as well, then $55,555 invested for two years will match the second installment that represents the balance of the proceeds:

$$\$55,555 \times (1 + .20)^2 = \$80,000$$

or

$$\$55,555 = \frac{\$80,000}{(1 + .20)^2}$$

In other words, the present value of the two-installment plan is the sum of $66,667 and $55,555, or $122,222:

$$\text{Present value} = \frac{\$80,000}{1 + .20} + \frac{\$80,000}{(1 + .20)^2} = \$122,222$$

This amount is less than the value of the $133,333 single-installment plan. Typically, investments that commit funds for two or more years require a return somewhat in excess of the one-year return. In this case, the value of the installment plan is even less.

This example suggests the most basic formula in financial mathematics—the present value formula. Let us denote by symbols the cash flow of the investment one period from now as C_1, the cash flow two periods from now as C_2, that of three periods from now as C_3, and so on; we will also represent the return on alternative investments, or *discount rate*, for one period as r_1, the two-period return as r_2 per period, and the three-period return as r_3 per period. The present value formula is:

$$\text{Present value} = \frac{C_1}{1 + r_1} + \frac{C_2}{(1 + r_2)^2} + \frac{C_3}{(1 + r_3)^3} + \cdots$$

where

C_1, C_2, C_3 = Cash flows for periods 1, 2, and 3.
r_1, r_2, r_3 = Rates of return for periods 1, 2, and 3.

This formula is completely general and can be applied to a wide range of investment problems. It appears complex yet is actually quite straightforward to apply, given access to personal computers with spreadsheet software.

While present value discounts all cash flows of the investment to the present, the analogous concept of future value brings the cash flows to the ending holding period of the investment. The measure of future value assumes all cash flows from the venture are reinvested in similar-risk ventures for the duration of the holding period. At that point, the resulting cumulative cash value is compared to what would have been obtained had the original investment been made elsewhere.

In the oil participation, the future value of the cash flows is simply $160,000, the value of the venture at the end of the year. This may be compared to $120,000, which is the amount that would have been obtained had the money been invested elsewhere. Thus the project is undervalued to the extent of $40,000 in terms of dollars next year or $33,333 in terms of dollars today:

$$\frac{\$40,000}{1 + .20} = \$33,333$$

This answer is the same as before.

Future value is often used in the context of evaluating money managers, where the question is asked, "To what value would a dollar have grown if given to this particular manager to manage?" For more general valuation problems it is less useful, since the holding periods of different investments are rarely comparable.

Much of the apparent complexity of financial mathematics arises from the use of shortcut versions of the present value formula. Such shortcuts generally antedate the ready availability of spreadsheet software and use simplifying assumptions to make the calculations easier. One such simplified assumption is that the interest rate is not affected by the period of the investment.[1] Each formula we shall discuss is in fact a special case of the present value formula. However, because these special cases *appear* so very different, they have in many cases taken on a life of their own.

Perpetuity Formula. The first special case is known as the *perpetuity formula*. It is sometimes convenient to make the simplified assumption that a particular investment will generate forever a steady cash flow.

---

[1] The way interest rates vary as a function of the period of the investment is called the *yield curve;* the assumption that all interest rates are the same is referred to as a *flat yield curve*.

> *Example:* Sure Thing Energy Associates Limited is expected to pay an annual dividend of $10 per share for the foreseeable future. How much is a share of Sure Thing worth today?

If the required return on equivalent investments is 20 percent regardless of the period of the investment, then $50 invested at that rate will also generate $10 annually for the foreseeable future:

$$\$50 \times .20 = \$10$$

or

$$\$50 = \frac{\$10}{.20}$$

Thus the present value of the dividends of Sure Thing is $50, and that is as much as one would pay for a share of Sure Thing. The perpetuity formula is:

$$\text{Present value} = \frac{C}{r}$$

where

$C = $ (Constant) cash flow received at the end of each period.

$r = $ (Constant) rate of return.

This formula is actually a special case of the earlier formula where there are an infinite number of cash flows (C_1, C_2, C_3, and so on) that are all the same and equal to C and where all rates of return (r_1, r_2, r_3, and all other rates of return) are equal to each other. The assumption that the investor will receive a given cash flow forever may seem a little extreme. Fortunately, it does little damage where cash flows are expected to persist for a long period of time (though not forever) and where the required rate of return is high. It is frequently used to value real estate investments and preferred stock issues that satisfy these conditions and where the simplicity of the formula recommends it to analysts.

The formula requires some modification where the cash flows increase over time. Suppose in the above example the dividends of Sure Thing were expected to grow at the rate of 5 percent per annum: $10 next year, $10.50 the following year, and so on. If one thinks about the amount of money that must be set aside at 20 percent to match this investment, then $50 would match *this* year's dividend, but would be $.50 short for the next dividend. However, $66.67 at 20 percent would yield $10 *plus* a 5 percent growth in the principal amount of $66.67, sufficient to pay out $10.50 next year and further increments in the following years. In other words,

$$\$66.67 \times .20 = \$10 + (\$66.67 \times .05)$$

Next year the principal will equal $70, which is 5 percent greater than $66.67. At that time,

$$\$70 \times .20 = \$10.50 + (\$70 \times .05)$$

For this reason $66.67 is the present value of the growing perpetuity. This amount must be set aside at 20 percent interest to match exactly the cash flows of the investment; it represents the maximum one would pay to acquire the sequence of growing dividends. In other words,

$$\$66.67 \times (.20 - .05) = \$10$$

or

$$\$66.67 = \frac{\$10}{.20 - .05}$$

and $66.67 is the maximum one would pay for a share of Sure Thing. In this particular application the formula for the present value of a growing perpetuity is:

$$\text{Present value} = \frac{C}{r - g}$$

where

C = Cash flow next period.
g = Rate of growth of cash flows.
r = (Constant) rate of return.

This formula is often referred to as the *dividend discount model,* or *dividend growth model,* where C is the next dividend, r is the required return by investors, and g is the expected rate of growth of future dividends. This stock valuation model is the most popular and appears in many guises (for example, if value and the initial dividend payment are each divided by the earnings of the firm and the formula is rearranged in terms of accounting identities, we have what is known as the *price-earnings ratio model*). After some tedious algebra, it is possible to see that this formula is also a special case of the original present value formula.

Annuity Formula. Another formula that is very commonly used in analysis is the *annuity formula*.

Example: Oiler Bank and Trust (OBT) has a note backed by an equipment lien that obliges Sure Thing to pay OBT 10 annual installments of $10,000, with the next payment due one year from today. How much is the note worth to OBT?

Assume again that the required return is 20 percent. The Sure Thing note could be thought of as two agreements:

1. An agreement by Sure Thing to make annual payments to OBT in perpetuity. Such an agreement would be worth $50,000 to OBT:

$$\frac{\$10,000}{.20} = \$50,000$$

2. An agreement by OBT to return the note to Sure Thing 10 years from now. This action would cost OBT $50,000 at that time (the value in 10 years' time of the continuing perpetuity) or $8,075 today:

$$\frac{\$50,000}{(1 + .20)^{10}} = \$8,075$$

Thus the note is worth $41,925 today, or $50,000 less $8,075.

An annuity that promises a fixed amount on a periodic basis for a finite period of time is simply the difference between a perpetuity and an appropriately discounted perpetuity. The formula follows:

$$\text{Present value} = C \times \left[\frac{1}{r} - \left(\frac{1}{r} \times \frac{1}{(1 + r)^N} \right) \right]$$

where
C = (Constant) cash flow per period starting next period.
N = Number of periodic payments.
r = (Constant) rate of return.

To see how this formula is applied, consider the two-installment example considered earlier, where $80,000 is received next year and the balance of $80,000 is received two years from today. The sum of $80,000 represents the fixed payment C, and $N = 2$ (two payments). Present value then is:

$$\text{Present value} = \$80,000 \times \left[\frac{1}{.20} - \left(\frac{1}{.20} \times \frac{1}{(1 + .20)^2} \right) \right]$$

$$= \$80,000 \times \left[5 - \left(5 \times \frac{1}{1.44} \right) \right]$$

$$= \$80,000 \times 1.5278 = \$122,222$$

This amount is the same as derived earlier and illustrates that the annuity formula is also a special case of the more general present value formula.

A Caution. The perpetuity, growing perpetuity, and annuity formulas are tools that can simplify present value arithmetic. But like all tools, they must be handled with great care. Because the formulas assume interest rates to be invariant to the term of the investment, analysts implicitly assume yield curves are level or "flat," when they employ them. This assumption can be particularly hazardous in bond analysis. The dividend discount model sometimes assumes dividends will grow at a constant, known rate into the future. If analysis were to show, for example, that the current growth of IBM was greater than that of the economy as a whole, uncritical application of this growth rate into the formula is tantamount to assuming that IBM will eventually swallow up the entirety of the U.S. economy. Furthermore, if IBM dividends were expected to grow at a rate equal to the rate of return, the formula would suggest IBM stock would have an infinite value. While it is possible to "jury-rig" the formulas to allow for some changes in interest rates with term to maturity and for different growth rates over the life of the investment, it is conceptually simpler to compute the present values directly, using the general formula in the context of spreadsheet or other computer software products.

Rate of Return Measurements

It is very common to compare investments according to their rates of return. In a single-period example, as noted in the oil participation case, the return is easily computed. Suppose the oil participation share is worth only $1,280 at year-end, where the remaining $320 represents an end-of-year distribution to shareholders. The annual rate of return measure is:

$$\text{Rate of return} = \frac{\$320 + \$1,280 - \$1,000}{\$1,000} = .60$$

The formula is:

$$\text{Rate of return} = \frac{\text{Income} + \text{Current value} - \text{Value last period}}{\text{Value last period}}$$

This return measure is sometimes called a *total return measure*, since it includes yield from current income as well as yield from capital appreciation (current value − value last period). The distinction between income and capital gains is not usually important for nontaxable pension funds[2] but is crucial for trust funds that draw a distinction between income and principal beneficiaries, for endowment funds where spending rules depend on the return measure, and for taxable investors whose income and realized capital gains are taxed at different rates.

Suppose the oil venture is to last two years and will be worth $1.6 million at that time:

	Value per Share	Income per Share
At start of venture	$1,000	$ 0.00
After one year	$1,280	$320.00
After two years	$1,600	$ 0.00

The total return for the first year is 60 percent and that for the second is 25 percent:

$$\text{Second-year return} = \frac{\$1,600 - \$1,280}{\$1,280} = .25$$

There are several approaches to obtaining a single return measure for this investment.

Arithmetic Return.   The average of successive returns is termed the *arithmetic return*. In the example the average of 60 percent and 25 percent is 42.5 percent:

$$\frac{.60 + .25}{2} = .425$$

---

[2]Some argue that assets are priced after consideration of taxes; hence, tax-exempt investors should prefer investments with a high income component.

The general formula for the arithmetic return is:

$$\text{Arithmetic return} = \frac{R_1 + R_2 + R_3 + \cdots + R_N}{N}$$

where

$R_1, R_2, R_3, \cdots R_N$ = Returns for periods 1, 2, 3, through N.
N = Number of periods.

The 42.5 percent number attempts to measure the "typical" annual return on investments of this type. It does not, however, measure the realized return to the investor over the holding period of the investment.

Geometric Return. The geometric return is the compounded value of successive returns (usually) expressed on an annual basis. In the oil venture, 100 shares of the venture are purchased at $1,000 per share. At year-end the shares are worth $128,000 in total, and the investor receives $32,000 in income. If this income is used to purchase 25 additional shares at $1,280 a share, worth a total of $32,000, the total investment is worth $200,000 (125 × $1,600) two years from today. In other words, the original investment has doubled in value. This doubling in value can be computed directly as:

$$(1 + .60) \times (1 + .25) = 2.00$$

This 100 percent return represents a two-year return. To *annualize* this number consider what rate of return compounded twice doubles the value of the original investment:

$$(1 + .4142)^2 = (1 + .60) \times (1 + .25)$$

Thus the geometric return is 41.42 percent. Using most pocket calculators it can easily be computed:

$$\text{Geometric return} = [(1 + .60) \times (1 + .25)]^{\frac{1}{2}} - 1 = .4142$$

Returns are often computed on a quarterly, monthly, or even daily basis. Annualization, taking the compound growth to the power of the reciprocal of the number of years under consideration, is a procedure for bringing these different return measures to a comparable basis.

The general formula for the geometric return is:

$$\text{Geometric return} = [(1 + R_1) \times (1 + R_2)$$

$$\times (1 + R_3) \times \cdots \times (1 + R_N)]^{\frac{1}{M}} - 1$$

where
$R_1, R_2, R_3, \ldots R_N$ = Rates of return for periods 1, 2, 3, through N.
N = Number of periods.
M = Number of years that comprise N periods.

Note that the 41.42 geometric return measure is less than the 42.5 percent arithmetic return. This will always be the case, and the measures differ more the greater the variability of returns.

Example: You expect Sure Thing preferred stocks to have a return of minus 50 percent next year but to double in value the following year. In other words, $1.00 invested today in Sure Thing would be worth $.50 a year from today and $1.00 the subsequent year. What is the holding period return on this investment?

Even though the arithmetic return is 25 percent (average of $-.50$ and 1.00), in two years the investment will be worth no more than its value today. Hence the geometric return is zero:

$$\text{Geometric return} = [(1 + -.5) \times (1 + 1)]^{\frac{1}{2}} - 1 = 0.0$$

This example demonstrates that when there are reports of extraordinary returns associated with investments for which the returns are highly variable, one should check carefully the method by which returns are computed.[3]

To get some idea of the difference between the methods of computing returns, Table 2–1 gives arithmetic and geometric return measures for broad classes of investments. Small stocks, whose returns are highly variable, have a much higher arithmetic than geometric return, as we would expect.

Internal Rate of Return. The internal rate of return answers the question "At what (constant) rate of return would the present value of the future cash flows of the investment exactly equal the current value of the investment?" Suppose, as before, a share of the oil venture is worth

---

[3]Typically, the arithmetic average is used with cross-sectional data while the geometric average is used with time-series data.

TABLE 2–1
Total Annual Returns by Investment Class, 1926–1984

	Arithmetic Return	Geometric Return	Standard Deviation*
Small stocks	18.2%	12.4%	36.3%
Common stocks	11.7	9.5	21.2
Long-term corporate bonds	4.6	4.4	7.6

---

*This measure is explained on page 28.
SOURCE OF DATA: Ibbotson Associates, *Stocks, Bonds, Bills and Inflation: 1985 Yearbook* (Chicago: Ibbotson Associates, Capital Management Research Center, 1986), pp. 94–99.

$1,000 today but will yield $320 next year and be sold for $1,600 the following year. The internal rate of return is that return r for which:

$$\$1,000 = \frac{\$320}{1 + r} + \frac{\$1,600}{(1 + r)^2}$$

It implies a return r of 43.5 percent. This number can be obtained by a process of trial and error, which has been automated in a number of financial calculators and spreadsheet software products. Where the investment under consideration is a bond, this internal rate of return is referred to as the *yield to maturity* of the bond.

The 43.5 percent number is greater than either the arithmetic or geometric rates of return for this example because the internal rate of return calculation implicitly assumes a flat yield curve; money can be invested *and reinvested* in the oil venture to yield a 43.5 percent return. Evidently the assumption was not valid in this example; after the first year, income can be invested to yield only 25 percent. The internal rate of return, interpreted as a yield to maturity, is a fundamental tool of bond analysis. This yield curve insight suggests caution in interpreting the measure where short rates differ substantially from long rates and particularly where the yield curve is thought not to be stable.

Time-Weighted versus Dollar-Weighted Rates of Return. An application where the difference between geometric and internal rates of return is of some importance is in the context of money manager performance measurement.

Example: Oilpro Securities Inc. and OilQuest are two money managers for the XYZ pension fund. They were both given $200,000 to manage; Oilpro was given the money as a lump sum, whereas OilQuest, being new to the business, was given the money in two annual installments of $100,000 each. Both managers invested 100 percent of the assets in the same oil venture, which experienced a 60 percent return in the first year and 25 percent in the second. How do their respective performances compare?

One common performance measure, called the *dollar-weighted* rate of return, is nothing more than the internal rate of return of the fund under management. The fund gave to Oilpro $200,000, which grew to $400,000 at the end of two years. The dollar-weighted return is that return r for which:

$$\$200,000 = \frac{\$400,000}{(1 + r)^2}$$

It implies a dollar-weighted return of 41.42 percent. On the other hand, OilQuest was given $100,000 initially and $100,000 after a year, which, given the 60 percent return in the first year and the 25 percent return in the second year, implied that the first part of the fund grew to $200,000 while the second part grew to $125,000, totaling $325,000, after two years. The dollar-weighted return for OilQuest is thus the return r for which:

$$\$100,000 = \frac{-\$100,000}{(1 + r)} + \frac{\$325,000}{(1 + r)^2}$$

The result is a dollar-weighted return of 37.08 percent.

The investment policies of the two managers were identical, yet Oilpro would appear the better manager by more than four percentage points per year! Yes, the fund was more valuable after two years left with that manager, but that is totally an artifact of the way in which the two managers were funded. The geometric return—in this context the *time-weighted rate of return*—does not suffer from this drawback and gives a 41.42 percent return to each manager regardless of the way in which the managers were funded. The comparison between the two measures becomes more difficult in the context where the money manager is funded and is required to make disbursements within a given reporting period. The concept of continuously compounded return assists us in this regard.

Continuously Compounded Return. The exact timing of cash flows is crucial in evaluating the performance of money managers. A manager who does not reinvest the proceeds from the sale of securities or the income from investments in a timely fashion would be guilty of mismanagement of the fund assets. Up to this point in the discussion it has been assumed that cash flows occur on a regular basis, at the end of every month or year for the holding period of the investment. This assumption, of course, is unrealistic. In any investment program, cash flows occur on an irregular basis throughout the year. The return that represents an appropriate basis of comparison is one that reflects the continuous reinvestment of these cash flows. Such a return is referred to as a *continuously compounded return*.

Suppose a particular investment is expected to earn an income equal to 10 percent of its current value over the course of the coming year. If the income comes in the form of a lump-sum payment at year-end, the return on the investment would be 10 percent. If the income comes in the form of two equal installments, one in the middle of the year and one at year-end, the investment should earn more than 10 percent, since a 10 percent return would assume that the interim installment was not reinvested.

If the interim income were reinvested in ventures earning a similar return, the annual return would be 5 percent compounded twice, or 10.25 percent. If, on the other hand, the income were to come on a daily basis, the annual return would be given by $\frac{1}{365}$ of 10 percent compounded 365 times, or 10.52 percent. The 10.52 percent annual return represents the maximum return measured on an annual basis from an investment yielding 10 percent when continuously compounded. In other words, a 10.52 percent annually compounded return corresponds to a 10 percent continuously compounded return.[4]

---

[4]The calculations that convert a particular continuously compounded rate to an equivalent annually compounded rate would appear a little cumbersome were it not for a convenient mathematical result. As we saw, $1.00 would grow to $1.1052 at a continuously compounded rate of 10 percent. The amount $1.1052 happens to equal $1.00 × $2.718282^{.10}$, where 2.718282 is the mathematical constant e, giving rise to the formula:

Annually compounded rate = $2.718282^{\text{Continuously compounded rate}} - 1.00$

Example: Oilpro placed an additional $100,000 in a short-term interest fund for seven months. This fund yielded a 10 percent return, continuously compounded, for the period in question. How much was Oilpro's investment worth at the time the funds were withdrawn?

As noted above, a dollar growing at 10 percent continuously compounded would equal $1.1052 at year-end. However, in this case the investment is only for seven months, or $7/12$ of a year. One way to compute the future value of the investment would be to take the 365th fraction of 10 percent compounded for $7/12$ of 365 days, or 213 days. A simpler approach is to convert the continuously compounded rate to the equivalent annually compounded rate of 10.52 percent and compound this value for the appropriate fraction of the year:

$$\$100,000 \times (1 + .10/365)^{213} = \$100,000 \times (1 + .1052)^{\frac{7}{12}} = \$106,008$$

Thus Oilpro ought to have been able to withdraw $106,008 from the short-term interest fund at the end of seven months.

The point of this example is to show that where rates of return can be considered continuously compounded, the future value (and present value) formula applies in the context of cash flows that occur throughout the year.

STATISTICS AND DATA ANALYSIS

Relationship to the Theory of Value

The advent of spreadsheet software has focused attention on the central role of analysis: where do the numbers come from? Earlier in this chapter, we showed how to derive measures of value, given information about future cash flows. Statistical methods process the available information into a form useful to the valuation process.

In the oil venture example the beginning $1.6 million number was taken as given. Is this a reasonable figure? Does it conform to what is known about the oil exploration business? The methods of statistics are obviously useful in this context, and we shall consider a variety of ways of processing the available data to derive simple summary measures of this data. In that example it appeared that only the opinion of the promoter supported the number. The interests of the promoter obviously differ from those of the investor, and statistical methods can be used to examine whether the number is unduly optimistic in light of prior claims by the promoter. Finally, the venture is quite risky. What effect can or should recognition of this risk have on the valuation process? Again statistical methods are useful in this context.

Statistical methods are crucial to the valuation process. Their usefulness falls under three headings:

- Reduction of large quantities of data into simple summary measures that describe the data and the relationships among the data.
- Statistical examination of hypotheses on which the valuation is based.
- Quantitative measurement of risk.

The remainder of this section will examine the first two issues, while the third will be studied in the next section.

Descriptive Statistics

The central task of descriptive statistics is to reduce a large amount of information into a comprehensible form. Statisticians use the term *measure of central tendency* to describe a single number that represents many numbers. The $1.6 million number could be said to be a measure of central tendency that reflects the recent history of returns to oil ventures; alternatively it could be thought of as representing the entire range of possible financial outcomes to this venture. It is evidently somewhat meaningless without some indication of how actual outcomes may differ from $1.6 million. Statisticians use the term *measure of dispersion* to describe the extent to which the actual numbers may differ from the measure of central tendency.

Measures of Central Tendency. The most familiar measure of central tendency is the *simple average*. Suppose that the $1.6 million number was based on an economic model that used data for 50 recent drillings to form some estimate of the cost of the project. These data are provided as Table 2–2.

The average cost was $256,770, which would appear to be a reasonable estimate for these purposes. The simple average obtained by adding up the data and dividing by the number of items is referred to by statisticians as the *sample mean*. This does not mean that this particular oil venture will cost $256,770. In fact, a number of recent oil wells cost

TABLE 2–2
Oil Venture: Drilling Costs

Well Number	Cost	Well Number	Cost
1	$473,760	26	$216,924
2	230,198	27	225,957
3	241,897	28	245,592
4	219,475	29	221,158
5	222,832	30	241,640
6	211,014	31	201,033
7	210,757	32	196,914
8	357,842	33	224,182
9	221,924	34	200,587
10	216,699	35	239,048
11	198,449	36	379,388
12	218,222	37	212,348
13	386,870	38	301,041
14	289,839	39	263,432
15	199,965	40	314,995
16	228,909	41	298,102
17	477,595	42	198,707
18	567,581	43	195,289
19	225,357	44	229,207
20	207,746	45	239,331
21	244,585	46	202,135
22	255,646	47	205,490
23	215,328	48	316,954
24	199,988	49	221,764
25	282,001	50	242,804

considerably more. Number 18 cost over $500,000. Furthermore, over half the wells in the study cost less than $256,770. What is going on here?

Table 2–3 shows the data presented in Table 2–2 ranked in order of the size of the cost of each well. Almost three quarters of the wells cost less than the average of $256,770. The abnormally high costs of Wells 1, 17, and 18 seem to have caused the average to be higher than the cost of most of the wells. Thus it could be argued that the average is not a reasonable single number to characterize the cost of this venture.

Another measure of central tendency is the *median*, a number chosen such that half of the data are above it and the remaining data are below it. In this example the median is $225,657, halfway between the cost of Wells 19 and 27. The costs of Wells 1, 17, and 18 are said to be *outliers* in the sense that they are extreme relative to the others. If we argue that

TABLE 2–3
Oil Venture: Drilling Costs Ranked by Cost

Well Number	Cost	Well Number	Cost
43	$195,289	27	$225,957
32	196,914	16	228,909
11	198,499	44	229,207
42	198,707	2	230,198
15	199,965	35	239,048
24	199,988	45	239,331
34	200,587	30	241,640
31	201,033	3	241,897
46	202,135	50	242,804
47	205,490	21	244,585
20	207,746	28	245,592
7	210,757	22	255,646
6	211,014	39	263,423
37	212,348	25	282,001
23	215,328	14	289,839
10	216,699	41	298,102
26	216,924	38	301,041
12	218,222	40	314,995
4	219,475	48	316,954
29	221,158	8	357,842
49	221,764	36	379,388
9	221,924	13	386,870
5	222,832	1	473,760
33	224,182	17	477,595
19	225,357	18	567,581

these values are not representative of the true cost of drilling a well, then they should not have significant impact on the measure of central tendency. The median has the property that it is not affected by the magnitude of outliers.

Still another measure of central tendency useful in certain applications is the most common value of the data, otherwise referred to as the *mode*. In the above example it would appear that there is no "common value" and each cost is different. However, if we classify costs into ranges of $50,000 and count the number of wells that fall into each cost classification, a pattern emerges.

A *histogram* is a graphical representation of such a classification of data. The histogram for the data contained in Table 2–2 is given as Figure 2–1. This histogram indicates that there are 6 wells that cost between $150,000 and $200,000, 30 that cost between $200,000 and $250,000, 5

FIGURE 2–1
Histogram of the Data Contained in Table 2–2

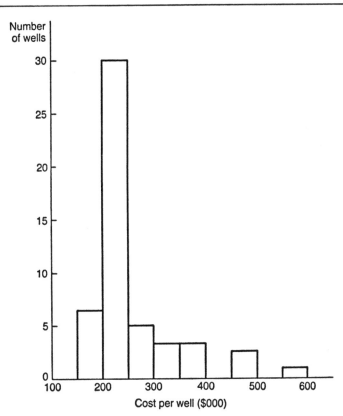

that cost between $250,000 and $300,000, and so forth. The *modal range* is $200,000 to $250,000. A reasonable value for the central tendency would lie in this range; the mode would be given by a weighted average of the midpoints of the adjacent ranges:

$$\text{Mode} = \frac{(6 \times \$175,000) + (30 \times \$225,000) + (5 \times \$275,000)}{6 + 30 + 5}$$

$$= \$223,780$$

The mode is perhaps the most intuitive of the measures of central tendency. Ultimately it is also the least satisfactory. There are two major problems with this measure:

1. The mode is sensitive to the precise classification chosen. Suppose the data were broken into ranges of $20,000. Thirteen wells cost between $200,000 and $220,000, and 12 cost between $220,000 and $240,000. By this classification the mode lies between $200,000 and $220,000,

2. Even given the classification of the data, the mode is not unambiguous. Suppose that instead of 1 there were 30 wells that cost between $550,000 and $600,000. In this case, the mode is ambiguous, and the distribution of the data is said to be *bimodal*. While evidently a problem for the mode, if this were the case it would also be a problem for the mean and median, both of which would then be intermediate between the two modes. A bimodal distribution frequently indicates that two or more sets of disparate data have been aggregated together. Gas wells are typically deeper and more expensive than oil wells. If the data pertained to both oil *and* gas wells, the distribution of the data would be bimodal, and the measures of central tendency for the aggregated data would be fairly meaningless.

A major property of both the median and the mode is insensitivity to extreme values in the data. This fact is said to be a major argument in favor of these measures over the simple average as a measure of central tendency. However, is this lack of sensitivity necessarily a good thing? Implicit in the decision to ignore these values is the assumption that Wells 1, 17, and 18 are somehow different from the other wells and should not enter into consideration. Suppose, however, that there was an equipment breakdown on Well 1, a lost bit on Well 17, and a flaming blowout on Well 18. To the extent that these are reasonable contingencies for the proposed well, they *should* enter into consideration. Unlike the median and the mode, the sample mean accounts for these contingencies relative to the frequency of their occurrence in the data, and for this reason it is not such an unreasonable measure of central tendency. Good practice, however, is to examine the facts surrounding each outlier.

Measures of Dispersion. The analyst interested in having one number represent an entire distribution of data ought to understand the extent to which the data can deviate from that measure of central tendency.

The *range*, the difference between the maximum and the minimum of the observed data ($372,292 in the Table 2–2 example), is one such measure of dispersion. It does indicate the range of variation in the data but is highly affected by outliers. A more satisfactory variant of this measure, the *interquartile range*, is defined by the difference between the *lower*

FIGURE 2–2
Boxplot of the Table 2–2 Data

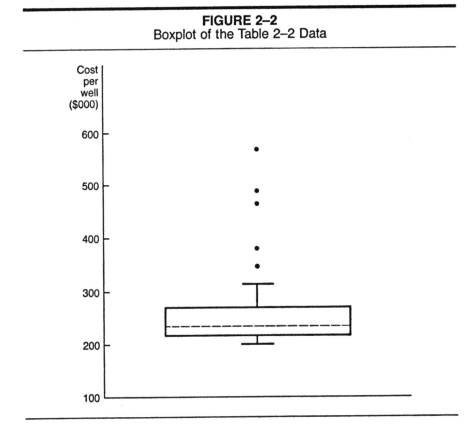

quartile, the number such that just 25 percent of the data are smaller, and the *upper quartile*, the number such that just 25 percent of the data are larger. In the Table 2–2 example, a quarter of the wells had a cost less than that of Well 6 ($211,014), and a quarter had costs exceeding $263,432 (the cost of Well 39). Thus half of the data lies within the interquartile range given by the difference between the two, $52,418. This number is best thought of as a measure of dispersion to be associated with the median. In fact, the relationship between the range, interquartile range, and median provides a succinct graphical representation of the entire distribution of the observed data, known as a *boxplot* (see Figure 2–2).

In the boxplot of the Table 2–2 data, the horizontal dashed line represents the median, the box the interquartile range, and the vertical lines extending from the boxes or "whiskers," the range. The whiskers extend

---

FIGURE 2–3
Boxplot of Annual Returns by Investment Class, 1926–1984

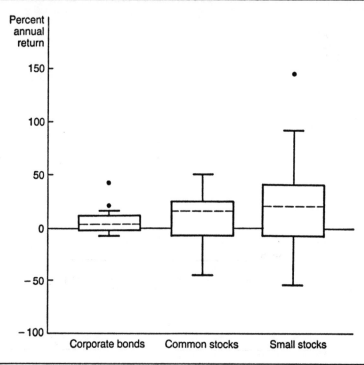

SOURCE OF DATA: Ibbotson Associates, *Stocks, Bonds, Bills and Inflation: 1985 Year-book* (Chicago: Ibbotson Associates, Capital Management Research Center, 1986), pp. 94–99.

to the range of the data or 1.5 times the interquartile range, whichever is smaller, to allow the outliers to be plotted separately.

Inspecting this boxplot we note that the upper tail of the distribution of the data—values in excess of the median—is much more extensive than the lower tail of the distribution. Where this is the case the distribution is said to be skewed to the right, or *positively skewed*. The relationship we observed between the sample mean, median, and mode is characteristic of such distributions. Where the lower tail is more extensive than the upper, the distribution is said to be skewed to the left, or *negatively skewed*.

Boxplots convey in abbreviated form information similar to that provided by the histogram. However, they are more useful than histograms in comparing distributions. By lining up boxplots against one another, one can gain an immediate visual impression of how distributions differ by their central tendencies, dispersion, and relative skewness. Figure 2–3 compares annual returns for three different classes of investment given in Table 2–1. We see immediately from this figure that small stock returns are more variable than common stocks in general, while corporate bond returns are less variable. While we saw in Table 2–1 that the average return (arithmetic return) is much higher for small stocks, the median return is not that much greater than for common stocks in general. It seems that small stock returns are more highly skewed, with a higher degree of dispersion, than are stocks in general, again suggesting that the high arithmetic returns for these stocks should be interpreted with care.

Boxplots are used in several types of analysis. They are frequently used to compare the distribution of return by money managers. In another application they summarize succinctly the results of simulation experiments such as those designed to uncover the differences between alternative policies for asset and liability planning.

Just as the interquartile range is a measure of dispersion generally associated with the median, the variance and standard deviation are measures of dispersion associated with the sample mean.

Variance measures the average deviation from the mean *squared* (the deviations themselves unfortunately average to zero). For the Table 2–2 data:

$$\text{Variance} = \frac{(\$473,760 - \$256,770)^2 + (\$230,198 - \$256,770)^2 + \cdots}{50}$$

$$= \$6,276,750,000$$

or more generally:

$$\text{Variance} = \frac{(X_1 - \overline{X})^2 + (X_2 - \overline{X})^2 + \cdots + (X_N - \overline{X})^2}{N}$$

where
$\overline{X}$ = Average value of the variable of interest.
N = Number of observations.[5]

The *mean absolute deviation* (MAD), on the other hand, averages the same deviations without respect to the sign of the deviation:

$$\text{MAD} = \frac{|\$473,760 - \$256,770| + |\$230,198 - \$256,770| + \cdots}{50}$$

$$= \$54,855$$

---

[5]Note that purists divide by $N - 1$ instead of by N to ensure that the estimate of the variance is an unbiased estimate of the true or underlying variance.

or

$$\text{MAD} = \frac{|X_1 - \overline{X}| + |X_2 - \overline{X}| + \cdots + |X_N - \overline{X}|}{N}$$

where
$\overline{X}$ = Average value of the variable of interest.
N = Number of observations.

and the vertical lines imply that the sign of the difference between the variable and its average value is ignored in the computation.

The variance is the most popular measure of dispersion. However, it is not expressed in dollar units. To remedy this problem, take the square root of this value. This square root is referred to as the *standard deviation*.

Standard deviation = Square root of variance
Standard deviation = $\sqrt{6,276,750,000}$ = \$79,226

Referring back to Table 2–1, the standard deviation of annual returns is a useful summary statistic for the dispersion of returns. Small stocks experience returns that are more variable than those of stocks in general, while government bonds have returns that are less variable.

As we shall see, the standard deviation and variance are particularly useful in the context of hypothesis tests and the definition of risk. For data analysis, however, they share the problem of sensitivity to outliers (these large values are squared before they enter the average and so will tend to dominate the measure). One approach to this problem is simply to exclude outliers. Standard deviations computed in this manner are called *trimmed standard deviations*. The MAD approach, which does not square deviations associated with large outliers, is less sensitive to this problem.

Measures of Association. Measures of central tendency and dispersion, boxplots and histograms describe a complex set of data in a simple way. They do not describe the relationships between different sets of data upon which valuation frequently depends. The simplest descriptive tool for analyzing the relationship between sets of data is the *scatter plot*.

Figure 2–4 gives scatter plots of the relationships between annual returns of different investment classes given in Figure 2–3. These scatter plots (sometimes called *draftsman plots* when organized in this fashion) show that there is a strong positive relationship between the returns on common stocks in general and the returns on small stocks: when common stock returns are high, small stock returns are also high. There is, however, less relationship between common stock returns and the returns on

FIGURE 2–4
Scatter plots of Returns on Common Stocks, Small Stocks,
and Corporate Bonds

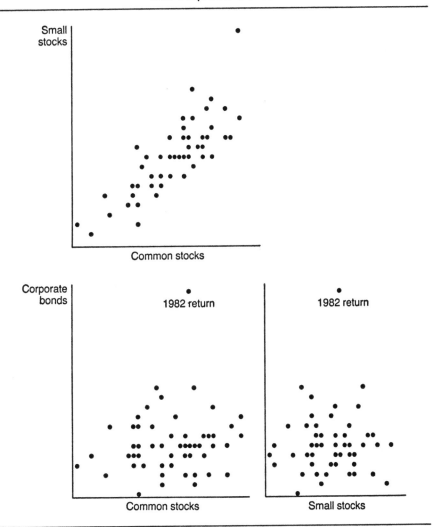

SOURCE OF DATA: Ibbotson Associates, *Stocks, Bonds, Bills and Inflation: 1985 Yearbook* (Chicago: Ibbotson Associates, Capital Management Research Center, 1986), pp. 94–99.

corporate bonds and still less between the returns on small stocks and on corporate bonds.

A measure that captures the extent to which data are associated is the *covariance*. In the case of small stocks and common stocks, when common stock returns (R_c) were above average, so too were small stock returns (R_s). Similarly, when returns were below average, so too were the returns on small stocks. Intuitively the covariance should be positive, and computing it as the average product of deviations from average should come out as a positive number:[6]

$$\text{Covariance between } R_c \text{ and } R_s = \text{Average value of } (R_c - \overline{R}_c) \times (R_s - \overline{R}_s)$$
$$= .0639$$
$$\text{Covariance between } X \text{ and } Y = \text{Average of } (X - \overline{X}) \times (Y - \overline{Y})$$

where

X = Value of the first variable of interest.
$\overline{X}$ = Average of the first variable.
Y = Value of the second variable of interest.
$\overline{Y}$ = Average of the second variable.

In a similar way, if the returns were negatively associated in the sense that when the change in one was positive the other was negative, the covariance would be negative. However, the actual magnitude of the number is difficult to interpret.

The *correlation coefficient* is a measure of association that is a little easier to interpret. It is obtained by normalizing the covariance by the standard deviations of the variables under consideration. In other words, in the example above:

$$\text{Correlation} = \frac{\text{Covariance}}{\text{Standard deviation } R_c \times \text{Standard deviation } R_s}$$
$$= \frac{.0639}{.212 \times .363} = .83$$
$$\text{Correlation between } X \text{ and } Y = \frac{\text{Covariance between } X \text{ and } Y}{S_X \times S_Y}$$

---

[6]Note that, as with the variance formula, in finding the average value of the product, purists divide by $N - 1$ instead of by N, the number of observations on the two variables.

where

X = First variable of interest.

S_X = Standard deviation of X.

Y = Second variable of interest.

S_Y = Standard deviation of Y.

TABLE 2–4
Correlation Matrix of Annual Returns, 1926–1984

	Common Stocks	Small Stocks	Corporate Bonds
Common stocks	1.00		
Small stocks	.83	1.00	
Corporate bonds	.15	.08	1.00

SOURCE OF DATA: Ibbotson Associates, *Stocks, Bonds, Bills and Inflation: 1985 Yearbook* (Chicago: Ibbotson Associates, Capital Management Research Center, 1986), pp. 94–99.

If two sets of data were perfectly correlated, in the sense that movements in one data series were exactly matched by corresponding movements in another, the correlation coefficient would be one. If there were no association the correlation would be zero. If the data were perfectly negatively associated, in the sense that movements in one series were matched by corresponding but opposite movements in the other, the correlation coefficient would be minus one. Table 2–4 gives what is termed the *correlation matrix* of the data depicted in Figure 2–4.

Table 2–4 can be compared directly to Figure 2–4. The returns on common stock seem to be closely associated with the returns on small stocks (correlation = .83) but less associated with the returns on corporate bonds (correlation = .15), while the degree of association between small stocks and corporate bonds (correlation = .08) is even more attenuated.

The correlation matrix is the most commonly used measure of association in investment analysis. However, it should be treated with care. Referring back to Figure 2–4, we see that much of the apparent positive association between common stock returns and corporate bond returns can be attributed to just one abnormally high return on bonds (43.79 percent experienced in 1982) that happened to occur at a time when the common stock return of 21.41 percent was slightly above average. If this one outlier were excluded, the evidence of a positive relationship between the total returns on stocks and bonds would be reduced.

FIGURE 2–5
Regression of Small Stock Returns on Common Stock Returns

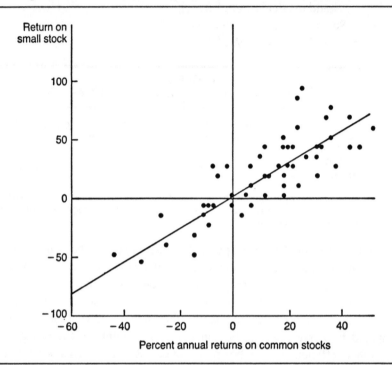

Percent annual returns on common stocks

Another common measure of association is the *simple regression*. It is very tempting to describe the relationship between returns on small stocks and on common stocks in general in terms of a line that best fits through the scatter plot of returns on the two classes of investment. Such a line, termed a *regression line,* is depicted in Figure 2–5. It is obtained by means of regression analysis, which minimizes the squared differences between the actual observations and the regression line. This technique is available in many statistical computer software packages. Such software takes as input the data for the variables in question, and provides as output estimates that are used to construct the line.

Output for a typical regression software package is given as Table 2–5. The "Coefficient" column describes the line drawn in Figure 2–5. "Intercept" is the starting value of the line: If one knew that the return on common stocks was 0.0 percent, one might predict that small stocks would earn a 1.698 percent return. In other words, in Figure 2–5, the line would

TABLE 2–5
Regression of Small Stock Returns on Common Stock
Returns: Sample Output

	Coefficient	Standard Error	t-Value
Intercept	1.698480	3.0786	0.5517
Common stock returns	1.416735	0.1272	11.1403

Residual standard error = 20.71715.
Multiple R-square = 0.6852.
N = 59
F-value = 124.1068 on 1, 57 degrees of freedom.

cross a vertical line drawn at zero common stock return, at a 1.698 percent return on small stocks. "Common Stock Returns" gives the slope of the line: We would expect that small stock returns would increase by 1.417 percent for every 1 percent rise in common stock returns. In the case of simple regressions involving asset or asset class returns, the 1.417 number is referred to as the *beta* of the asset. In short, the relationship between small stock returns and common stock returns may be represented as:

$$R_s = 1.698 + 1.417 \times R_c + e$$

where the line is given by the 1.698 and 1.417 numbers and *e* represents the error, or *residual*, which gives the difference between the actual small stock return and the return that would be predicted given the line.

The multiple R-square item (sometimes referred to as R-squared or simply R^2) is a simple summary measure of the relationship between small stocks and the returns on common stocks. It says that 68.53 percent of the variability in small stock returns can be explained by the variability of common stock returns. It is also the square of the correlation coefficient between small stock and common stock returns (.6853 = .83 × .83).

The residual also indicates how well the regression line explains the observed data. The standard deviation of these residuals is also a measure of the extent to which the relationship describes the data. This standard deviation is referred to as the residual standard error (sometimes also referred to as the standard error of the regression), which in this instance is 20.72 percent. Even if we were to know the return on common stocks in general, there is a large degree of uncertainty about possible returns on small stocks. The remaining statistics, the standard error and *t*-value columns and the F-value item give indications as to the reliability of these results and will be discussed separately below.

One might conclude from this analysis that small stock returns are "caused" by common stock returns. However, one could argue equally well that small stocks "cause" common stock returns. The truth lies somewhere in between. Both small stocks and common stocks in general are affected by the state of the economy, and there is a certain degree of variability the investor cannot avoid by simply switching from small stocks to a broadly diversified common stock portfolio. It is this exposure to common factors of variability that we shall see is at the heart of an appropriate definition of the risk faced by investors.·

Hypothesis Tests

Data analysis provides procedures to describe a set of data; hypothesis tests provide techniques for examining theories or hypotheses about how the data came into being. In the oil example at the beginning of the chapter the given $1.6 million was a reasonable estimate of how valuable the oil venture would be at year-end. Suppose that the promoter of the venture had been involved in 30 recent ventures, each of which struck oil. The estimated value of each venture at the initial offering and the ultimate value at the end of each project are given in Table 2–6.

These estimates do not appear to have been very reliable. The standard deviation of the difference between the estimate and the ultimate value of the oil venture (the last column in Table 2–6) is $277,460. When confronted with this data, the promoter might argue that the oil exploration business is very risky. It is difficult to estimate with any degree of precision the actual worth of an oil well before it is drilled. However, there were 20 out of 30 cases in which the estimated value was too high. In addition, the average difference was −$166,366. Are these data sufficient to conclude that the promoter systematically overestimates the ultimate value of the oil ventures in the offering prospectus?

In this context it is useful to draw a distinction between the *empirical distribution* (the distribution of the observed data) and what is termed the *theoretical distribution* (the distribution that could be said to give rise to the observed data). The data in Table 2–6 pertain to the empirical distribution of the errors the promoter makes in estimating the ultimate value of the well. These data are essentially retrospective. They are relevant to current decisions only to the extent that they allow us to infer future conduct of the promoter. The promoter might argue that the reason the ultimate value fell short of expectations to the average amount of $166,366 was bad luck on Ventures 14 and 28 rather than a predisposition on the part of the promoter to overestimate systematically. After all, the

TABLE 2–6
Estimated and Actual Value of 30
Related Oil Ventures ($000)

Venture	Estimate	Actual	Difference
1	$1,600	$1,425	$ – 175
2	1,800	1,440	– 360
3	1,600	1,587	– 13
4	1,600	1,746	146
5	1,500	982	– 518
6	1,500	1,128	– 372
7	1,600	1,147	– 453
8	1,600	1,662	62
9	1,600	1,610	10
10	1,300	1,531	231
11	1,700	1,688	– 12
12	1,700	1,841	141
13	1,500	1,248	– 252
14	1,800	1,161	– 639
15	1,600	1,545	– 55
16	1,400	1,732	332
17	1,700	1,712	12
18	1,800	2,069	269
19	1,700	1,568	– 132
20	1,600	1,255	– 345
21	1,700	1,572	– 128
22	1,600	1,706	106
23	1,800	1,509	– 291
24	1,600	1,143	– 457
25	1,700	1,258	– 442
26	1,500	1,174	– 326
27	1,600	1,241	– 359
28	1,700	959	– 741
29	1,600	1,673	73
30	1,600	1,297	– 303

– $166,366 average difference was based on results for only 30 oil ventures. If we had data for other ventures, the promoter would claim, we would find that the difference would eventually average to zero. In other words, the data in Table 2–6 merely represent 30 cases drawn from a theoretical distribution for which the mean difference is zero. If this were the case, the estimates would be said to be *unbiased.*

Unfortunately, we do not get to observe the theoretical distribution directly. To assess the promoter's claim, we need to *infer* its properties from the empirical distribution. The promoter claims that the estimates are unbiased, that the true mean difference in fact is zero. In the parlance of statistics this is said to be the *null hypothesis:*

Null hypothesis: Mean difference = $0.00

This null hypothesis is to be set against our initial reaction, that the promoter has a predisposition to overestimate the value of oil ventures. In other words, the *alternative hypothesis* is:

Alternative hypothesis: Mean difference < $0.00

This formalization of null and alternative hypotheses is referred to by statisticians as a *hypothesis test*, or *significance test*. The object is to examine how far the sample mean is from the null hypothesis and to measure the significance of the difference.[7]

One of the attractive features of the sample mean as a measure of central tendency is that we know something of the way in which it is affected by the exigencies of a particular sample of data. The sample mean will of course vary around the true mean of the data from one particular sample to the next. It is highly unlikely that in another sample of 30 oil ventures the average error would turn out to be exactly −$166,366. The sample mean varies with each sample, and its variance turns out to be the variance of the underlying data divided by the number of items of data on which the sample mean is based. It is not surprising that the reliability of the sample mean as an estimate of the true or underlying mean should increase with the size of the sample used to estimate it: As the sample size increases, the sample mean will close in on the true mean of the underlying data.

$$\text{Mean of sample means} = \text{Mean of data}$$
$$\text{Variance of sample means} = \frac{\text{Variance of data}}{N}$$

The standard deviation of the sample mean is given by the square root of the variance and is referred to as the *standard error*. For the example given above, the standard error of the mean is:

$$\text{Standard error} = \sqrt{\frac{\$277,460^2}{30}} = \$50,657$$

---

[7]In this particular application, we care only about large negative differences. Statisticians refer to such tests as *one sided* or *one tailed*. If the issue were the general reliability of the promoter, we would be as concerned with large positive differences as well. The test would then be referred to as *two sided,* or *two tailed.*

or in general:

$$\text{Standard error} = \text{Square root of } \frac{\text{Variance}}{N}$$

where N = Number of observations used to estimate the mean of the data.

The standard error is then a natural measure of the extent to which the sample mean differs from the mean under the null hypothesis. We see that $-\$166,366$ differs from the null hypothesis of zero to the extent of 3.28 standard errors. This 3.28 number is referred to as the t-value or t-statistic:

$$t\text{-value} = \frac{-\$166,366 - \$0.00}{\$50,657} = -3.28$$

or in general

$$t\text{-value} = \frac{\text{Sample mean} - \text{Null hypothesis mean}}{\text{Standard error of sample mean}}$$

Since the t-value has a theoretical distribution[8] approximated by a normal or bell-shaped distribution for which a difference greater than 1.65 standard errors occurs less than 5 percent of the time (this number can be found from tables published in most elementary statistics books), a difference of 3.28 standard errors is "large."[9]

Thus the average error is too large to be accounted for by the exigencies of the particular sample of 30 oil ventures. In the parlance of statistics, we say we reject the null hypothesis of a zero mean error at a *5 percent level of significance*. In plain English, we say the promoter significantly overestimates the ultimate value of the oil ventures he promotes.

The same analysis can be used to evaluate claims by a money manager that he or she can outperform some popular index of returns. In this instance, the average error (the difference between the fund return and the index return) is referred to as the *alpha*, or value added, of the fund. The null hypothesis is that the true alpha is zero, and the alternative hypothesis is that the true alpha is positive, that the money manager can indeed out-

---

[8]Actually, the exact distribution is what is termed a student-t distribution with $(30 - 1)$ "degrees of freedom." For about 30 or more degrees of freedom, this is for all practical purposes identical to the well-known normal distribution.

[9]A t-value of 3.28 is large by any reckoning. The 1.65 number refers to a one-tailed test; in a two-tailed test, where we allow for the possibility that the main difference can be large in either a positive or negative direction, the critical number is 1.96. Treat with caution any finding of "significance" that depends on this distinction!

perform the index. Unfortunately, the variability of returns is frequently so great that an extensive track record is necessary to show evidence that the manager can significantly outperform the index, at least using this simplest form of analysis. Risk adjustment procedures and procedures for reducing the apparent variability of returns lie at the heart of sophisticated procedures for performance measurement.

Multiple Regression Analysis

In the oil drilling example of Table 2–2 there was no adjustment for the fact that the different wells might not have been drilled to the same depth. It seems reasonable to suppose that drilling costs increase with the depth of the well. If we have some idea of how deep the well might be, we might be able to get a more precise idea of the costs of this particular oil venture.

Using annual estimates of the cost per well and the average depth of all onshore oil, gas, and dry wells drilled in the United States from 1959 through 1984, we find that cost per well (in dollars) is indeed positively correlated with the depth of the well (in feet) with a correlation coefficient of .348. Further, regressing cost per well on the average depth per well, we find the results given in Table 2–7. In that table, the standard error and t-values have the same interpretation as in the previous section, where the t-value pertains to the hypothesis that the coefficient in that particular row is in fact zero. The F-value, which in this particular case represents the t-value squared, provides another way of testing this hypothesis.

Thus we find that not only is there evidence of a positive association between depth and the cost per well but the association is significant. We might conclude from Table 2–7 that the best estimate of cost of the well is given by taking $72.5784 per foot of the projected depth of the well minus the amount $192,588.

This interpretation of the results is correct as far as it goes, but it does not go far enough. Regression analysis is no substitute for thought. To see how deceptive such analyses can be, consider the relationship between the predictions of the regression model (sometimes referred to as the *fitted values*) given by:

Estimated costs = −$192,588 + ($72.5784 × Depth of well)

and the residuals or errors given by:

Residual costs = Actual costs − Estimated costs.

TABLE 2–7
Results from Regression of Cost per Well on Average
Depth of Well
(all onshore oil, gas and dry wells, United States,
1959–1983)

	Coefficient	Standard Error	t-Value
Intercept	− 192,588.0000	110,368.0000	− 1.7450
Depth	72.5784	22.8501	3.1763

Residual standard error = 132790.9.
Multiple R-square = 0.1214.
N = 75.
F-value = 10.08872 on 1, 73 degrees of freedom.
SOURCE OF DATA: American Petroleum Institute, *Basic Petro-leum Data Book* Vol. 5 (Washington, D.C.: American Petroleum Institute, May 1985, Table 9).

This relationship is plotted in Figure 2–6. On careful examination, we see that the model makes systematic, predictable errors for both oil and gas wells and that the model seriously underpredicts high costs for both well classifications (the errors are positively skewed). What is going on here?

The Table 2–7 results cover a period of rising costs for all types of productive activity. The producer and wholesale price indexes of the U.S. Bureau of Labor Statistics increased threefold from 1959 to 1983. Drilling technology became more sophisticated over that period, and costs per well rose as a result. The rise in energy prices in the late 1970s and early 80s prompted more than twice the number of wells to be drilled in 1982 than were drilled in 1975, straining the labor and material resources and again causing costs to rise. These effects would appear to swamp the modest changes in the depth per well over that interval.

How can these different effects be isolated? Just as simple regression examines the relationship between one variable and another, multiple regression examines the relationship between one variable and potentially many others. In addition to depth per well, we may consider additional variables: time (the date of the observation, 1959, 1960, . . . 1983); the total number of wells drilled in the United States each year; whether the well was a gas well (zero if the datum in question belonged to an oil or a dry well, one if it pertained to a gas well); and whether the well turned out to be dry. Variables of this sort that classify the data are referred to as *dummy variables*. The variation in producer prices can best be accounted for by expressing all costs in *constant dollar* amounts. That is, each cost

---

FIGURE 2–6
Plotting Residuals against Fitted Values for Table 2–7 Results

---

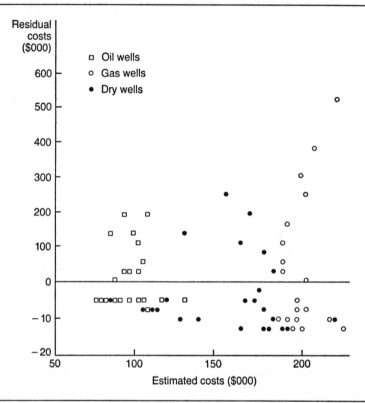

SOURCE OF DATA: American Petroleum Institute, *Basic Petroleum Data Book* Vol. 5 (Washington, D.C.: American Petroleum Institute, May 1985, Table 9).

---

figure is expressed as a fraction of the producer price index for the year in question.

Results from regressing constant dollar costs against depth, time, the number of wells, and the well classification are contained in Table 2–8. This table reveals that:

1. Each additional foot of depth costs $89.17, other things equal.
2. Costs per well have increased an average of $5,753.83 per annum.
3. Every additional well drilled increases the cost per well $3.28.
4. At any given depth, the average gas well costs $52,063 more than an oil well, and a dry well costs $5,789 less.

5. These numbers are significant at the 5 percent level (from the *t*-values), but the gas differential is only barely significant if we consider a one-tailed test.

TABLE 2–8
Regressing Constant (1983) Dollar Costs against Depth, Time, Number of Wells, and Well Classification, 1959–1983

	Coefficient	Standard Error	t-Value
Intercept	−11,636,450.0000	1,482,837.0000	−7.8474
Depth	89.1725	18.7627	4.7527
Time	5,753.8280	777.8590	7.3970
Number of wells	3.2795	.3594	9.1251
Gas	52,063.1400	29,894.9600	1.7415
Dry	−5,789.7840	18,156.3300	−3.1889

Residual standard error = 35611.66.
Multiple *R*-square = 0.9224.
N = 75.
F-value = 164.2498 on 5, 69 degrees of freedom.

In short, these results imply that expected costs will be given by the formula:

$$\text{Expected costs} = -11,636,450 + (\$89.17 \times \text{Depth})$$
$$+ (\$5,753.83 \times \text{Year})$$
$$+ \left(\$52,063 \times \begin{cases} 1 \text{ if well is gas} \\ 0 \text{ otherwise} \end{cases}\right)$$
$$- \left(\$5,789 \times \begin{cases} 1 \text{ if well is dry} \\ 0 \text{ otherwise} \end{cases}\right)$$

This formula explains 92 percent of the observed variability in costs.[10]

These results look impressive, but again one should look at the residuals from the regression, plotted in Figure 2–7. Things do not look good. Even though the model explains a higher percentage of the variability in costs, the errors for oil well costs appear even more predictable than before. Furthermore, there is a distinct pattern to the residuals. They seem

---

[10]The F-value in the case of multiple regression tests the hypothesis that *all* coefficients equal zero. The critical value depends on the 'degrees of freedom' given as 5 and 69, and are tabulated in most statistics texts. In this instance, the critical value for testing at the 5 percent level is 2.5. The observed value is 164.2, which is greater than 2.5, so we say the regression is "significant."

FIGURE 2–7
Residuals Plotted against Fitted Values for Multiple Regression
in Table 2–8 ($000)

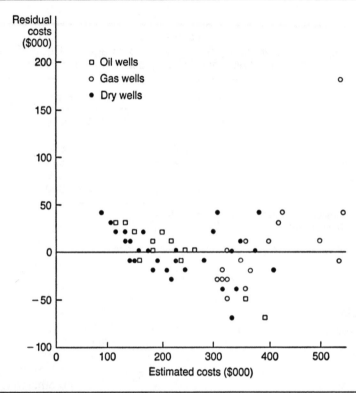

SOURCE OF DATA: American Petroleum Institute, *Basic Petroleum Data Book* Vol. 5 (Washington, D.C.: American Petroleum Institute, May 1985, Table 9).

---

to fan out.[11] When estimated costs are low the residuals appear less variable than when estimated costs are high. In addition, the residuals tend to be positive when estimated costs are very low or very high.

These are typical symptoms calling for a logarithmic or ratio transformation of the data. While the variability of the error measured in dollars may appear to increase with expected costs, perhaps the variance measured in terms of the *percentage error* is more stable.

Table 2–9 summarizes results from such a regression, which is a little more difficult to interpret. The time coefficient (note that time was *not* in

---

[11]Statisticians refer to this phenomenon as *heteroscedasticity*.

TABLE 2–9
Results from Regressing the Logarithm of Constant Dollar
Costs against Time, Well Classification, and the Logarithms
of Depth and the Number of Wells, 1959–1983

	Coefficient	Standard Error	t-Value
Intercept	−55.2329	2.4604	−22.4488
Logarithm of depth	1.8852	0.1966	9.5901
Time	0.0240	0.0016	14.8721
Logarithm of number of wells	0.4194	0.0342	12.2769
Gas	0.0565	0.0656	0.8566
Dry	− 0.3122	0.0414	− 7.5459

Residual standard error = 0.07508.
Multiple R-square = 0.9714.
$N = 75$.
F-value = 468.7797 on 5, 69 degrees of freedom.

logarithm form) is interpreted to mean that there is an average growth in constant dollar costs of 2.4 percent per year, other things equal. Costs depend on depth to the extent of the depth taken to the power 1.88, and they depend on the number of wells to the extent of that number raised to the power .412. A gas well increases costs (by a ratio equal to the antilog of .0565) but by an insignificant amount (note the small t-value). However, dry wells are significantly cheaper (to a ratio equal to the antilog of − .3122). The scatter plot of residuals to fitted values (in terms of the logarithms) given in Figure 2–8 shows that this regression, finally, appears well specified.[12]

UNCERTAINTY AND VALUATION

Factor Methods and the Theory of Value

This chapter started with the proposition that investments can be characterized by the cash flows they generate and that valuation is a problem of comparing alternative cash flows. In the oil venture example, it was assumed that the venture would be worth exactly $1.6 million one year from

---

[12]The intercept, the logarithm of the constant term, would be close to zero if expressed in dollar terms.

FIGURE 2–8
Residuals Plotted against Fitted Values (in Terms of Logarithms) for
Regression in Table 2–9

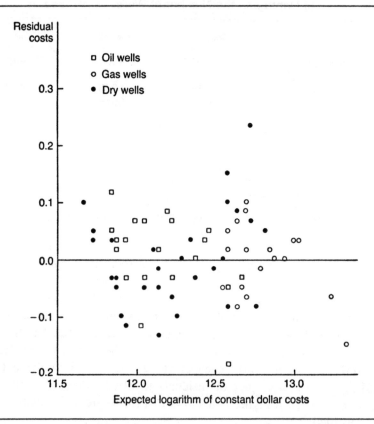

SOURCE OF DATA: American Petroleum Institute, *Basic Petroleum Data Book* Vol. 5
(Washington, D.C.: American Petroleum Institute, May 1985, Table 9).

today. In reality, of course, there is considerable uncertainty about what
such a venture would be worth at that time. The Table 2–6 numbers are
perhaps a more realistic representation of what the venture may be worth.
It is indeed possible that investors may lose part or all of their investment
by year-end. What effect can or should this uncertainty, or risk, have on
the valuation process?

Oil exploration is a very risky process. In a largely undeveloped field,
there is considerable uncertainty about whether a given well will actually

strike oil and, if so, what the flow rate and proven reserves will turn out to be after the well is drilled. For this reason the value of the well before it is drilled may appear somewhat imponderable. However, suppose the investor already owns shares in a well that is being drilled in an immediately adjacent area. The ultimate value of that well is also highly uncertain; but whatever it turns out to be, it should be very highly correlated with the ultimate value of the well in question. If the investor could sell those shares for $1,333 per share today and buy shares in the new venture for $1,000 per share, he would be better off by $333 per share today and as well off a year from today. At $1,000 per share, the shares of the new venture are significantly undervalued. Valuation remains a problem of comparing alternative cash flows.

This oil well example may appear a little too neat. Surely there are few examples where investments exist that are exact duplicates, in a sense, of the investment in question. Most investors hold portfolios of securities rather than individual securities. In the Table 2–6 example, the uncertainty concerning the ultimate value of the venture, measured by the standard deviation of the error estimating this value, was on the order of $277,460. If the investor chose instead to hold a portfolio consisting of an equal investment in each of the 30 ventures, he or she would thereby *diversify* the risk. This diversification would be as if the investor held a share in the mean value of the different ventures; as we saw, the standard deviation would fall to $50,657. By holding a sufficiently large portfolio, such an investor can be shielded from the exigencies of a particular venture. The investor should not be in a position to care if a bit is lost or there are labor problems with a particular crew. These things should average out. Even if the well is dry, the dry well represents only one 30th of the original investment. What the investor cares about is the risk that cannot be diversified away. If oil prices fall, *all 30* oil ventures will be worth less. It is at this portfolio level that investments can be matched and hence valued in terms of their exposure to common factors of variation in the economy as a whole.

Factor methods provide techniques and procedures for evaluating the impact of factors of variation that affect all securities. The well-known *capital asset pricing model* can be thought of as corresponding to a model where there is only one factor of variation affecting the returns on all securities. In this model, securities are valued so that their return over and above the Treasury bill, or *riskless* return, is expected to be proportional to the degree to which they are exposed to all common stocks, the so-called *market factor*. This model is referred to as a *single-factor model*. The *arbitrage pricing theory* introduced by S. A. Ross[13] derives similar results for the case where there is more than one factor affecting the returns on securities, called a *multiple-factor model*.

Single-Factor Models

In single-factor models, it is assumed that the uncertain returns on different securities are related only to the extent that they are all related to some common market factor. In other words, investors can reduce their risk by diversifying their portfolios; but there is an essential risk that cannot be diversified away, a risk that arises from the uncertainty of the economy as a whole. This market factor can thus be measured by the returns on a broadly diversified portfolio, usually identified with a capitalization-weighted portfolio such as the Standard & Poor's 500. This insight gives rise to the *market model* introduced by W. Sharpe.[14]

In Table 2–5, a simple regression appeared to capture the relationship between the returns on a portfolio of small stocks R_s, and the returns on a broadly diversified common stock portfolio R_c:

$$R_s = 1.698 + (1.417 \times R_c) + e$$

This is an example of a market model where, in this context, the error (e) is termed the *nonsystematic,* or *idiosyncratic,* component of returns. The 1.417 number is referred to as the beta of the small stock portfolio. The nonsystematic component of returns can be diversified away within a large portfolio. The beta, which measures the extent to which the returns on the security depend on the market factor, thus represents a measure of the risk that cannot be diversified away. The beta of a broadly diversified market fund is one. An asset or portfolio more risky than the market has a beta greater than one. As we would expect, small stocks are riskier than the market as a whole, with a beta of 1.417. A beta less than one indicates a security less risky than the market as a whole. (Public utility stocks typically fall into this latter category.)

To estimate beta, one could simply use a regression analysis like the one presented in Table 2–5. Most investigators usually regress *monthly* or

---

[13]See S. A. Ross, "The Arbitrage Theory of Capital Asset Pricing," *Journal of Economic Theory*, 3, December 1976, pp. 343–62.

[14]See W. Sharpe, "A Simplified Model for Portfolio Analysis," *Management Science*, 9, January 1963, pp. 277–93.

daily returns, where available, to obtain the most precise estimate of this quantity. There are several caveats to this approach. In periods when interest rates are highly volatile (such as the late 70s and early 80s in the United States), a large part of the variability in stock returns could be accounted for by this phenomenon. If this is the case, then the returns on the security and on the market should be measured in excess of the yield on Treasury bills with the same time to maturity as the holding period over which the returns are defined. Beta is not stable over extended periods of time, since the operations of firms change. Sixty months of data is the maximum that should be used to estimate this parameter, and there are a variety of ways one can adjust beta to account for changes in the firms that issue the securities in question.

There are a variety of services that provide periodic estimates of beta for a wide range of equities. These data can be used to construct the beta of a portfolio as a weighted average of the betas of the component equity securities in the portfolio, using as weights the percentage of the current value of the portfolio invested in each equity issue. Few services provide estimates of beta for other than equity issues.

The major advantage of this class of single-factor models is that it is very easy to use in a variety of applications. It is well understood, and the data used in its estimation are readily available, at least for the equity markets. The major disadvantage is that it may not be descriptively accurate. If there exist more than one factor of variation affecting broad classes of securities, then the beta measure will systematically over- or underestimate the risk of particular securities. Furthermore the implicit assumption that the S&P 500 is the "market" is at least to be questioned. It is not clear that such a portfolio is sufficiently diversified, as it contains only equity issues and excludes small equity issues at that.

Multifactor Models

Multifactor models attempt to address the principal drawbacks of the single-factor models: the assumption of only one factor and the reliance on the return on a particular market composite as the single factor. However, they do so at the cost of some increase in the difficulty of estimation and application.

Formally, the multifactor model can be expressed as:

$$\text{Return on asset} = \text{Constant} + (b_1 \times \text{Factor 1}) + (b_2 \times \text{Factor 2})$$
$$+ \cdots + \text{Idiosyncratic component of return}$$

where

Factor 1, Factor 2, and so forth represent factors of variation in the economy as a whole that are common across all assets.

b_1, b_2, . . . represent the extent to which the particular asset in question is exposed to each of the factors. (The factors and factor exposures are analogous to the market factor and beta of the single-index model.)

Idiosyncratic component of returns represents the part of returns that is not related to the common factors and that can be diversified away in large portfolios.

The relationship between single- and multifactor models is similar to the relationship between simple and multiple regression. In fact, multiple regression may be used to estimate the coefficients of the multifactor model. To do this, one would first specify the factors of variation such as unexpected changes in unemployment, interest rates, and inflation. Then, for each asset, one would regress the time series of returns on that asset against the factors specified by the investigator. The coefficients obtained from such a time-series regression analysis would represent the factor exposures b_1, b_2, and so forth, for each asset under study.[15] However, it is difficult to specify all the potential common factors of variation on some a priori basis.

Another approach to estimating the multifactor model is to use *factor analysis,* which does not require the investigator to specify in advance what the factors of variation represent. Such analysis can be performed using many standard computer software packages. If a multifactor model generates observed returns, we should be able to infer factor exposures from the extent to which the time series of returns for different securities are correlated with each other. This is precisely what factor analysis does. It takes as input the correlation matrix of security returns and as output returns the factor exposures for each asset. In the parlance of factor analysis, the factor exposures are called *factor loadings,* and the factors themselves are referred to as *factor scores.* Given the ready availability of computer software, this procedure is very easy to apply. However, the results of such analysis are sometimes difficult to interpret. In addition, the factors identified by such an approach may not be particularly stable over time.

---

[15]This approach has been outlined in N. Chen, R. Roll, and S. A. Ross, "Economic Forces and the Stock Market," *Journal of Business,* 59, July 1986, pp. 383–403.

These procedures assume there is a large quantity of historical data on security returns. For this reason, the formalization of multifactor models has been largely restricted to the study of equity markets. However, the insights of the approach are clearly not limited to such markets. The study of term structure issues (in the case of bond markets) and real estate issues are amenable to this kind of analysis.

Where there is insufficient data for explicit estimates of factor exposures using multiple regression or factor analysis, other methods are available. One group of authors has considered input/output analysis as a way of relating the returns on different securities in a multifactor context by examining the interrelationship between the cash flows underlying each security.[16] Scenario analysis that asks "what if" questions that relate the possible returns of the security to the state of the economy within a top-down securities analysis approach can be best thought of in terms of such a multifactor model.

The factor exposures estimated for single- or multifactor models represent measures of risk specific to each security. These measures of risk reflect the extent to which the returns on that security relate to factors of variation in the economy as a whole. With sufficient data they can be estimated by regressing the *time series* of returns on the security against a *time series* of factor values. In the case of the single-index model the factor values represent returns on some market index. In the case of the multifactor model the factor values represent unexpected changes in macroeconomic factors, which in the case of factor analysis are in turn measured by the factor scores.[17]

The importance of each of these measures of risk can be weighed by the extent to which investors in the capital markets require a premium over and above the riskless return in order to bear such risks. Both the capital asset pricing model and the arbitrage pricing theory predict that the return investors expect to receive is given by the riskless return plus a measure of the quantity of risk (given by the risk exposures of the particular security) times a measure of the "price" of risk (given by the risk premiums that may differ according to the measure of risk but are constant across securities). In principle, with sufficient data, the risk premiums can be

---

[16]See P. Estep, N. Hanson, and C. Johnson, "Sources of Value and Risk in Common Stocks," *Journal of Portfolio Management*, Summer 1983, pp. 5–13.

[17]The measure of risk specific to a *portfolio* of assets is given at a point in time by a weighted average of the measures of security risk, where the weights are simply the percentage of the portfolio invested in each of the assets. In other words, the beta of a portfolio is simply the "portfolio" of the betas.

estimated by regressing the *cross section* of average security returns against the *cross section* of factor exposures.[18] Cross-section regressions of this type can be used to estimate the investor's required return on risky investments. In addition such regressions are used in the context of performance measurement to measure the performance that may be attributed to the risk borne by a particular money manager (see Chapter Eight).

CONCLUSION

This chapter is meant to serve as an overview of the quantitative methods used in the context of financial analysis. The mathematics of valuation and statistics and data analysis are tools to which every analyst should have ready access. This is not to say that every analyst needs to make frequent use of these tools, and it is not to suggest that use of the tools will unambiguously lead to large and positive returns. In the remainder of this book, we show how the tools can be applied in a variety of specialized areas of analysis.

REFERENCES

American Petroleum Institute. *Basic Petroleum Data Book* Vol. 5. Washington, D.C.: American Petroleum Institute, May 1985.

Chen, N.; R. Roll; and S. A. Ross. "Economic Forces and the Stock Market." *Journal of Business,* 9, July 1986, pp. 383–403.

Estep, P.; N. Hanson; and C. Johnson. "Sources of Value and Risk in Common Stocks." *Journal of Portfolio Management,* Summer 1983, pp. 5–13.

Ibbotson Associates. *Stocks, Bonds, Bills and Inflation: 1985 Yearbook.* Chicago: Ibbotson Associates, Capital Management Research Center, 1986.

Ross, S. A. "The Arbitrage Theory of Capital Asset Pricing." *Journal of Economic Theory* 3, December 1976, pp. 343–62.

Sharpe, W. "A Simplified Model for Portfolio Analysis," *Management Science,* 9, January 1963, pp. 277–93.

---

[18]Strictly speaking, this regression should be in the form of a *weighted least-squares* regression where the weights are given by the reciprocal of the estimated standard deviation of the idiosyncratic component of each security's return. In other words, the constant term, measures of risk, and average return for each security should be divided by the standard deviation of the idiosyncratic term prior to running the regression. If this is not done, the residuals from the cross-sectional regression will be said to be *heteroscedastic* (see footnote 10).

CHAPTER THREE

Quantitative Methods in Equity Analysis

H. Russell Fogler

INTRODUCTION

This chapter demonstrates the application of quantitative methods to equity analysis. It begins with a discussion of equity valuation within the context of a "bottom-up" philosophy whereby securities are evaluated on the basis of company-specific information. This discussion is followed by a section on factor analysis, which provides a "top-down" perspective whereby securities are evaluated according to their sensitivity to macroeconomic factors.

EQUITY VALUATION

ABC, the broadcasting network, had a total return of 82 percent for the first six months of 1985. Could this return have reasonably been anticipated by careful quantitative analysis?

The first step in addressing this question is to estimate the "theoretical or intrinsic value" of ABC by using what Wall Street calls a dividend discount model (DDM).

The basis for the DDM is simply the present value (PV) formula described in Chapter Two:

$$PV = \frac{C_1}{1 + r_1} + \frac{C_2}{(1 + r_2)^2} + \ldots + \frac{C_N}{(1 + r_N)^N} + \frac{P_N}{(1 + r_N)^N}$$

where *PV* is the present value of future cash flow streams from both dividends in each period ($C_1, C_2, \ldots C_N$) and a final projected price in period *N* (labeled P_N). In many applications the discount rate is assumed constant so that each cash fund is discounted at the same rate of *r*. For example, if ABC's 1984 dividend of $1.60 per share were projected to grow annually at 10 percent for the next five years, then the dividend discount model for January 1985 would have looked as follows:

$$P_{\text{Jan. 85}} = \frac{1.76}{1 + r} + \frac{1.94}{(1 + r)^2} + \frac{2.13}{(1 + r)^3} + \frac{2.34}{(1 + r)^4}$$
$$+ \frac{2.57}{(1 + r)^5} + \frac{P_N}{(1 + r)^5}$$

As the above equation illustrates, three forecasts are needed to calculate present value:

1. Price in the horizon year *N*.
2. Dividends up to the year *N*.
3. Discount rate *r*.

Thus the relevant question is "How accurately can these inputs be forecasted?"

Future price is the most difficult of the three forecasts. According to theory, P_N is the present value of all future dividends after *N*; that is, $D_{N+1}, D_{N+2}, \ldots D_\infty$. Also, the future discount rate (*r*) must be forecasted. In practice, forecasts are made of either dividends (D_N) or earnings (E_N) first, and then price is estimated by assigning an "appropriate" requirement for yield, price-earnings ratio, or capitalization rate. While we are often counseled that $P_N/(1 + r)^N$ becomes very small if *N* is very large, most practitioners set *N* at approximately five years because it is highly uncertain to forecast further ahead. Moreover, it is common to estimate several values for P_N with associated probabilities, thus incorporating one's uncertainty.

The forecast of dividends is somewhat easier. Usually, past history is available, management can be queried, and flow of funds can be projected for a given scenario. In our example, ABC had been paying a $1.60 a year for five years, so an increase in dividend was reasonable to expect, assuming that the cash was available. A growth rate of 10 percent is assumed in our example, since the dividend payout ratio was less than 25 percent of earnings and ABC's yield was relatively low in December 1984.

The forecast of *r* is more complex than dividends, although not nearly as difficult as forecasting final price (which of course requires a forecast of future discount rates as well)! First, one must determine if a single rate is to be used or whether a different rate should be used for each year. If multiple rates are to be used, an explicit interest rate forecast must be developed. One procedure is to examine the current yield curve for bonds and then to calculate the implied forward discount rate. Finally, given two stocks with identical dividend forecasts, if one stock is riskier, then that stock should have a lower valuation; thus r must be adjusted upward for company risk.

With the above caveats in mind, let us begin by estimating future dividends and earnings for the dividend discount model. We will accept our previous dividend forecast for ABC. Thus our next step is to forecast a final price five years from now (P_5). Two valuation methods will be examined for this task.

Constant growth model. If future dividends are assumed to grow at an assumed rate (g), then the present value formula becomes:

$$PV = \frac{C(1 + g)}{1 + r} + \frac{C(1 + g)^2}{(1 + r)^2} + \ldots + \frac{C(1 + g)^N}{(1 + r)^N} + \frac{P(1 + g)^N}{(1 + r)^N}$$

and it can be shown that if N is assumed to approach infinity the above formula is equal to:

$$PV = \frac{D}{r - g}$$

Let us suppose that $r = 13$ percent (we will explain why later); then we can estimate price in year five as:

$$P_5 = \frac{2.57}{.13 - .10} = \$85.67$$

Price-earnings model. A simpler version of the same idea is the price-earnings (P/E) model. If a company retains or holds back a percentage of its earnings (ABC, for example, pays out $1.60 from earnings of $6.39, or about 25 percent, and therefore retains about 75 percent), the above equation becomes:

$$PV = \frac{(1 - b)E}{r - g}$$

where b is the percentage of present earnings (E) held back or retained. Thus:

$$P/E = \frac{1 - b}{r - g}$$

and the price-earnings ratio in year five is estimated as:

$$P_5/E_5 = \frac{.25}{.13 - .10} = 8.33$$

If the 1984 earnings of $6.39 grew at 10 percent per year (versus 4.28 percent for 1980 through 1984), then E_5 would equal $10.29 and the forecasted price (P_5) would be $85.72. Furthermore, if we assume 13 percent is a fair rate of return for this investment, the present value would be:

$$PV = \frac{1.76}{1.13} + \frac{1.94}{1.28} + \frac{2.13}{1.44} + \frac{2.34}{1.63} + \frac{2.57}{1.84} + \frac{85.67}{1.84} = 53.88$$

Disappointingly, using this analysis we would *not* have bought ABC for our portfolio in December 1984. The present value of $53.88 is below the market price of $64.00.

An alternative use of the DDM is to calculate the internal rate of return from buying the stock now and holding it for five years, with the implicit assumption that the stock can be sold at the forecasted price. Thus, assuming we could buy ABC at $64 a share in December and assuming from the constant growth model above that the price five years from now equals $85.67, the equation to be solved is:

$$64 = \frac{1.76}{1 + r} + \frac{1.94}{(1 + r)^2} + \frac{2.13}{(1 + r)^3} + \frac{2.34}{(1 + r)^4} + \frac{2.57}{(1 + r)^5} + \frac{85.67}{(1 + r)^5}$$

or

$$r = 8.98 \text{ percent}$$

This approach also implies that ABC is an unattractive investment.

It may be worthwhile to take another look at ABC from a different perspective. First of all, ABC had been changing its financial complexion. It's long-term debt of $220.3 million in 1980 had been reduced to $140.5 million in 1984. This reduction, about $16 million a year, occurred while the equity base grew from $870.1 million to $1,352.3 million. Moreover, this reduction made a lot of sense. The early 1980s were years of very high interest rates, and ABC earned less on new investments than the rate of interest on new debt, thus effecting negative leverage.

"Excess debt capacity" seems to have evolved, assuming an optimal debt-equity mix exists (which is subject to debate). One conservative way to adjust for this debt capacity effect is to make the following assumption: If ABC simply stopped reducing its debt by approximately $16 million a year and paid dividends instead, its current dividend would rise from $1.60 to $2.15 in 1985 and grow at 10 percent. Using our previous techniques, our estimates would become:

Dividends to 1989 at 10 percent growth: $2.15, $2.37, $2.60, $2.86, $3.15.

Earnings per share 1989 at 10 percent growth: $10.29.

Price in 1989—constant growth model:

$$P_o = \frac{3.15}{.13 - .10} = \$105.00$$

Price in 1989—price-earnings model:

$$P/E = \frac{1 - b}{r - g} = \frac{.3365}{.13 - .10} = 11.216$$
$$P_5 = P_5/E_5 \times E_5$$
$$= 11.216 \times 10.29 = \$115.41$$

With the above estimates, the present value equation can be used to estimate either a fair price in December 1984 or the rate of return earned at a price of $64 per share. For example, using the more conservative estimate of P_5:

$$PV = \frac{2.15}{1.13} + \frac{2.37}{1.28} + \frac{2.60}{1.44} + \frac{2.86}{1.63} + \frac{3.15}{1.84} + \frac{105.00}{1.84} = \$66.01$$

and

$$\$64 = \frac{2.15}{1 + r} + \frac{2.37}{(1 + r)^2} + \frac{2.60}{(1 + r)^3} + \frac{2.86}{(1 + r)^4}$$
$$+ \frac{3.15}{(1 + r)^5} + \frac{105.00}{(1 + r)^5}$$
$$r = 13.74 \text{ percent}$$

Thus, after more detailed analysis, ABC would have been expected to earn a 0.74 percent return after risk adjustment. This return, of course, assumes

---

TABLE 3–1
DDM Estimates for ABC

| | PV Estimates | |
Assumptions	Original	Revised
1. $D_o = 1.60$, $P_s = \$85.67$	\$53.88	\$58.88
2. $D_o = 2.15$, $P_s = \$105.00$	66.01	71.01
3. $D_o = 2.15$, $P_s = \$115.41$	71.76	76.76

---

that no transaction costs are incurred to purchase ABC. Thus the market value of ABC in December 1984 appears fair at first glance.

Further analysis is warranted, though. How sensitive is the foregoing valuation to the assumptions used in applying the DDM? For example, what if $P_5 = \$115.41$ had been used? What if ABC becomes a takeover candidate? How would this development affect our assessment of its relative attractiveness?

The impact of different terminal prices can be handled easily by recomputing the present values and internal rates of return under new assumptions. For example, if P_5 were assumed to equal $\$115.41$, then $PV = \$71.76$ and $r = 15.73$ percent.

Issues such as what price might be paid in a merger are more difficult to deal with. In general the above present values and rates of return would need adjustment for potential synergies. For example, ABC appears to have approximately \$150 million of unused debt capacity based on its 1980 debt-equity ratio. This translates into about \$5.00 per share on its approximately 29.1 million shares. Thus, if a takeover were announced today, we would expect about \$5 per share more. And if one *assumes* that the above projections and risk would remain unchanged after borrowing \$150 million, then estimates in Table 3–1 show the resulting present values.

One approach for dealing with these uncertainties is to assign probabilities to the various outcomes. These probabilities, of necessity, are subjective—the result of experience, research, and even intuition. For example, assume that the probability distribution in Figure 3–1 reflects our assessment of the probable distribution of terminal price. Our analysis would have suggested ABC as a buy in December 1984. The mean price of the distribution is \$67.23 with a standard deviation of \$7.91. But the probability of results above the December price of \$64 is 80 percent versus a 20 percent probability for results below the current price.

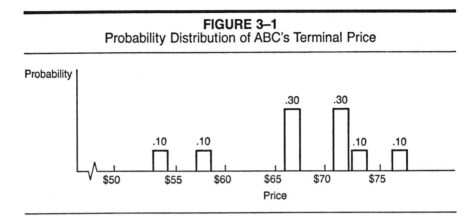

FIGURE 3–1
Probability Distribution of ABC's Terminal Price

The subsequent takeover battle and buyout of ABC by Capital Cities Communications at $121 per share reflected projected synergies well above the implicit estimates in the above analysis. It would be erroneous to infer that through the quantitative analysis described above, one could have anticipated the takeover and the resultant extraordinary return. An event as significant as the takeover but unfavorable could have occurred and caused ABC's return to be sharply negative. Over time and with diversified portfolios, unpredictable events should cancel each other out so that the fruits of careful quantitative analysis and sound judgment are manifested. The ABC example reflects both value added through analysis and extraordinary luck. The two should not be confused.

The function of security analysis and valuation may be to "skew" the distribution in your favor, realizing that incredible upside potential can seldom be foreseen but downside risks can be reduced.

DDM Assumptions

In models, simplifying assumptions are made, and these assumptions must be remembered. Sometimes their impact can be incorporated as part of the probability distribution, as was illustrated above. In other cases you may simply adjust your interpretation of extreme results. Yet in all cases of using DDMs the following assumptions should be recognized.

Assumption: No Yield Bias. Table 3–2 shows performance results for the best and worst 25 stocks annually on the Value Line data tape from 1973 to 1979. For example, reading from the last column, the S&P 500 averaged a 5.4 percent return, but the best performers earned 92 percent

TABLE 3-2
Best- and Worst-Performing Stocks
(standard deviations in parentheses)

	1973	1974	1975	1976	1977	1978	1979	Average
1. S&P 500 performance	−14.66	−26.47	37.20	23.84	−7.18	6.56	18.44	5.39
2. Best stocks:								
a. Performance	66	49	188	106	47	77	108	92
	(28)	(27)	(43)	(28)	(10)	(26)	(24)	
b. Valuation	187	355	838	590	447	333	340	441
	(263)	(347)	(501)	(290)	(359)	(270)	(328)	
c. Five-year earnings growth	28	17	29	41	30	21	20	27
	(24)	(21)	(13)	(24)	(16)	(20)	(25)	
d. Dividend yield	2.88	5.69	7.30	5.30	4.67	4.32	4.33	4.93
	(1.59)	(2.47)	(3.70)	(2.50)	(2.03)	(2.09)	(2.18)	
e. Price-earnings (P/E) ratio	16.43	6.88	4.86	7.34	9.49	7.24	6.81	8.44
	(6.44)	(5.66)	(3.14)	(5.63)	(7.72)	(2.74)	(2.41)	
f. Beta	0.91	1.13	1.19	1.14	1.05	1.17	1.08	1.10
	(.46)	(.33)	(.28)	(.22)	(.26)	(.25)	(.19)	
3. Worst stocks:								
a. Performance	−20	−58	−14	−16	−33	−77	−18	−34
	(6)	(2)	(8)	(6)	(4)	(26)	(10)	
b. Valuation	38	53	120	128	62	147	50	85
	(132)	(125)	(160)	(165)	(87)	(319)	(160)	
c. Five-year earnings growth	5	7	10	14	6	9	−1	7
	(22)	(17)	(15)	(12)	(12)	(27)	(14)	
d. Dividend yield	1.28	2.40	2.98	2.38	2.82	4.33	5.59	3.11
	(1.24)	(1.64)	(2.68)	(1.30)	(1.01)	(1.42)	(2.47)	
e. Price-earnings (P/E) ratio	24.38	16.92	13.43	18.99	13.13	9.34	10.04	
	(13.71)	(9.45)	(8.63)	(11.73)	(3.95)	(3.95)	(3.59)	
f. Beta	1.37	1.12	1.10	1.17	1.12	1.00	1.08	1.14
	(.39)	(.29)	(.25)	(.17)	(.13)	(.17)	(.24)	

SOURCE: B. D. Fielitz and F. L. Muller, "A Simplified Approach to Common Stock Valuation," *Financial Analysts Journal*, November–December 1985, pp. 34–41, Table 2. Performance, growth, and dividend yields are expressed as percents.

versus −34 percent for the worst performers (lines 2a and 3a). Lines 2b and 3b contain scaled values from a relatively simple DDM with an average value of 441 for the best performers versus 85 for the worst performers. Other studies also show that even simple DDMs differentiate successfully between the best and worst performers. But how can such simple approaches work in a reasonably efficient market? Part of the answer may be that certain biases worked well in many years, as discussed below.

Could the above results have been explained simply by buying stocks with high dividend yields and low P/E ratios? After all, "anomalies" of unexplained high returns came from small, high-yield, and low-P/E stocks throughout the 1970s and early 1980s (although anomalous returns might be reduced if transactions costs were charged for rebalancing). Possibly! The average value for dividend yield and P/E respectively was 4.93 percent and 8.44 for the best performers versus 3.11 percent and 15.18 for the worst performers. Perhaps the DDM is biased in that it systematically selects high-yield, low-P/E stocks. The success of the DDM may therefore depend on whether or not these attributes are in favor.

Assumption: Investor and Model Time Horizons Are Equal. The horizon problem arises from the fact that users of DDMs typically hold stocks for much shorter time periods than those implied by the model.

The source of such bias is easily seen by returning to the earlier example of ABC, when a takeover bid was assumed to add $5 to the present value of our forecasts. The adjustment of adding the $5 directly assumed that the takeover occurred today. If it had occurred in one year, the $5 would have only been $4.42 (that is, $5 ÷ 1.13). Or, if it occurred two years from now, the value would have dropped to $3.92 (that is, $5 ÷ 1.13²). And more importantly no single rate of return could be determined unless a specific date was assigned for the takeover bid because, for example:

$$\$64 = \frac{2.15}{1 + r} + \frac{71.01}{1 + r}$$

is *not* equal to

$$\$64 = \frac{2.15}{1 + r} + \frac{2.37}{(1 + r)^2} + \frac{71.01}{(1 + r)^2}$$

Assumption: $r - g$ Is Estimated Accurately. When applying quantitative methods, one should always ask "My analysis is most sensitive to what numbers?" In the dividend discount model, the denominator of

$(r - g)$ is the answer. For instance, in our ABC example assume three estimates of r: 12 percent, 13 percent, and 14 percent. Using our previous dividend forecast,

$$P_5 = \frac{\$2.57}{.12 - .10} = \$128.50$$

$$P_5 = \frac{\$2.57}{.13 - .10} = \$85.67$$

$$P_5 = \frac{\$2.57}{.14 - .10} = \$64.25$$

Thus inaccuracy of 2 percent in estimating either r or g leads to terminal price forecasts that are 100 percent different. This is especially critical, as both r and g are difficult to estimate. Let us consider the value r, for example.

Using the capital asset pricing model framework, one must estimate two parameters: the security's beta and the market return. At the end of December 1984, Treasury bills were yielding about 8 percent. Historically, common stocks have yielded about 7 percent over Treasury bills, but because real rates were about 2 percent higher than normal a 5 percent risk premium seems reasonable, so that the market's expected return is 13 percent. Additionally, although Value Line's five-year regression of weekly price changes estimated ABC's beta at 1.15, we estimated it at 1.00 based upon the changing financial structure (again, judgment is necessary). Thus the security market line that shows return as a function of beta would have looked like the line in Figure 3–2. And since ABC's beta is assumed to be 1.00, the required return equals

$$r = R_f + [b_{ABC} (R_m - R_f)]$$
$$= 8 + [1.00 (13 - 8)] = 13.00 \text{ percent}$$

Now let us consider our estimates of g. In our forecasts for ABC, we assumed that future dividends would grow at 10 percent for the next five years and then continue at that rate into the future. Sometimes a third stage is assumed if a company is in a rapid growth phase. For a rapidly growing small company, for example, it might be assumed that there would be no dividends for the next three years, then rapid growth in dividends for five years, and then average growth after that. Such a model is called a three-stage model because it explicitly specifies three different growth rates (see Figure 3–3). Of course, with personal computers available, it is easy to create whatever dividend stream is most appropriate. The greater

---

FIGURE 3–2
ABC: Estimated Security Market Line (SML)

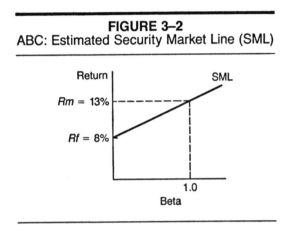

---

problem is the horizon problem discussed previously, as growth stocks require longer horizons than other stocks.

Assumption: No Estimation Error and Information Content. All of the problems and biases mentioned above are part of *estimation error*. Estimation error explicitly recognizes that we do not have perfect information; therefore *all* of our estimates have error.[1] The obvious question is "What can be done to reduce the error?" Combining information from

---

FIGURE 3–3
Dividend Growth in a Three-Stage Model

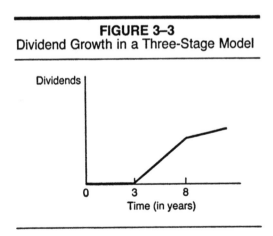

---

[1] For how to adjust for estimation error, see Daniel Rie, "How Trustworthy Is Your Valuation Model?" *Financial Analysts Journal,* November–December 1985, pp. 42–48.

various sources may be useful if the sources are not perfectly correlated, as discussed below.

Because there is estimation risk to one estimate, why not create a portfolio of estimates? For example, if several analysts have different DDM estimates of a stock's return, why not "average" these estimates? Two assumptions are implicit: (1) Each estimate has some predictive ability. (2) The estimates are not perfectly correlated over time; that is, they do not miss at the same time in the same direction. A simple measure of information content could be the historical correlation between an analyst's forecasts versus the actual outcomes. If this calculation were made for several analysts while also computing the correlation between them, then their estimates can be averaged to minimize overall forecast error. This approach has been termed the *information coefficient* approach, as coefficients between 0 and 1 are used to measure the degree of an analyst's forecasting ability. Then, having calculated the correlation between analysts, an optimal weighting procedure is calculated.[2]

Regression Analysis

Suppose you hypothesize that ABC's monthly returns are caused mainly by movements in the overall market. A positive residual error may suggest an overvalued stock, whereas a negative residual error may suggest undervaluation. Testing this hypothesis by regressing ABC's monthly returns against the Standard & Poor's 500 Stock Average's returns for 1980 through 1984 showed:

$$R_{ABC,t} = .74 + .56 \times R_{S\&P,t} + e_{ABC,t}$$
$$(.73) \quad (2.47)$$

where

$R_{ABC,t}$ and $R_{S\&P,t}$ = Monthly returns of ABC and the S&P 500 Index, respectively.

$e_{ABC,t}$ = Residual error in month t.

Numbers in parentheses are the t-statistics for rejecting a hypothesis that the true intercept and slope are zero. Thus, in months when the S&P return was zero, ABC's return would have averaged 74 basis points, although the variation was so great that no statistical significance is apparent

---

[2]Keith Ambachtsheer and James L. Farrell, Jr., "Can Active Management Add Value?" *Financial Analysts Journal,* November–December 1979, pp. 39–47.

from the t-statistic. The coefficient of .56 on ABC's sensitivity to S&P's returns has a t-statistic of 2.47, which is significant at the 5 percent level (but not at the 1 percent level). Thus we might conclude that it is likely some relationship exists, but it is not as strong as we would like. The R^2 for the regression was only 9.5 percent, thus further reducing our confidence in the explanatory power because only 9.5 percent of the variation in ABC's return was attributable to the S&P 500's return.

Table 3–3 presents ABC's residual errors as well as residual errors from similar regressions for CBS, Cox Communications, and Salomon Brothers' Bond Index. Three features stand out. First, a number of large outlying observations occurred for ABC's errors. The average monthly return was just over 1 percent, so absolute errors of 10 percent or larger are substantial. Second, no consistent trend of over- or underprediction is evident, despite our earlier analysis that suggested ABC's financial risk was declining over time. And third, several of ABC's largest residuals were correlated with the residuals of the Salomon Brothers Bond Index, but none were correlated with the residuals of Cox Communications.

With the above observations in mind, three approaches might help to improve the explanatory power of the model: (1) use the same model with "better" data, (2) use a "better" estimating procedure than least-squares regression, or (3) add more variables to the model. Better data might involve using weekly data instead of monthly data. For example, Value Line's beta of 1.15 was estimated from five years of weekly price changes for ABC against the price change of the New York Stock Exchange Index; such weekly data might not have as many large outliers and thus might be more reliable. Another method of improving data is to transform it; for example, when asset size is entered into regression models it is generally transformed by using its logarithm.

In contrast to obtaining better data, another method of estimation may be more appropriate. Beta estimates tend to drift toward the market beta of 1.0 (very low historical betas tend to rise, and very high betas tend to decline).[3]

Bayesian estimation captures this drift tendency, with the resulting estimates including the expected drift. "Stein estimators" are another method for reducing drift, and these estimates cause stocks with great

---

[3]Many commercial services use adjustment procedures to capture this drift tendency. For a short discussion and details, see Meir Statman, "Betas Compared: Merrill Lynch versus Value Line," *Journal of Portfolio Management*, Winter 1981, pp. 41–44.

TABLE 3–3
Residuals from Regressions on the S&P Index, 1980–1984

		Residual Errors			
Year	Month	ABC	CBS	Cox Communications	Salomon Brothers Bond Index
1980	1	− 12.41	− 5.75	− 6.09	− 9.58
	2	− 13.10	− 6.05	− 3.04	− 7.41
	3	7.13	5.05	5.11	2.68
	4	− 19.54	− 8.55	7.10	12.05
	5	8.94	4.51	4.49	2.94
	6	− 4.48	− 4.96	− 6.15	2.09
	7	− 0.21	3.18	4.27	− 7.70
	8	4.34	− 1.35	19.44	− 5.44
	9	4.78	− 0.78	− 2.00	− 4.00
	10	− 10.26	− 5.14	− 8.68	− 2.96
	11	− 14.08	− 6.95	1.93	− 4.56
	12	− 4.70	− 2.72	2.24	3.57
1981	1	7.27	10.11	5.52	− 0.36
	2	7.16	8.34	1.53	− 3.73
	3	3.34	− 3.05	16.99	1.04
	4	− 1.91	9.29	− 3.40	− 7.72
	5	0.64	− 2.66	5.96	5.59
	6	− 4.18	− 2.21	− 5.43	− 0.28
	7	− 3.65	− 0.65	− 8.13	− 4.31
	8	1.59	− 4.55	5.33	.− 1.94
	9	5.94	3.36	1.85	− 0.91
	10	19.98	4.24	6.75	3.40
	11	− 8.80	− 10.23	− 8.76	10.97
	12	− 1.36	− 2.82	2.92	− 5.24
1982	1	− 3.50	− 4.82	− 2.18	− 1.47
	2	− 6.66	2.35	0.04	4.26
	3	13.16	− 6.02	− 1.32	2.10
	4	7.74	1.28	− 12.19	1.59
	5	0.61	− 3.57	− 5.90	1.85
	6	5.04	− 3.42	− 9.54	− 2.27
	7	2.07	5.35	10.38	6.76
	8	8.42	10.01	3.72	2.52
	9	4.21	0.28	1.58	4.81
	10	− 4.79	4.25	3.15	4.42
	11	12.17	16.53	0.58	− 1.39
	12	2.39	− 6.53	1.82	0.27
1983	1	− 9.00	− 4.79	0.28	− 3.03
	2	0.54	2.56	− 1.85	2.84
	3	11.92	9.44	− 3.34	− 1.36
	4	− 0.62	0.20	0.38	2.30
	5	− 5.91	− 8.72	− 1.48	− 2.10

TABLE 3–3 *(concluded)*

Year	Month	ABC	CBS	Cox Communications	Salomon Brothers Bond Index
				Residual Errors	
	6	− 1.27	− 2.06	0.75	− 1.14
	7	− 6.33	1.20	−12.11	− 1.14
	8	− 5.31	1.16	− 4.64	− 0.24
	9	3.65	9.70	3.19	3.11
	10	− 1.70	− 2.71	− 2.34	− 0.70
	11	− 4.37	− 2.34	− 8.36	0.12
	12	− 1.01	− 1.74	− 2.75	− 1.14
1984	1	4.85	− 0.26	− 5.25	2.91
	2	− 9.76	− 0.88	1.33	− 1.85
	3	11.34	12.16	− 0.70	− 2.99
	4	− 0.70	1.20	12.21	− 1.84
	5	− 0.08	4.61	− 2.45	− 2.97
	6	8.10	6.27	11.97	− 0.40
	7	1.05	2.18	− 8.60	8.31
	8	3.31	− 4.33	−10.30	− 3.24
	9	− 0.93	− 0.91	1.86	2.61
	10	− 7.89	− 5.81	− 0.68	6.39
	11	− 8.10	− 6.43	2.55	1.35
	12	4.84	− 0.69	− 4.26	− 1.01

variability to have their return reduced toward the average return.[4] Still another approach is to reestimate beta based on a cross-section sample of many companies, comparing their fundamental accounting ratios. Each company's beta is the dependent variable, and the independent variables are attributes such as payout, earnings variability, company size, and growth rate.[5] This last estimation procedure, of course, both changes the estimation procedure and adds more variables. The next section addresses this addition of variables.

[4]See Joe Lavely, Gordon Wakefield, and Bob Barrett, "Toward Enhancing Beta Estimates," *Journal of Portfolio Management*, Summer 1980, pp. 43–46.

[5]For example, see Vinay V. Marathe, "Portfolio Beta Estimation," in *The Investment Manager's Handbook*, ed. Sumner N. Levine (Homewood, Ill.: Dow Jones–Irwin, 1980), pp. 202–21.

Multiple Regression Analysis

Multiple regression analysis may help to explain more of the variation in a company's returns and improve one's confidence that a high residual error indicates an overvalued stock whereas a negative residual error indicates undervaluation. Such a procedure allows relative comparison of all stocks in your data base. And with readily available data bases for personal computers, this research can be both efficient and inexpensive.

Burton Malkiel and John Cragg developed and tested the following model in the late 1960s:[6]

$$\frac{P}{NE} = a_o + a_1 g + \frac{a_2 E_{t+1}}{NE} + \frac{a_3 D}{NE} + a_4 I$$

where

P = End-of-year market price per share.

NE = Average "normalized" earnings estimates of security analysts.

g = Average predicted future long-term annual growth of earnings per share.

E_{t+1} = Average predicted earnings per share for the next year.

D = Total dividends paid per share.

I = Predicted instability index of the future earnings stream.

The earnings variables (NE, E_{t+1}, g, and I) were predicted by security analysts. Seventeen investment firms (four brokerage houses, five banks, five mutual funds, two pension fund managers, and one life insurance company) participated except for the growth estimates, which were supplied by only nine of the analysts.

The coefficients (the a's) of this equation were estimated by multiple regression analysis of 178 large corporations for the years 1961 to 1965, and the results presented in Table 3–4 permit several interesting observations:

1. *Signs are consistent and significant.* One desirable feature in regression analysis is a consistency of signs over various years. Also, the coefficients are generally significant on all the variables, and the signs are as one would expect (positive on earnings and dividends, negative on risk).

2. *Coefficients change over time.* Although the sign remains consistently positive or negative, the magnitude of the coefficients shifts, some-

---

[6]See Burton G. Malkiel and John G. Cragg, "Expectations and the Structure of Share Prices," *American Economic Review*, September 1970, pp. 601–17.

times considerably. For example, 1961 was the year when investors were enthusiastic about growth, while in 1962 the market experienced a 25 percent setback in five months and many growth stocks suffered sharp losses. As can be seen, the coefficients on the growth variable were highest in 1961, while the risk coefficient was the lowest; just the opposite results occurred in 1962 after the bear market.

3. *Predicted long-term growth contributes most to P/E ratios.* The *t*-values of the long-term growth variable were extremely large in all five samples. This high correlation could, however, reflect a feedback effect—that is, a high price-earnings ratio reinforcing the analysts' tendency to predict high growth.

4. *Explanatory power is relatively high.* The R^2 of approximately 80 percent indicates that about 80 percent of the variation in the price-earnings ratios for that year can be explained by variation in the other variables.

5. *Short-term growth variable adds stability.* The variable E_{t+1}/NE is the percentage growth expected next year, in contrast to g, which is the expected long-term growth rate. While it is not evident from Table 3–4, Malkiel and Cragg also showed that the yearly variation in the equation's coefficients was substantially reduced by adding this short-term growth variable.

While the above five statements summarize Table 3–4's results, important insights were offered by other parts of their work as well as other studies. For example, financial leverage was found to be at least as significant a risk measure as earnings instability, and beta was not as effective as either; however, high correlations existed between all three of these risk measures.

Multiple regression analysis is a useful tool for identifying attributes that proxy for the systematic components of a company's return and, by extension, the part of return that is company-specific, residual return. If one believes in the reversal of company-specific returns, then multiple regression analysis might help to distinguish undervalued and overvalued companies.

FACTOR ANALYSIS

The foregoing discussion focused on analysis to uncover information specific to a particular company. This type of research activity is referred to

---

TABLE 3–4
Multiple Regression Model

$$\frac{P}{NE} = a_0 + a_1 g + \frac{a_2 E_{t+1}}{NE} + \frac{a_3 D}{NE} + a_4 I$$

Coefficients

Year	a_0	a_1	a_2	a_3	a_4	R^2
1961	−27.96	+2.91	+31.78	+4.57	− .58	.77
		(.21)	(5.76)	(3.96)	(.70)	
	13.56	5.51	1.15	− .83		
1962	+3.42	+1.61	+6.88	+3.21	−2.20	.79
	(.12)	(2.87)	(2.32)	(.41)		
1963	−11.33	+2.29	+15.11	+8.11	−1.14	.80
	(.14)	(2.82)	(2.70)	(.39)		
	16.30	5.35	3.01	−2.88		
1964	−9.29	+1.87	+15.20	+7.03	−1.13	.78
	(.14)	(1.94)	(2.40)	(.41)		
	13.05	7.83	2.92	−2.75		
1965	−11.15	+2.42	+13.78	+4.22	− .81	.83
	(.12)	(1.85)	(2.34)	(.38)		
	19.59	7.46	1.81	−2.14		

Note: Numbers in parentheses below coefficients are standard errors, and numbers below parentheses are *t*-values.

SOURCE: Burton G. Malkiel and John G. Cragg, "Expectations and the Structure of Share Prices," *American Economic Review*, September 1970, p. 612, Table 5.

---

as bottom-up analysis. The following discussion concentrates on an approach that is called top-down. As this term suggests, factor analysis is concerned with identifying systematic factors that affect security returns. This approach requires one to anticipate the factor returns and then to find companies that will benefit by their exposure to these factors.

In estimating the beta of ABC, its returns and residuals seemed related to at least two factors: the S&P index's return and CBS's return. Thus we might have hypothesized a two-factor model to explain returns:

$$R_{ABC,t} = R_{f,t} + b_{ABC,1} f_{1,t} + b_{ABC,2} f_{2,t} + e_{ABC,t}$$

where

$R_{ABC,t}$ = ABC's return in time period t.

$R_{f,t}$ = Return on a riskless asset during t.

$b_{ABC,i}$ specifies the percentage change in ABC's return for a given level of f_i.

$e_{ABC,t}$ is a random error term.

$f_{1,t}$ might represent the excess market return over the riskless rate, as proxied by Standard & Poor's index.

$f_{2,t}$ might be an index of excess returns on major broadcasting stocks.

Factor analysis is a mathematical procedure for calculating indexes that best explain the variation within a sample set of data. Table 3–5 contains a set of such indexes for several stock and bond indexes, as well as individual stocks. Each of the coefficients might be considered as a "beta" that varies between plus and minus one. For example, the first factor index has a correlation of 97 percent with the S&P 500 Index. Hence this might be thought of as the market effect. ABC's returns have a correlation of 37 percent with the index. The second factor is harder to interpret; its heaviest loadings are Salomon Brothers Bond Index, ABC, CBS, EXXON (negative), Schlumberger (negative), American Brands, and Atlantic Richfield (negative). This second index may reflect oil and commodity price inflation, as a drop in such prices might raise bond prices, lower interest rates, and reduce oil company profits relatively. The third index may be long-term interest rates (the Bond Index and American Brands load positively), while the fourth may be short-term rates.

The above analysis has some very important implications—or good news! Because the indexes were calculated by principal components analysis, they successively explain the greatest amount of remaining variation, independent of the other indexes. The amounts of variation explained by each of the four indexes were 43 percent, 11 percent, 8 percent, and 6 percent—a cumulative total of 68 percent of the variation in the indexes and stocks. Thus we start to see that there are a few really important factors in the return-generating process. Numerous other studies also document the presence of three or four general factors related to market effects, interest rates, inflation, and so on.[7]

Unfortunately such factor indexes have important limitations—the bad news! First, although they explain past movements exactly, it is hard to know what economic forces are influencing them (hence a large number of "maybes" in examining these indexes). Second, because they explain

---

[7]See Nai-fu Chen, Richard Roll, and Stephen A. Ross, "Economic Forces and the Stock Market," *Journal of Business*, 59, July 1986, pp. 383–403.

TABLE 3–5
First Four Factor Loadings

	Factor 1	Factor 2	Factor 3	Factor 4
Standard & Poor's 500 Index	0.97	−0.04	0.09	−0.01
Cash equivalents	−0.30	0.09	0.29	0.61
Salomon Brothers Bond Index	0.30	0.43	0.57	0.05
American Stock Exchange Index	0.86	−0.22	0.00	−0.09
New York Stock Exchange Index	0.98	−0.04	0.08	0.02
Wishire 5000 Index	0.98	−0.06	0.05	0.03
ABC	0.37	0.61	−0.32	0.33
CBS	0.58	0.48	−0.24	0.19
Cox Communications	0.59	0.21	−0.15	0.23
Exxon	0.64	−0.52	0.31	0.02
Schlumberger	0.65	−0.47	0.26	0.20
American Brands	0.44	0.40	0.50	0.02
Avon Products	0.43	0.33	0.06	0.36
Chase Manhattan Bank	0.75	−0.19	0.18	0.02
Diamond Shamrock	0.75	−0.19	0.18	0.02
Charming Shoppes	0.60	0.13	−0.34	0.24
Manor Care	0.64	0.30	−0.23	0.26
Gerber Scientific	0.69	−0.06	−0.27	0.33
Atlantic Richfield	0.49	−0.54	−0.02	0.44
Variance explained	0.43	0.11	−0.08	0.06
Cumulative variance	0.43	0.54	0.62	0.68

Note: The above loadings and indexes were calculated by *principal components* analysis, which can be considered a special case of factor analysis. In principal components, no specification of the number of factors is made; rather, successive sources of variation are calculated until all variation is explained. By contrast, factor calculations parcel variation into systematic factor-explained variation and residual idiosyncratic variation. Generally, the factor interpretations will not depend on the technique chosen if samples are large, although the loading estimates will vary.

the past movements exactly, indexes (other than the first) are often nonstationary over time.[8] Third, to be very accurate, one needs to prespecify the exact number of factor indexes, and there is no way to do this precisely.[9]

---

[8]See Stephen R. Cosslett and H. Russell Fogler, "Factor Nonstationarity in Large Samples: A Note" (Unpublished manuscript, 1986).

[9]Various statistical tests are available to test the hypothesis that *k* factors are sufficient to explain returns. Yet, if the true process has five factors but the fifth's explanatory power is small, the tests may not reject a hypothesis that the true underlying process is a four-factor process.

The Theory Behind the Factors[10]

Factor models have just two purposes: (1) to attribute portfolio returns and (2) to adjust returns for systematic risk.

Factor models for attributing return are merely linear equations that express the statement:

$$R_i = E_o + b_{i1}f_1 + b_{i2}f_2 + \ldots + b_{iK}f_K + e_i$$

where R_i is the return on the ith stock, E_o is the expected return, plus the price change represented by the ith stock's return sensitivities (b_{ik}) to k factors multiplied by the factors' changes (f_k), plus e_i, which is some idiosyncratic return not explained by the other terms.

Factor models for risk adjusting are also linear equations but with systematic factors only; thus

$$R_i = E_o + b_{i1}f_1 + b_{i2}f_2 + \ldots + b_{is}f_s + e_i$$

where S is the number of systematic factors. *Systematic factors* are sources of variation that cannot be diversified away. For example, an economic depression affects virtually all stocks, as does unanticipated inflation; thus overall economic activity and inflation would be systematic factors. *Unsystematic factors* are sources of variation that can be diversified away. For example, building stocks may be highly correlated, but one's portfolio can hold just one or two such stocks in combination with other stocks that do well when building stocks do poorly (possibly stocks that do well when interest rates rise). Finally, according to theory, higher *systematic* risk causes higher long-run returns, so that the return expected in the future (ex ante return) will be related to these systematic factors:

$$E_i = g_o + g_1 b_{i1} + g_a b_{ia} + \ldots g_s b_{is}$$

where E_i represents the stock's *ex ante expected return*, g_o represents the implied riskless rate and g_1 through g_n represent the market prices of risk, the quantities of which are represented by the stock return sensitivities b_{i1} through b_{is}. In a present value model, the ex ante expected return determines the appropriate discount rate r to be used in the analysis.

What are the systematic factors? Frankly we do not know, and ulti-

---

[10]For a simple discussion of the relationship of the arbitrage pricing theory to factor models, see H. Russell Fogler, "Common Sense on CAPM, APT, and Correlated Residuals," *Journal of Portfolio Management,* Summer 1982, pp. 20–28.

mately this is an empirical issue.[11] The most obvious sources of greatest nondiversifiable variation can be hypothesized from our extended dividend discount model. Obvious candidates are changes in real economic activity, interest rates, inflation, and dividends. Evidence suggests that at least three or four systematic factors exist. Two popular four-factor name tags are (1) growth–cyclical–stable–energy and (2) real production–inflation–credit premium–term structure slope.[12] Yet, while research on verifying systematic factors may continue for long into the future, use of simple and straightforward factor models for return attribution and portfolio management are currently very effective.

How to Use Factor Models for Attributing Return

Suppose you wanted to attribute the S&P return to its factor composition. To do so, you would need the average effect of each factor (that is, the *factor sensitivity* coefficient) and the characteristics of the S&P index's factors. These values are presented in Table 3–6.

With only four common factors (beta, yield, size, and price), the small unexplained return of 0.64 percent is rather good. Of course, you may ask "Why is there any error for a portfolio as large as the S&P average?" There are several important causes:

- *Only a few factors were included.* Many common factors and sector/industry factors generate returns. Only four sector effects were included, as a first-step regression showed that the other sector effects were not statistically significant.

---

[11]Two concepts are crucial to understanding the empirical issue. First, theory is based on return-risk trade-off for expected (ex ante, or future) return, although hypothesis testing can only be conducted with actual (ex post, or after the facts are in) data. Second, *any* two or more sets of data can be used to explain ex post results, *if* the data sets have the same number of dependent factors. This is a subtle point that is best illustrated by the two equation systems:

$$2X + 3Y = 12 \qquad 1A + 1B = 12$$
$$2X + 1Y = 8 \qquad 2A + 1B = 8$$

Although the solution values for (X,Y) are different than for (A,B), both systems are equal to (12,8); then both systems can be said to "explain" (12,8).

In our world of uncertainty the empirical issue becomes a choice of variables—which variables $(X,Y$ versus $A,B)$ provide the most stable relationship with the greatest explanatory power.

[12]See, for example, James L. Farrell, Jr., *Guide to Portfolio Management* (New York: McGraw-Hill, 1983), pp. 205–13; Chen et al., "Economic Forces."

TABLE 3–6
Factor Sensitivity Coefficients of the S&P Index

	Factor Sensitivity	S&P Average, Third Quarter 1986	Return Attribution
Starting point (intercept)	15.22%		15.22%
Beta	− 5.67	1.00	− 5.67
Yield	− .58	4.18	− 2.42
Size (in natural logarithm)	− 1.06	14.85	−15.74
Price	.12	.39	4.68
Sectors:			
Capital goods	2.76	.05	.14
Materials and service	1.96	.10	.20
Energy	2.55	.14	.36
Financial	− 3.76	.07	−.26
Consumer nondurables	0	.29	.00
Utilities	0	.13	.00
Transportation	0	.03	.00
Consumer durables	0	.04	.00
Technology	0	.15	.00
Unexplained return			.64
S&P return			− 4.13%

- *The estimates were from a different set of stocks than the S&P.* The sample was 1,249 companies with equity capitalization over $25 million.
- *Ordinary least-squares regression was used.* Each stock was weighted equally although the S&P total return depends on the capitalization weight of each stock. Also, all estimates have some sampling error as well as implicitly assuming independence and normality in the residuals (an unlikely result, given the effects from missing factors).
- *Rounding and averaging may cause some slight amount of error.* Although this effect is almost negligible, one should remember the logarithm of an average size will be less than the average of the logarithms of size.

Given the above limitations, should such factor attribution be discarded? The answer is no, not if it adds useful information. But one must be careful in using it. First, the amount of return explained (R^2) in *individual stocks* was only about 8 percent, which is similar to the results found by others in cross-sectional regressions although about 40 percent

TABLE 3–7
Factor Sensitivities of an Equally Weighted Portfolio

	Portfolio	S&P
Expected return (DDM forecast)	12.57%	13.10%
Yield	3.09%	4.28%
P/E ratio	12.86	11.14
Growth	9.60%	8.30%
Factor price sensitivities		
Real GNP	26.53	21.48
Short-term interest rates	−2.77	−2.76
Inflation	−10.09	−8.37
Oil prices	.64	1.20
Defense spending	−1.26	−1.20

is explained over a number of years. And for *portfolios* the explanatory power will be much higher. Also, if a "normal portfolio" is specified as a manager's benchmark, then a manager's ability can be understood by examining how much more or less return is attributed to each factor in his portfolio relative to the factor exposure of the benchmark. Such analysis may help to distinguish whether a portfolio's return is attributable to luck or to skill.[13]

Building a Portfolio with Factor Bets

In Table 3–7, which illustrates an equally weighted portfolio, the factor sensitivities indicate relative return sensitivity to changes in each economic factor.[14] For example, the real GNP sensitivity indicates that a change of 1 percent in real GNP would cause a 26.53 percent change in our portfolio's price versus a change of 21.48 percent in the price of the S&P index. These factor sensitivities were estimated by simulating alternative economic scenarios and measuring the resulting return changes as forecasted by a dividend discount model.

Several portfolio characteristics are immediately evident. For example, the portfolio has a lower expected return than the S&P 500 (12.57 percent

[13]For a discussion of the theory of such performance measurement, see Mark Kritzman, "How to Detect Skill in Management Performance," *Journal of Portfolio Management*, Winter 1986, pp.16–20.

[14]This section is abstracted from Michelle Clayman et al., *Stockfacts* (New York: Salomon Brothers, 1985), pp. 35–40.

TABLE 3–8
Four Screens for Portfolio Adjustments

Screen	Factor Sensitivity	Expected Return
1. High oil sensitivities		
Rowan Cos	0.54	
Texaco	0.50	
Halliburton	0.30	
Texas Instruments	0.15	
Nalco Chemical	0.05	
2. High GNP sensitivities (Low Expected Returns)		
Rexnord	1.42	12.73
Advanced Micro Devices	1.25	12.36
Intel	1.25	11.69
Motorola	1.25	12.93
LTV	1.12	0.00
Abbott Laboratories	1.10	13.11
Halliburton	1.04	12.70
Hewlett-Packard	1.04	12.70
New York Times Co–Class A	1.03	12.03
3. High defense sensitivities		
General Dynamics	0.36	14.83
Boeing	0.28	13.57
Lockheed	0.24	14.34
Advanced Micro Devices	0.02	12.36
Intel	0.02	11.69
Texas Instruments	0.01	11.82
Sundstrand	0.01	13.72
4. High expected returns		
Boeing		13.57
Citicorp		16.77
Clorox		13.83
General Dynamics		14.83
General Signal		13.92
International Business Machines		13.74
ITT		14.65
Kimberly-Clark		13.96
Lockheed		14.34
Ned Bancorp		16.12
J. C. Penney		13.89
Security Pacific		15.66
Sundstrand		13.72
United Technologies		14.58
Warner-Lambert		13.51

versus 13.10 percent). It has slightly more GNP sensitivity, slightly lower oil sensitivity, and slightly higher defense sensitivity.

After examining the portfolio, suppose that we decide upon the following objectives:

- Raise expected return without increasing exposure to GNP.
- Reduce the oil sensitivity.
- Raise the defense sensitivity.
- Turn over not more than 20 percent of the portfolio.

Thus both specific security returns (bottom-up analysis) and economic factor bets (top-down economic analysis) must be combined at this portfolio construction phrase.

Table 3–8 contains four screens. The first screen identifies the oil-sensitive stocks, and the second screen contains GNP-sensitive stocks with low expected return. The third screen shows the defense-sensitive stocks, and the final screen has companies with high expected returns.

Suppose we sell Rowan Companies, Halliburton, Advanced Micro Devices, Intel, and Motorola, replacing them with General Dynamics, Sundstrand, NED Bancorp, Kimberly-Clark, and Warner-Lambert. Recalculating our portfolio statistics, we would find that the new portfolio's expected return exactly equals that of the S&P 500. The energy sensitivity is zero, while GNP price sensitivity is reduced slightly. The portfolio's defense sensitivity is higher. This means that if there were no changes in economic expectations, the portfolio could be expected to perform in line with the S&P 500. If, however, expectations for defense spending were to rise or expectations for GNP and oil prices were to fall, then the portfolio would be likely to perform better than the S&P 500.

As the portfolio was actively tracked from the end of the third quarter 1984 to the end of the first quarter 1985, the original portfolio has a total return of 9.5 percent, while the restructured portfolio was up to 15.2 percent (the corresponding return for the S&P 500 was 11.0 percent). In this case the alteration of the portfolio's economic sensitivities along with the identification of "cheap" stocks from the DDM added 470 basis points in incremental return. Obviously factor analysis can make a difference but does not guarantee superior performance.

CONCLUSION

Whereas equity valuation allows one to construct portfolios from a bottom-up perspective, factor analysis provides the technology to construct portfolios from the top down. If one is skillful at anticipating the direction of factors, it is possible to identify companies that will benefit by their exposure to various factors. These approaches are not mutually exclusive. Rather, valuation and factor analysis can be used in conjunction with each other and especially in conjunction with sound judgment.

REFERENCES

Ambachtsheer, K., and J. L. Farrell, Jr. "Can Active Management Add Value?" *Financial Analysts Journal,* November-December 1979, pp. 39-47.

Chen, N.; R. Roll; and S. A. Ross. "Economic Forces and the Stock Market" *Journal of Business,* 59, July 1986, p. 383–403.

Clayman, M.; T. Estep; S. Hamilton; P. Joblansky; K. McMahon; A. Sasdi; S. Start; and C. Ciaccio. *Stockfacts.* New York: Salomon Brothers, 1985.

Cosslett, S. R., and H. R. Fogler. "Factor Nonstationarity in Large Samples: A Note." Unpublished manuscript, 1986.

Farrell, J. L., Jr. *Guide to Portfolio Management.* New York: McGraw-Hill, 1983.

Fielitz, B. D., and F. L. Muller. "A Simplified Approach to Common Stock Valuation." *Financial Analysts Journal,* November-December 1985, pp. 34–41.

Fogler, H. R. "Common Sense on CAPM, APT, and Correlated Residuals." *Journal of Portfolio Management,* Summer 1982, pp. 20–28.

Kritzman, M. "How to Detect Skill in Management Performance." *Journal of Portfolio Management,* Winter 1986, pp. 16–20.

Lavely, J.; G. Wakefield; and B. Barrett. "Toward Enhancing Beta Estimates." *Journal of Portfolio Management,* Summer 1980, pp. 43–46.

Malkiel, B. G., and J. G. Cragg. "Expectations and the Structure of Share Prices." *American Economic Review,* September 1970, pp. 601–17.

Marathe, V. V. "Portfolio Beta Estimation." In *The Investment Manager's Handbook,* ed. Sumner N. Levine. Homewood, Ill.: Dow Jones-Irwin, 1980, pp. 202–21.

Rie, D. "How Trustworthy Is Your Valuation Model?" *Financial Analysts Journal,* November-December 1985, pp. 42–48.

Statman, M. "Betas Compared: Merrill Lynch versus Value Line." *Journal of Portfolio Management,* Winter 1981, pp. 41–44.

Quantitative Methods in Fixed-Income Analysis

Roger G. Ibbotson and Margaret A. Corwin

Fixed-income securities are contracts that usually entitle the holder to a series of cash flows or interest payments as well as a return of principal. This chapter addresses the quantitative methods that may be used to analyze such contracts. The first part of the chapter addresses bond valuation issues and the measurement of returns. The second part addresses bond yields. The final section addresses portfolio considerations and how interest rate sensitivity can be managed.

VALUATION OF FIXED-INCOME SECURITIES

Elements of Bonds

The *par value* of a bond is the value printed on the face of a bond certificate. This principal (face) amount is the amount that must eventually be repaid and approximates the amount borrowed by the issuer. The most common par value of U.S. government and corporate bonds is $1,000. In

---
NOTE: This chapter is adapted with permission from a chapter in Roger G. Ibbotson and Gary P. Brinson, *Investment Markets: Gaining the Performance Advantage* (New York: McGraw-Hill Book Company. Copyright (c) 1987, McGraw-Hill, Inc.).

this country, bond prices are usually quoted in a price per $100 of face value; United Utilities' 10 percent bonds, maturing in 20 years, might sell for $90 or about 90 percent of face value, which means they have an actual price of $900 per $1,000 bond.

As the United Utilities example illustrates, a bond's market *price* is usually not equal to its face value. This price is determined in the market by the bond's coupon rate, maturity date, call provisions, tax status, and default risk, as well as prevailing interest rates. Each of these factors is considered in turn.

In addition to a return of principal, most bonds promise a series of cash payments. The amount of those payments is determined by the *coupon rate*, usually expressed as a percentage of the principal (par) amount. For example, the United Utilities bond with a 10 percent coupon produces 10 percent interest on the $1,000 face value, or an annual interest of $100. If the bond sells above or below $1,000 the coupon remains at $100. The bond would have an annual yield greater than 10 percent if the bond were to sell for less than $1,000. If the bond sold above $1,000 the annual yield would be less than 10 percent. Coupons are usually paid semiannually, and such yields are slightly higher because the interest compounds.

When bonds are sold between interest dates, they are usually priced to include part of the interest payment that the new owner will receive. Consequently the seller must allocate part of the purchase price to *accrued interest*. The *flat price* of a bond is the quoted price plus accrued interest.

A bond's *maturity date* is the date on which the issuer must repay the bond's principal value. Long-term debt is usually considered to be any obligation repayable more than 10 years from the date of issue, while medium-term debt is longer than 1 year and less than 10 years. Short-term debt is debt due in less than one year.

Types of Bonds

A bond's principal and interest payments can take one of three forms: a coupon bond, a zero coupon bond, or an annuity. The focus of this chapter will be on the first two, which are generally thought of as bonds.

Coupon bonds, the most common type, have already been described. Typically these are issued near face value. Coupon bonds also pay a fixed dollar amount of interest determined by the coupon rate. Such payments are made to bondholders, usually semiannually, until maturity.

A *zero coupon,* or *discount, bond* is a bond issued below its par value, or at a discount. For example, a $1,000 zero coupon bond that matures in three years might sell for $780 for an annual yield to maturity of 8.6 percent. Its return comes from an increase in principal value alone, for this type of bond pays no interest on face value. The price of such a bond without default risk is the present value of the face amount, assumed to be received with complete certainty. Some corporate bonds and all U.S. Treasury bills (but not Treasury notes or bonds) are issued at a discount. Some investors find "zeros" advantageous because most are not callable before maturity and because, over the investment horizon, they have no reinvestment risk. Zeros were developed for investors with well-defined time horizons. Strictly speaking, zeros are called *original-issue discount* bonds that distinguish them from coupon bonds selling below face value, since bond traders sometimes refer to the latter as *discount* bonds.

An *annuity* is the third type of bond payment scheme. A house mortgage and an insurance annuity contract are examples of annuities. Each payment contains principal and interest. Payments are level over a finite term, and there is no "balloon" payment of principal at maturity. The amount of principal and interest changes because the interest is computed on a decreasing outstanding balance; the interest portion is less and the principal portion greater with each payment.

The Present Value Formula

As with other investments, the value of a bond can be expressed as the present value of the payments to which the bondholder is entitled. Suppose an investor purchased a bond paying an annual coupon, on the coupon payment date. Expressed in terms of a par value of 100, the present value is given by

$$PV = \frac{c}{(1 + r_1)} + \frac{c}{(1 + r_2)^2} + \frac{c}{(1 + r_3)^3} + \ldots + \frac{100 + c}{(1 + r_T)^T}$$

where
c = Coupon.
$r_1, r_2, \ldots r_T$ = Appropriate discount rates for one year, two years, through T years.
T = Time to maturity of the bond.
The value of 100 in the last term of the formula reflects the repayment of principal at maturity. In many applications it is assumed that all the discount rates are equal. In that case the (single) discount rate that sets the present value equal to the current price of the bond is said to be the *yield to maturity* (or simply the *yield*) of the bond.

Few bonds actually pay annual coupons, and rarely are bonds purchased on coupon payment dates. For this reason it is sometimes convenient to express the present value formula as:

$$PV = [c \times d(t_1)] + [c \times d(t_2)] + [c \times d(t_3)]$$
$$+ \ldots + [(100 + c) \times d(T)]$$

where $d(t_1)$, $d(t_2)$, . . . $d(T)$ represent the appropriate *discount factors* associated with payments received t_1, t_2, through T years from today. These discount factors are given by the formula:

$$d(t) = \frac{1}{(1 + r_t)^t}$$

where t now refers to the year or fractional part of the year at which the payments occur.[1]

It is evident from the present value formula that the value of a bond varies inversely with the interest rates that are represented as the discount rates in the formula. As interest rates decline, the value of the bond rises because the fixed coupon and principal payments associated with the bond become more valuable. Likewise, when interest rates rise, these payments become less valuable, and bond prices fall.

Bond Yields and Returns

Yield to Maturity. A bond's yield to maturity (or simply its yield) is its internal rate of return, or the single discount rate that equates the present value of future income to the bond's current market value. This calculated return of a bond relates to three factors:

1. The money received in the form of a periodic coupon payment.
2. The difference between purchase price and redemption value.
3. The number of years to maturity.

---

[1]Since many bonds pay coupons on a semiannual basis the industry convention is to assume that rates are expressed on a semiannual compounded basis. In other words:

$$d(t) = \frac{1}{\left(1 + \frac{r_t}{2}\right)^{2t}}$$

This is a complication we shall ignore for the remainder of the chapter.

In bond trading, yields to maturity are typically quoted on a semiannual compounding basis.

Consider again the United Utilities bond with a 10 percent coupon, a face value of $1,000, a term of 20 years, and a market value of $900. (For ease of explanation, assume annual coupons instead of the more prevalent semiannual coupons observed in the marketplace.) The present value of the bond's income is the value of an income stream of $100 annually plus the value of the $1,000 principal payment 20 years later. (The interest has a present value of $781.85, while the principal has a present value of $118.15, summing to $900.) If the security's market value is $900, its yield to maturity is determined by iteration, or trial and error—that is, by trying various discount rates to see which rate equals that market value. Using present value tables or a calculator in such a process, the discount rate is found to be about 11.3 percent. Thus the bond's yield to maturity is about 11.3 percent. A bond's yield to maturity changes if interest rates change, if its default risk increases, or if expectations about inflation change.

Expected Return. A bond's yield to maturity would be the bond's *expected return* if there is no expected default and if interest rates are constant through time. If default is expected the bond's expected return will be less than its yield to maturity because of the expected loss from default.

Yet there is a problem with thinking about yields as constant returns. The calculation assumes that the same rate is used to discount all payments, but bondholders may demand different rates over different future periods. The yield is really an average and hides the variability of rates at which interest payments might be reinvested. The return expected by investors may vary from period to period in the future.

Actual Return. A bondholder's *actual return* is the amount of money received from holding the bond over a period, divided by the investment at the beginning of the period. Only if the bond is held to maturity is the bond's actual return equal to its expected return or yield. If sold before maturity the bond's actual return includes the capital gain or loss on its sale. If interest rates change at any time during the period, interest payments may be reinvested at rates higher or lower than expected.

Consider yet again the United Utilities bond, this time one year later. The coupon is still 10 percent, and the face value is still $1,000. But now the remaining term is 19 years, and the market price is $950. Assuming the bond is then sold, its actual return can be calculated as the difference between purchase price ($900), and the sale price ($950), or $50, plus the income from the period ($100), both divided by the purchase price. Therefore, the actual return is 16.7 percent in that year, while its yield to maturity at the end of the year has fallen to 10.6 percent.

Aftertax Return. So far the before-tax returns on bonds have been described. To obtain the *aftertax returns,* the taxes on interest income and on capital gains or losses from principal must be taken into account. The interest income from coupon bonds, determined by the coupon rate, is all subject to tax. Likewise the increase in a discount bond's principal value over its purchase price must be treated as interest income. In addition the difference between a bond's purchase price (less accrued interest if any) and its sales price is taxed at capital gains rates, which are usually lower than ordinary rates.

Discount Yield. The yields on short-term bonds are often quoted as discount yields. This is the annual interest over par, divided by the time to maturity. For example, a bond with a 7 percent coupon selling at 93 with one year to maturity is quoted as having a yield of 7 percent, which is approximately $70/$1,000 divided by 1, which equals 7 percent. A more correct computation would be $70/$930 divided by 1, or 7.5 percent. Because long-term bond yields include compound interest, short- and long-term bond yields are not directly comparable. Of course short-term bond yields can be converted to the yield to maturity and then referred to as *bond equivalent yields,* which are comparable.

Current Yield. Sometimes people measure a bond's *current yield,* which is the ratio of its promised or current income to its current market price. Again, this is not to be confused with a bond's yield to maturity. If the 10 percent United Utilities bond sells for $950 its current yield would be the coupon ($100) divided by the market value ($950), or a current yield of 10.5 percent in contrast to its yield to maturity of 10.6 percent. In this example the yield to maturity is higher than the current yield because the investor expects a $50 capital gain at maturity, which is included in the yield to maturity.

Note that a bond's coupon rate is different from its current yield. The coupon rate is the bond's return as a percent of its par (principal) amount, while its current yield is the income return on the investment at the market price. Yield to maturity, however, measures the total expected return—including both income and capital gain or loss—on the overall investment. To reiterate: when the term *yield* is used in this chapter, yield to maturity is implied.

A Bond's Duration

The duration of the bond is a weighted average of the times when payments are due. Each payment's weight is determined by its present value as a percentage of the present value of the bond as a whole. Consider two bonds, both with four-year terms and 12 percent yields to maturity. The first is a four-year zero coupon bond with a price of $635.50. This bond had a duration of four years because there is a single payment at maturity that makes up 100 percent of its present value. By contrast, the second is a four-year bond with a 9 percent coupon and a price of $908.87. This bond has a shorter duration—3.5 years—because each coupon payment (compounded annually to simplify the illustration) figures into the weighting. The calculation of these bond durations is shown in Table 4–1.

The formula for duration is:

$$\text{Duration} = t_1 \times \frac{c \times d(t_1)}{PV} + t_2 \times \frac{c \times d(t_2)}{PV}$$
$$+ \ldots + T \times \frac{(100 \times c) \times d(T)}{PV}$$

where

$d(t_1)$, $d(t_2)$, . . . $d(T)$ = Discount factor for payments to be received t_1, t_2, through T years from today, c is the coupon.

PV = Present value of the bond.

Since the present value of the bond is nothing more than the sum of the discounted payments to be received from the bond, the formula says simply that duration is a weighted average of the time until payment dates, where the weights are given by the fraction of the present value arising from that period's payment.

Duration thus measures the average time investors have money owed to them in present value terms. In Table 4–2, the effects of increasing maturity and decreasing coupon rates on a bond's duration are illustrated. When a bond's yield and coupon are held constant but its maturity is increased, its duration increases but much more slowly than the bond's maturity in years. While a 5-year, 12 percent bond has a duration of 3.9

TABLE 4–1
Different Durations of a Four-Year Discount and a Four-Year Coupon Bond
(with annual compounding)

(1) Type of Bond	(2) Time (years)	(3) PV of Payment	(4) PV of Payment as Fraction of PV of Bond	(5) (2) × (4)
Discount bond				
Coupon = 0 percent	4	$635.50	1.00	4 years
Annual yield to maturity = 12 percent				
Coupon bond				
Annual coupon = 9 percent				
Annual yield to maturity = 12 percent				
Interest	1	$ 80.36	.088	.088 years
	2	71.75	.079	.158
	3	64.06	.071	.213
	4	57.20	.063	.252
Principal	4	635.50	.699	2.796
Total		$908.87	1.000	3.5 years

years, a similar 10-year bond has a duration of 6.1 years, and a comparable 20-year bond has a duration of only 8.0 years.

The higher the bond's coupon rate, the shorter its duration. This is because the higher the coupon rate, the larger the coupons' weights relative to the present value of the bond. A 30-year bond with a coupon of 12 percent has a duration of 8.6 years, while a 30-year bond with a coupon

TABLE 4–2
Maturities and Durations of Selected Bonds
(with semiannual compounding)

Coupon	Yield to Maturity	Maturity	Price	Duration
12%	12%	5 years	$1,000.00	3.901 years
12	12	10	1,000.00	6.079
12	12	20	1,000.00	7.975
12	12	30	1,000.00	8.566
6	12	30	515.14	9.196
0	12	30	33.40	30.000

of 6 percent has a duration of 9.2, and a 30-year discount bond, with a zero coupon, has a duration of 30 years.

While the expression for duration given above is completely general, in practical applications measures of duration differ according to assumptions that are made about the appropriate discount rates. They also differ according to uses to which measures of duration are put.

If the discount factors are computed assuming the discount rates are all equal to the yield to maturity (ytm) on the bond:

$$d(t) = \frac{1}{(1 + \text{ytm})^t}$$

then the resulting measure of duration is referred to as *Macauley's Duration* after Frederick Macauley who originally developed this measure[2]. So called *second generation* duration measures compute the discount factors $d(t)$ on the basis of the zero coupon yield curve, using methods to be discussed later in this chapter.

The extent to which bond prices are affected by changes in interest rates depends on the length of time investors have their funds committed to such investments. Thus duration is a natural measure of interest rate sensitivity. For this purpose, analysts use a measure of *adjusted duration* given as duration divided by one plus the yield to maturity of the bond, since it can be shown that the percentage change in bond price is approximately equal to the adjusted duration times the change in yield to maturity. Take a bond with a duration of five years, a coupon of 12 percent, and a yield to maturity of 12 percent, selling at par, or 100. If the yield to maturity rises 10 basis points, or .10 percent, to 12.10 percent, the price will fall approximately 5/1.12 times .10 percent, or .446 percent, to 99.554.

Analysts should treat this measure of adjusted duration with some care. Since duration falls as interest rates rise, the measure *overestimates* the fall in prices as interest rates rise, and *underestimates* the rise in prices when interest rates fall. This property, known as *convexity*, needs to be adjusted for when interest rates change by more than an insignificant amount. Another limitation of adjusted duration as a measure of interest rate sensitivity is an implicit assumption that short term rates of interest

---

[2]Frederick Macauley, *Some Theoretical Problems Suggested by the Movement of Interest Rates, Bond Yields, and Stock Prices Since 1865* (New York: National Bureau of Economic Research), 1938.

move in lockstep with long-term rates. More advanced measures of duration are being developed to account for these difficulties.[3]

DETERMINANTS OF BOND YIELDS

Bonds with the same yield to maturity are not necessarily equivalent. Bonds differ according to coupon rate and time to maturity. They also differ with respect to credit risk, taxable status, call terms, conversion options, and other special features. The interpretation of the yield to maturity depends on an understanding of the effect these variables have on the value of bonds.

Yield Curves—The Term Structure of Interest Rates

The yield to maturity measure is easiest to interpret where the appropriate discount rates that enter into the present value formula are in fact the same for all maturities. The appropriate discount rates typically rise with time to maturity. Investors seem to demand a difference in yield between long-term and short-term bonds even where there is no risk of default and the bonds are otherwise equivalent. If two bonds have the same yield to maturity and are the same except for time to maturity, such an investor would prefer the shorter time to maturity. The reason is that the later payments would be valued less than they would be if the discount rates were the same for all maturities. The yield curve describes the way that rates vary with time to maturity.

The yields to maturity on default-free bonds of various maturities are shown together in Figure 4–1 to portray what is called the yield curve on Treasury securities. In June 1986, 30-day Treasury bills are shown to yield about 6.1 percent while five-year notes yield about 8.1 percent, the 2.0 percent difference being the yield spread between these two securities. The yield curve on such riskless securities is also called the *term structure of interest rates*.

The yield curve, or term structure, takes three basic forms, as also shown in Figure 4–1. In an upward sloping curve, such as the June 1986 curve, short-term rates are lower than long-term rates. When the curve is

---

[3]Other complications arise where the bonds in question may be called by the issuer prior to maturity. Adjustments for these option-like characteristics (see Chapter 6) are described in Alden Toevs 'Hedging Interest Rate Risk of Fixed Income Securities with Uncertain Lives' in Robert Platt (ed.) *Controlling Interest Rate Risk* (New York: John Wiley & Sons), 1986, pp. 176–96.

FIGURE 4-1
Term Structure of U.S. Treasury Yields

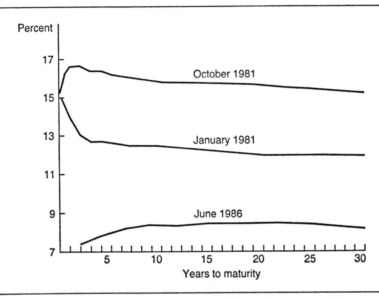

SOURCE: Ibbotson Associates, *Stocks, Bonds, Bills and Inflation: 1986 Yearbook* (Chicago: Ibbotson Associates, Inc., 1986).

downward sloping, as in the January 1981 curve, short-term rates are higher than long-term rates. The curve can also be humpbacked, as it was in October 1981; here short-term rates are low, medium-term rates are high, and long-term rates are in between. The shape of the yield curve can indeed change over time. However, the upward sloping curve depicted for June 1986 is found most frequently.

Economists are interested in this curve chiefly because it contains within it some indication of the future course of interest rates. To give a concrete example, suppose that at a recent Treasury bill auction, one-year Treasury bills were sold to yield 6 percent to their maturity in one year. At the same time, a zero coupon Treasury stripped certificate is trading at a price to yield 8 percent to its maturity in two years. This yield spread reflects the fact that the yield curve is upward sloping.

Under what conditions would the average investor consider the two investments equivalent? If the investor were to invest in the two-year paper, $100 of initial investment would grow to $116.64 in two years:

$$\$116.64 = \$100 \times (1 + .08)(1 + .08)$$

On the other hand, the investor who invested in the Treasury bill would have to reinvest the proceeds at the end of the year to match the two-year investment. In fact, the investor would require a return of 10.04 percent on the reinvested funds to match the two-year investment:

$$\$116.64 = \$100 \times (1 + .06)(1 + .1004)$$

In other words, for a 6 percent, one-year investment to exactly match an 8 percent, two-year investment, the investor would require an annual return of 10.04 percent one year from today. The 10.04 percent number implied by the yield spread between 6 percent on one-year investments and 8 percent on two-year investments is referred to as a *forward rate*. The current rate of 6 percent is referred to as the *spot rate*.

One theory that would explain the upward-sloping yield curve is that investors expect interest rates to rise. In other words, they expect the spot rates in the future to match the forward rates implicit in the yield curve. This view, known as the *expectations hypothesis,* is necessarily incomplete, as few investors can assess precisely what will happen with interest rates in the future. Investing in the two-year instrument ties up money for that period of time. Investors are unable to take advantage of favorable changes in interest rates and are, moreover, subject to the possibility of capital loss if interest rates rise and they have to sell their investment prior to maturity. Hence, investors require some kind of premium on longer-term paper to account for this risk. This view, known as the *liquidity preference hypothesis,* would predict that the forward rate exceeds the market's expectation of the future expected spot rate by the measure of this premium. This view would predict that the yield curve would be upward sloping even if expected spot rates were equal to the current spot rates and would explain why yield curves generally slope in an upward direction. The fact that yield curves are sometimes sloped downward, as in January 1981, is a strong indication that the market expected interest rates to decline. Finally, there is the *preferred habitat theory* that suggests that the market may be dominated by individuals and institutions with very particular maturity preferences. This view might explain why it is that the yield curve sometimes exhibits "bumps" in its shape.

Credit Risk and Default Premiums

Other than the time to maturity, the credit or default risk is usually the most important characteristic of a bond. U.S. government bonds are usually assumed to be default free. If a bond is subject to default, the promised yield to maturity must be high enough not only to cover this probability but also to provide compensation for taking default risk. The total of these compensations is the *default premium*. If the expected loss from default is 1 percent and if the compensation for taking default risk is 1 percent, then the total default premium would be 2 percent. When a riskless bond yields 10 percent, the corresponding yield on a bond subject to the default probability described above would be 12 percent. The expected return would be approximately 12 percent conditional on no default but only 11 percent after allowing for the probability of default.

The yield spread between a bond and a comparable government bond is in large part a measure of the market's assessment of default risk. In addition, various rating agencies rate the creditworthiness of most bonds. For example, Moody's rates bonds Aaa, Aa, Baa, and so forth, with the lower-rated bonds having the higher likelihood of default.

Taxable Status

Major categories of bonds are treated differently for tax purposes. The income from municipal bonds is exempt from U.S. federal income tax and also, in many cases, from state and municipal taxes. The income from U.S. Treasury issues is typically subject to federal taxes, and the income from corporate bonds is also subject to state taxes. This difference alone explains a yield spread between municipal bonds and other bonds of a similar risk.

To the extent that capital gains are taxed at rates that differ from those applied to income, high-coupon bonds have different aftertax returns than low-coupon bonds. Historically, corporates with low coupons have low yields that may in part be explained by the fact that investors expected part of their return in the form of capital gains that were taxed at a lower rate. In the past, bond premiums and discounts were treated asymmetrically for tax purposes;[4] for the same yield to maturity, other things equal, the investor would prefer the bond trading at a discount to one trading at a premium.

Even among U.S. Treasury issues, there are important differences in tax status. Aside from the wide range of coupon rates, premiums, and discounts, some Treasury issues have special estate tax characteristics. Known as flower bonds these bonds are redeemable at par to pay estate taxes in the event that the holder dies. One type of flower bond requires

---

[4]With the notable exceptions of Treasury bills and original issue discount bonds.

the bond to be held at least six months prior to the death of the holder, while another requires only that the bond be held at the time of death. While these bonds typically have a long term to maturity, few investors would purchase them with the intent of holding them to maturity. For this reason the high price and low yield to maturity of such bonds are deceptive.

Callable Bonds

Most long-term bonds are callable by the issuer after some grace period. Corporates are usually callable at par plus the coupon, and government bonds with call provisions are callable at par.[5]

The call term is in fact an option that the issuer holds. The option has value; the bond sells at a lower price and has a higher yield to maturity than a comparable bond issued without the call terms. The issuer will tend to call the bonds if interest rates fall and he or she can refinance at a lower rate. Call terms make bond valuation complex, since a delayed option has to be valued. The theory of options discussed in Chapter Six can be applied in this context.

Convertible Bonds

Convertible fixed-income securities are corporate bonds or debentures that may be exchanged at a specified price for a certain number of shares of the corporation's common stock. Convertible bonds have two characteristics: a claim on a preset stream of cash flows and an option to purchase the common stock of the firm. The value of a convertible bond is thus related to these two components: the bond's value as a straight debt instrument and the value of the option on the firm's stock. Such instruments have unlimited potential for price appreciation. As the value of the corporation's stock increases, so will the value of the convertible debt security. This security also provides investors with limited downside risk, or limited loss of principal. The risk of loss is minimized because the value of a convertible bond is bounded below by the value of a straight bond; if the firm's stock falls in price so as to make the option worthless the convertible bond is still worth the same amount as other nonconvertible debt securities of the corporation.

---

[5]Most Treasury bonds are not callable.

Convertible bonds are sometimes sold as a way to "have your cake and eat it too." To be sure, the conversion terms are valuable; but they are also built into the price, giving convertibles lower yields than they would otherwise have. The conversion feature is in fact an option; and again, the theory of options discussed in Chapter Six can be used to value the privilege of conversion.

DATA ANALYSIS

Historical Returns

In the previous section, we discussed the extent to which the yield to maturity could be used to compare and analyze different bond issues. Another approach is to compare these issues on the basis of their historical returns. Historical returns are not the same as the yield to maturity, since total returns include both the yield to maturity and the return in excess of yield. Stated another way, total returns include both income and capital gains or losses over specified holding periods.

The total returns on U.S. Treasury and corporate bonds, and cash equivalents, are measured annually from 1960 to 1984 and presented in Table 4–3. The geometric mean or compound annual return, the arithmetic mean return, and the annual standard deviation are given for each bond category.

The period 1960–1985 was generally a period of rising interest rates. Therefore capital losses were incurred on net, especially for those who held longer-term bonds. The capital losses on longer-term bonds more than offset the higher yields earned over the period. Thus, over the 25-year period, cash equivalents tended to outperform notes and intermediates, which in turn tended to outperform longer-term bonds. The other important variable explaining the historical returns is credit risk. The higher credit risk of corporates caused them to have higher returns. This risk was rewarded over the period, since there were very few defaults. Thus commercial paper outperformed Treasury bills, corporate intermediates outperformed Treasury notes, and long-term corporates outperformed Treasury bonds.

Correlations

Table 4–4 presents the correlation matrix of total annual returns for the 10 bond categories. Note that the highest correlations of bond returns are for

TABLE 4–3
U.S. Bond Market: Total Annual Returns, 1960–1984

	Compound Return	Arithmetic Mean	Standard Deviation
Corporate			
Intermediate-term	6.37%	6.80%	7.15%
Long-term	5.03	5.58	11.26
Corporate total (including preferreds)	5.35	5.75	9.63
Government			
Treasury notes	6.32	6.44	5.27
Treasury bonds	4.70	5.11	9.70
U.S. agencies	6.88	7.04	6.15
Government total	5.91	6.10	6.43
Cash equivalents			
U.S. Treasury bills	6.25	6.29	3.10
Commercial paper	7.03	7.08	3.20
Cash total	6.49	6.54	3.22

SOURCE: Roger G. Ibbotson, Laurence B. Siegel, and Kathryn S. Love "World Wealth: Market Values and Returns" *Journal of Portfolio Management,* Fall 1985.

those bonds with similar maturities. Treasury bills and commercial paper have a correlation of .99, Treasury notes and corporate intermediates have a correlation of .90, and Treasury bonds and long-term corporates are also correlated .90. To a somewhat lesser extent corporates correlate with each other across maturities. Naturally the total categories are highly correlated with their subcomponents.

These results demonstrate quite clearly that interest rate sensitivity at different maturities is the primary factor responsible for bond returns over any given period. Despite the differences between government and corporate issues, bonds that promise similar cash flows have returns that are similar to the extent that they are subject to the same interest rate factors.

Regression Analysis

In order to analyze further how bond returns relate to each other and to economic phenomena, regression analysis is used. First, the excess returns over Treasury bills (held to be riskless) are computed for total corporate bonds and total government bond portfolios. These excess returns are regressed on the excess returns on a portfolio consisting of all bonds; the

TABLE 4–4
U.S. Bond Market: Correlation Matrix of Total Annual Returns

	Treasury Notes	Treasury Bonds	Total U.S. Agencies	Intermediate Government Bonds	Long Corporate Bonds	Total Corporate Bonds	Corporate Bonds	Treasury Bills	Commercial Paper	Total Cash
Treasury notes	1.000									
Treasury bonds	0.904	1.000								
U.S. agencies	0.962	0.904	1.000							
U.S. total government bonds	0.972	0.950	0.964	1.000						
Intermediate-term corporate bonds	0.900	0.865	0.848	0.887	1.000					
Long-term corporate bonds	0.858	0.912	0.808	0.859	0.941	1.000				
U.S. total corporate bonds	0.865	0.902	0.809	0.863	0.960	0.996	1.000			
Treasury bills	0.395	0.111	0.328	0.325	0.336	0.094	0.135	1.000		
Commercial paper	0.394	0.115	0.348	0.330	0.313	0.070	0.108	0.990	1.000	
U.S. total cash	0.400	0.119	0.340	0.332	0.339	0.096	0.136	0.999	0.995	1.000

SOURCE: Roger G. Ibbotson, Laurence B. Siegel, and Kathryn S. Love "World Wealth: Market Values and Returns" *Journal of Portfolio Management*, Fall 1985.

results are reported in Table 4–5. Note that the alphas, the intercepts from these regressions, are near zero, and the betas that represent the slope coefficient are quite significant. The beta of corporate bonds is 1.33 and the beta of governments is only .84. At least one explanation for the higher beta of the corporate bond portfolio is the fact that this portfolio has a longer average term to maturity.

Each of the bond categories is regressed on the inflation rate. Note that the betas of the cash equivalents are positive while the other betas are negative—and more negative the longer the maturity. Recall that the total returns consist of a yield component plus the return in excess of yield. Yields tend to go up with inflation, leading to higher income but to capital losses. Cash equivalents are good inflation hedges, while long-term bonds are negative hedges against inflation for short-term investors.

Estimating the Term Structure

Most accounts of the mathematics of bond valuation assume the analyst can simply observe the term structure of interest rates and use this information to compute the discount factors that appear in the present value formula. Figure 4–2 gives the yield curve as measured by the yields to maturity on Treasury bills, bonds, and notes implied by the mean of bid and ask price quotations as of December 31, 1985.[6] While it is clear from this figure that the yield curve is upwardly sloping, a number of bonds with the same maturity seem to trade at different yields. As one example two Treasury bonds, both set to mature on November 16, 1986, trade to yield 6.3 percent and 7.6 percent, respectively. Should the analyst use the 6.3 percent number or the 7.6 percent number? Some of these differences can be explained. The bond yielding 6.3 percent trades at a discount, whereas most of the other bonds trade at a premium; the 6.3 percent number reflects some of the tax advantages associated with bonds that are purchased at a discount. Some differences may be due to pricing errors and would represent arbitrage opportunities, although many other differences simply reflect the fact that many bonds are not frequently traded. The mean of the bid and ask prices does not always represent an accurate assessment of what the bond could actually trade for in the market. Finally, some of the differences may simply reflect quotation errors.

---

[6]The yield to maturity of flower bonds and other bonds with special tax treatments are excluded from this figure as are the yields to maturity of callable bonds. These bonds have yields to maturity that systematically differ from those of other bonds, for reasons outlined earlier in this chapter.

TABLE 4–5
Bond Regressions: Total Annual Returns

Dependent Variable	Independent Variable	Alpha (Percent)	Alpha T Statistic	Beta	Beta T Statistic	Adjusted R²	Standard Deviation of Residuals	First-Order Autocorrelation of Residuals
Corporate bonds	U.S. total bonds	- 0.05	- 0.10	1.33	18.35	0.933	2.56	- 0.28
Government bonds	U.S. total bonds	0.12	0.36	0.84	18.61	0.935	1.60	- 0.28
U.S. corporate bonds								
Intermediate-term	Inflation	7.45	2.82	- 0.16	- 0.39	- 0.037	7.43	0.37
Long-term	Inflation	10.42	2.61	- 0.91	- 1.46	0.046	11.23	0.18
Total corporate bonds	Inflation	9.49	2.75	- 0.70	- 1.31	0.029	9.69	0.26
U.S. government bonds								
Treasury notes	Inflation	6.72	3.44	- 0.05	- 0.18	- 0.042	5.49	0.15
Treasury bonds	Inflation	8.59	2.46	- 0.66	- 1.21	0.019	9.81	- 0.01
U.S. agencies	Inflation	7.33	3.22	- 0.05	- 0.15	- 0.042	6.40	0.05
Total government bonds	Inflation	6.58	2.76	- 0.09	- 0.24	- 0.041	6.70	0.14
U.S. total bonds	Inflation	7.56	2.88	- 0.31	- 0.75	- 0.018	7.38	0.22
U.S. cash								
Treasury bills	Inflation	3.11	3.77	0.60	4.66	0.464	2.32	0.74
Commercial paper	Inflation	3.63	4.48	0.65	5.14	0.514	2.28	0.74

SOURCE: Roger G. Ibbotson, Laurence B. Siegel, and Kathryn S. Love "World Wealth: Market Values and Returns" *Journal of Portfolio Management*, Fall 1985.

FIGURE 4–2
Yield Curve of Treasury Bills, Bonds, and Notes, December 31, 1985

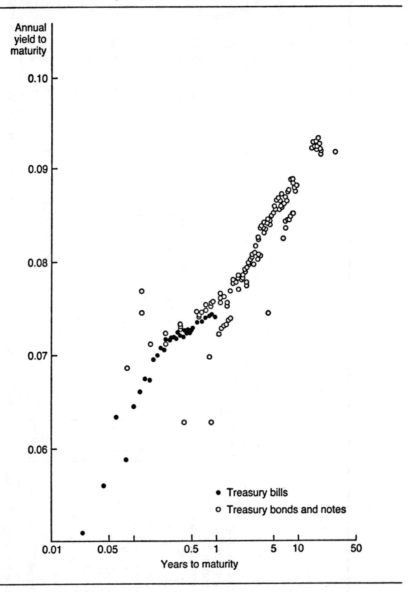

One obvious approach to the problem is to fit some kind of smooth curve to the data represented in Figure 4–2. Few yield curves rise as steadily as does the one depicted in that figure; as indicated earlier in this chapter, yield curves can take quite a variety of shapes. For this reason simple linear regression procedures are often not appropriate. Many analysts simply fit a smooth curve by eye through the points depicted in such figures; others employ more sophisticated procedures that use computer technology to do essentially the same thing. Such procedures are called spline smoothing (we shall refer to them later in this section).

This approach is not altogether satisfactory for several reasons. On a purely practical level it is sometimes difficult to fit a smooth curve to this data. Figure 4–3 illustrates the difficulties associated with fitting such a curve to the Treasury bill data. It is much easier to fit the discount factors directly to this data. Since Treasury bills are zero coupon bonds, the price today expressed as a fraction of par is the discount factor associated with the time to maturity of that bill:

$$\text{Price today} = \text{present value} = \$1 \times \frac{1}{(1 + r_t)^t} = d(t)$$

where

r_t = Yield of the Treasury bill to a maturity of t.

$d(t)$ = Discount factor associated with this maturity.

Figure 4–4 illustrates the Treasury bill discount factor as a function of the time to maturity for the same data reported in Figure 4–2. Unlike the yield to maturity the discount function is a smooth function of time and can be easily estimated. Since many applications only use the yield to maturity as a way of obtaining the discount function, it seems sensible to estimate the discount function directly.

Unfortunately the Treasury bill data extend only out as far as one year to maturity. The yield to maturity on coupon bonds represents a complicated average of yields to maturity on each of the coupons associated with the bond. As such it cannot be used to construct discount factors.[7] This is

---

[7]However, it is possible to write the value of the coupon bond as the sum of discount factors times the payments to be received at each of the coupon payment dates. If each of the discount factors can be expressed as a function of the time to each coupon payment date, it is possible to use econometric methods to estimate the discount factors on the basis of coupon bond prices as well as on the basis of discount bond prices. This procedure is discussed in Stephen J. Brown and Philip H. Dybvig, "The Empirical Implications of the Cox, Ingersoll, Ross Theory of the Term Structure of Interest Rates," *Journal of Finance* 41 (1986), pp. 617–30.

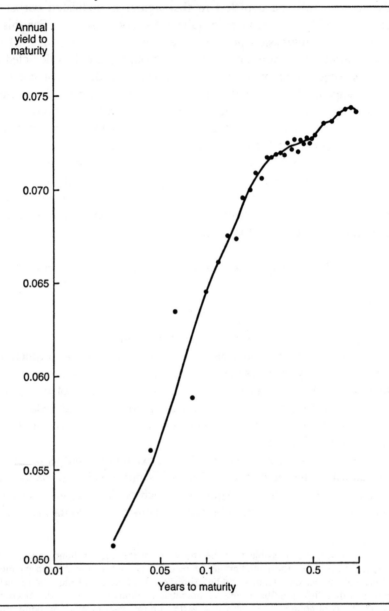

FIGURE 4–3
Treasury Bill Yield Curve, December 31, 1985

FIGURE 4–4
Treasury Bill Discount Factors, December 31, 1985

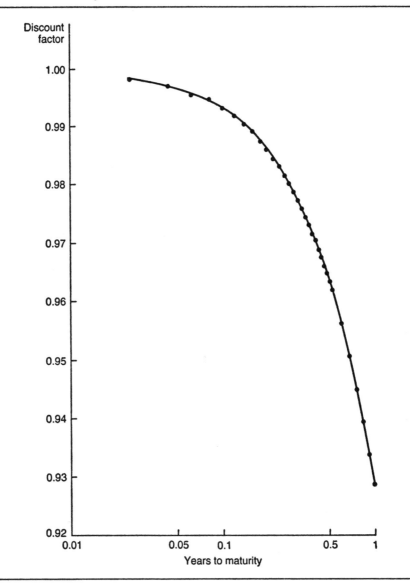

another argument against fitting a smooth curve to coupon bond yields: such yields are often difficult to interpret. Recently rights to the coupon and principal repayment of par have been issued separately in the secondary markets as zero coupon CATS, TIGRs and STRIPS. With such data, one can estimate the discount factors directly for more than one year to maturity.

To this point we have not discussed in detail the methods to be used for fitting smooth curves to this kind of data. There are almost as many procedures as there are statistics software packages that implement them. The most common family of procedures falls under the general rubric of spline smoothing. The idea behind spline smoothing is a very simple one. If one were to consider the discount factor $d(t)$ as a cubic function of the time to maturity:

$$d(t) = a + bt + ct^2 + dt^3$$

it would be possible to estimate coefficients a, b, c, and d directly, using multiple regression methods. Within certain ranges of the time to maturity, the fitted function might approximate relatively closely the actual discount function, to work adequately for all possible times to maturity. The spline procedure estimates the cubic function for ranges of the time to maturity, constraining the coefficients so that the function encounters a smooth transition between ranges.

This procedure has been criticized by H. G. Fong and Oldrich Vasicek on the grounds that the approximation has no basis in theory and does not seem to be adequate at long times to maturity.[8] They suggest fitting exponential functions in place of the cubic functions within each of the ranges of time to maturity. This approach does not necessarily address the problem of imposing ad hoc smoothness constraints on the functions to be estimated. One approach is to base these constraints on an equilibrium theory of interest rates.[9]

An alternative approach that does not involve the necessity to impose any constraints on the data has been suggested. Instead of fitting a yield curve or a discount function to the data as a smooth curve, the analyst

---

[8]H. Gifford Fong and Oldrich Vasicek, "Term Structure Modeling," *Journal of Finance* 37 (1982), pp. 339–48.

[9]See Stephen Brown and Philip Dybvig, "Empirical Implications of the Cox, Ingersoll, Ross Theory of the Term Structure of Interest Rates," Journal of Finance 41, (July 1986), pp. 617–32.

should estimate the sequence of forward rates as a series of constants, one for each series of periods out into the future.[10]

FACTORS THAT AFFECT BOND MARKETS

Horizon Premiums

A bond's maturity—or more precisely its duration—significantly affects its sensitivity to prevailing interest rates. Long-term bond prices are more sensitive to interest rate changes than those of short-term bonds. As previously indicated, the difference between the yields in long- and short-term bonds or between any two bond yields is called a yield spread. Investors seem to demand such a spread, or premium, for assuming the interest rate risk of long-term bonds. This spread is called the bond *maturity premium, horizon premium,* or *liquidity premium.*

In economic terms the yield on a default-free bond is equal to the expected inflation plus the expected real interest rate plus the bond's horizon premium. With inflation of 6 percent, a real interest rate of 3 percent, and the bond's horizon premium of 1 percent, such a default-free bond should yield 10 percent. The horizon premium constitutes the compensation for interest rate risk.

Inflation and Real Returns on Bonds

Changes in expected inflation cause changes in nominal interest rates and consequently in bond yields. The economist Irving Fisher was the first to observe that the nominal rate of interest must equal the real rate of interest plus the prospective rate of inflation. Thus, if investors generally revise their estimates of expected inflation downward by 1 percent, the nominal interest rate may also fall by 1 percent.

In practice, changes in expectations about inflation often do cause a shift in bond yields. In fact the change may affect bonds of different durations in different ways. If investors expect that near-term inflation will increase, the yields on bonds of short duration rise. If investors do not increase their expectations about long-term inflation as much, yields on bonds of longer duration will increase but less sharply.

---

[10]Thomas Coleman, Lawrence Fisher, and Roger Ibbotson, "Estimating Forward Interest Rates and Yield Curves from Government Bond Prices: Methodology and Selected Results" (Working paper, Yale University, 1986, unpublished).

Bond Dedication and Immunization Strategies

Liabilities in essence are the obligation to make payments in the future. An individual might be planning to put a child through college, or a pension fund manager might anticipate paying pension benefits to retirees. Both invest their assets in the interim to meet these future demands. Shrewd investors have observed that by matching the duration of such assets to that of anticipated liabilities, the risk of insufficient wealth to meet these obligations is reduced.

Dedication. When the liability is known and its amount fixed, certain assets can be set aside, or *dedicated*, to meet that liability. To continue the above examples, the parent may buy a zero coupon bond to assure that funds will be available when a child reaches college age, and the pension fund manager may buy bonds with interest payments that exactly match the monthly amount of expected retirement obligations to retired employees. For example, a portfolio of zero coupon bonds with durations of six, seven, and eight years can be used to meet a series of liabilities with maturities of six, seven, and eight years.

Immunization. If liabilities of differing amounts mature at different times, the matching of cash flows can be complicated or impossible. In this situation it is possible to immunize the liabilities with a portfolio. The objective of the procedure known as *immunization* is to insulate the investor from adverse changes in interest rates. Obviously this objective can be accomplished by dedication strategies but is a little more difficult to achieve using coupon bonds, as one is concerned with minimizing the risk associated with reinvestment of the coupon payments.

Fortunately it is possible to immunize a coupon bond portfolio by so arranging the portfolio that the duration of the portfolio matches the desired holding period of the investor. In this procedure, if interest rates rise investors benefit by the fact that they can reinvest coupons at a higher rate, but they incur a capital loss. On the other hand, if rates fall investors reinvest at a lower rate but experience a capital gain. If the investor were to hold bonds to maturity, capital risk is minimized but reinvestment risk is high. If, on the other hand, the investor were to roll over investments on a short-term basis, reinvestment risk is minimized but capital risk is high. There is thus a trade-off. Under certain conditions, to be discussed later, reinvestment risk and capital risk are equal and exactly offsetting at the duration of the bond (as discussed earlier, duration can be thought of as the midpoint of the bond payments measured in present value terms). Thus, if the investor chooses a portfolio such that the duration exactly matches the desired holding period, perhaps dictated by the liabilities the investor faces, such an investor will be *immunized* against unforeseen changes in interest rates.

This analysis assumes that the long-term rates, which chiefly affect the capital risk component, move in lockstep with the short rates that affect reinvestment risk. Investors who look to duration-based immunization as a way of locking in abnormally high short rates are liable to be disappointed. If short rates fall, leaving long rates largely unaffected, reinvestment value will fall without a corresponding rise in capital value.

Immunization and Interest Rate Elasticity. When long and short interest rates change by the same amount, the yield curve shift is parallel. In this case, as discussed before, only a bond's *adjusted duration* need be known in order to determine the effect on a bond's price. Typically, however, long-term rates are more stable than short-term rates. Thus the short end of the yield curve is more volatile and sensitive to interest rate changes. In economic terms, short-term rates are more interest rate elastic than long-term rates.

Empirically, short rates usually adjust by a greater amount than long rates. For every 1 percent change in the yield to maturity on a 1-year bond, 2-year bond yields change about 0.8 percent on average. For longer-term bonds, the changes are smaller: 5-year bond yields change about 0.4 percent relative to 1-year bonds, and 15-year bond yields change only 0.2 percent.

When elasticity factors are computed, long-term bonds are less elastic than short-term bonds. If the factor was one for short-term bonds, the factor will be less than one for long-term bonds. When such factors are multiplied by a bond's duration, the expected change in price can be determined. Specifically, the expected change in price is equal to the elasticity factor (expressed as a negative number) times the bond's adjusted duration times the expected short-term change in yield.

CONCLUSION

The analysis of fixed-income securities is especially amenable to quantitative methods because unlike equities, for example, their cash flows are highly predictable. Therefore, the linkage between present value concepts and bond valuation is fairly direct. This convenient linkage, together with some data analysis, leads to several observations and suggests certain fixed-income strategies.

The yield to maturity of a bond best measures its approximate expected return. This is true especially for a default-free bond over the life of the bond, ignoring reinvestment risk. For bonds with default risk, the bond's expected return will be below its promised yield to maturity, because there is some probability that the bond will default.

The actual return on a bond equals its yield to maturity plus the return in excess of this yield, whether positive or negative. Gains and losses on bonds occur primarily because of changes in prevailing interest rates.

The adjusted duration of a bond measures its price sensitivity to changes in its yield to maturity. Long-term bond prices are more sensitive to changes in yield to maturity than short-term bonds. On the other hand this is partially offset by the empirical fact that short-term interest rates fluctuate more than long-term interest rates.

Dedication and immunization are techniques to protect a bond portfolio's nominal value from changes in interest rates over a given horizon. When the liabilities are fixed, zero coupon bonds can be dedicated so that their maturities match the horizon. In this way nominal risk is eliminated at the end of the horizon.

Immunization is desirable when there are many liabilities with complicated payment schedules and when coupon bonds are used to match these liabilities. As interest rates change, there is a trade-off between the bond's price and the rate at which coupon payments are reinvested. Immunization is a mathematical procedure for balancing such trade-offs.

REFERENCES

Brown, S. J., and P. H. Dybvig. "The Empirical Implications of the Cox, Ingersoll, Ross Theory of the Term Structure of Interest Rates." *Journal of Finance* 41 (June 1986), pp. 617–30.

Coleman, T.; L. Fisher; and R. Ibbotson. "Estimating Forward Interest Rates and Yield Curves from Government Bond Prices: Methodology and Selected Results." Working paper, Yale University, 1986, unpublished.

Fong, H. G., and O. Vasicek. "Term Structure Modeling." *Journal of Finance* 37 (1982), pp. 339–48.

Ibbotson, R. G., and G. P. Brinson. *Investment Markets: Gaining the Performance Advantage*. New York: McGraw-Hill, 1987.

Macauley, F. *Some Theoretical Problems Suggested by the Movement of Interest Rates, Bond Yields, and Stock Prices Since 1865*. (New York: National Bureau of Economic Research), 1938.

Toevs, A. "Hedging Interest Rate Risk of Fixed Income Securities with Uncertain Lives" in Platt, R. *Controlling Investment Rate Risk*. (New York: John Wiley & Sons), 1986, pp. 176–96.

CHAPTER FIVE

Quantitative Methods in Real Estate Analysis

Susan Hudson-Wilson

INTRODUCTION

Valuation in the context of real estate can be very complex and difficult. However, the general principles of valuation are similar to those that apply in other investment contexts. Moreover the general perception that real estate markets are inefficient creates opportunities for those with special knowledge of such markets or special access to pertinent information. Use of quantitative methods will aid though not, of course, guarantee performance.

This chapter begins by introducing some of the issues of property valuation, using a simplified property analysis that focuses on the application of concepts of present value and measures of return. (This treatment is not meant to be exhaustive; the interested reader is referred to other texts for further reading on these issues.[1]) The chapter then addresses some of the ways in which methods of statistics and data analysis are used in the valuation context and concludes with a brief review of portfolio design considerations.

---

[1]See, for example, Paul F. Wendt and Alan R. Cerf, *Real Estate Investment Analysis and Taxation* (New York: McGraw-Hill, 1979).

PROPERTY VALUATION ISSUES

Valuation

There are several traditional approaches to valuation in real estate analysis. These are known as the cost approach, the market data approach, and the income approach. They are used to obtain an appraisal meant to approximate market value closely if the property were to be sold today for what is referred to as its highest and best use. The highest and best use reflects the most valuable use to which the property may be put. In other words, an apartment building may be worth more to a prospective purchaser who intends to convert it into a condominium than to a purchaser who intends to operate it as a rental building. It is as a condominium (net of the costs of conversion) that the property should be valued.

The cost approach represents an approach to valuation that stresses the physical value of the structure and the land over the economic value of the property's leasing and management and the value of the alternate uses to which the property can be put. Essentially the appraiser calculates the replacement cost of the property and subtracts an amount that reflects the fact that the property is not newly constructed. The adjustment tends to be somewhat subjective and typically does not allow for the income that can be generated by the property. This approach cannot be used for the valuation of the land component, for which a separate calculation has to be made.

The market data approach is closer to a concept of market value of the highest and best use of the property. In this approach, comparable properties are defined for which market prices are available. An adjustment (or a series of adjustments) is made for the fact that the property in question is not exactly the same as the properties to which it is compared. The adjustment process is again somewhat subjective.

The income approach values the highest and best use in terms of the present value of the cash flows resulting from such a use. Most of the simple applications assume that the cash flows are to be received in perpetuity either by the owner of the property or by the person to whom the property is eventually sold. This is a simple application of the perpetuity formula discussed in Chapter Two:

$$\text{Present value} = \frac{C}{r}$$

In this context the cash flow quantity C is often referred to as *stabilized net operating income* (NOI), and the discount rate r is referred to as the *capitalization rate.* If we were to assume that the cash flow *C* were to grow at a constant rate *g* over time, then the appropriate formula would be:

$$\text{Present value} = \frac{C}{r - g}$$

and the quantity *(r − g)* would be interpreted as the capitalization rate.

The capitalization rate is generally held to include some kind of risk premium. To estimate this quantity, many analysts invert the present value formula above to find the capitalization rates that may be inferred from the prices at which properties currently trade:

$$\text{Capitalization rate} = \frac{\text{Cash flow}}{\text{Present value}} = \frac{\text{Net operating income}}{\text{Current price of property}}$$

and properties can be compared on the basis of their implied capitalization rates. The analysis of capitalization rates is analogous to the analysis of the equity price-earnings model discussed in Chapter Three (the capitalization rate can be thought of as the reciprocal of the price-earnings ratio).

Net operating income is generally defined as rental and nonrental income (gross potential income) less an allowance for vacancy and other losses and for operating expenses that include maintenance and repair expenses, payroll, real estate taxes, utility costs, insurance, and so forth. While it is typically measured net of extraordinary items (is "stabilized"), it in many instances is only a benchmark of value, as it is difficult to estimate many of the expense items with any degree of precision. For this reason, some analysts neglect the corporate tax liability associated with the cash flow.

A variant of this approach is known as the *gross income multiplier,* where the expense items are neglected altogether and the measure of cash flow is simply the gross rental and nonrental income from the property in question.

The simplifications used to construct cash flow measures are often made necessary by the paucity of data in many real estate applications. Of what value is analysis based on such numbers? So long as the measures of income are proportional to some well-defined measure of aftertax cash flows, it is perfectly appropriate to use the implied capitalization rates for comparison purposes. However, where simplifications are used, valuations derived from such numbers should be treated with a due degree of caution.

Such valuations are appraisals of value for the "typical" investor and are presumably reflected in the price at which the property could be sold. They may not represent measures of value for a particular investor. To value a property from that perspective, it is necessary to construct pro forma income statements for each year of the holding period. This enables the analyst to estimate accurately revenues and expenses and to assess the corporate tax consequences for a particular investor. The aftertax cash flows for each year of the holding period, plus some estimate of the value of the property if sold at the end of that period, are discounted at the required rate of return for that investor. A simple example should make this clear.

Simplified Valuation Example. This example represents a significantly "stripped-down" case. An actual valuation would be concerned with real estate and corporate income taxes, the expertise of the property manager, construction costs, value per square foot, and the nature of the sale (timing, leverage, partnerships, etc.). Later we will add some complexity to the problem, but it should be clear that there is a significant subjective element to real estate valuation that can only be captured imperfectly by use of quantitative methods.

The hypothetical property under analysis is a 100,000-square-foot office building in Burlington, Massachusetts. There are three "credit" tenants leasing 100 percent of the space under 10-year, triple-net leases at fixed rental rates of $17 per square foot. In other words, the tenants are regarded as financially secure and pay all of the expenses associated with the space rented in addition to the rent itself. Inflation and vacancy are assumed to be zero, and a $.10 per square foot structural reserve[2] constitutes the only expense to the building's owner. The asking price for the building is $18,777,777, or $187 per square foot. (See Table 5–1.)

Assume that the investor contemplating a purchase has determined that the building will be worth $16,900,000 in five years, the assumed holding period. The investor has arrived at this conclusion by capitalizing the fifth-year net operating income at a rate of 10 percent. That is, the fifth-year net cash flow of $1,690,000 ($17.00 per square foot rent times 100,000 square feet minus the structural reserve) has been set equal to 10 percent of the market value of the building. This calculation assumes that the current use reflects the highest and best use at that point in time.

This investor, having determined the future value of the office building, determines the present value of the property by discounting the cash flows and the future value (called *reversion*), using his required rate of

---

[2]This is a reserve to fund the maintenance of the building's exterior. It is treated as an expense, so it is deducted from gross potential income.

TABLE 5–1
Annual Pro Forma Income Statement

	Years 1 through 5
Lease 1 (20,000 square feet)	$ 340,000
Lease 2 (30,000 square feet)	510,000
Lease 3 (50,000 square feet)	850,000
Gross potential income	1,700,000
Less:	
Vacancy factor.....................	0
Reserve (.10 per square foot)	10,000
Net operating income................	$1,690,000

return. The required rate is generally determined as the risk-adjusted opportunity cost of the funds available for the purchase of the property. The case under analysis is a relatively low-risk transaction, so the required, or *hurdle*, rate of return would reflect this fact. The investor would set the fifth-year capitalization rate equal to the required rate in order to be consistent. Setting the hurdle rate at 10 percent and calculating the present value yields a present value of $16,900,000. Given the need to earn at least a 10 percent rate of return and given the assumed future value, the investor would be willing to pay up to $16,900,000 for the property. If the investor were able to conclude the transaction for less, the internal rate of return would rise above the required rate.

Recall the asking price of $18,777,777. The investor and the seller are nearly $2 million apart because of different perceptions of risk or different assessments of the highest and best use. The investor may be a new entrant to the real estate markets or may have owned real estate through a time period in which even credit tenants were not a sure thing.

Another way to view this example is to assume that the property is being offered at a lower price, say $17,000,000. The investor would then capitalize fifth-year NOI as before and could calculate the internal rate of return (IRR) on the investment and compare this rate with the hurdle rate. In this case, an asking price of $17,000,000 would yield an IRR of 9.84 percent, which is below the investor's required return. Unless the investor could complete the transaction at the present value price of $16,900,000, the investor's return requirement would not be met, even at this lower price.

Finally, let us assume that the asking price of the property is known, as is the investor's required rate of return. Assume the asking price is $17,000,000, and the required rate of return is 10 percent. Given these two pieces of information, the future value (after five years) of the property may be calculated. This future value represents the *required future value*, given the asking price and the cash flows, in order for the investor to attain his required rate of return. The required future value of $17,061,051 may then be compared with the likely future price as determined by capping fifth-year NOI, (that is, the "market" price of $16,900,000). In this case, if the investor were to purchase the property at the asking price and then seek to attain his required rate of return, he would need to set a selling price in the fifth year that would be above the market price. Thus the prospective investor would be attempting to set a lower cap rate (and so a higher price) than that which the market would be likely to bear. The investor's cap rate would be 9.9 percent (divide NOI by the required selling price) while the previously determined market cap was 10 percent. Again, unless the investor can attain a lower initial purchase price or can adjust the required rate of return downward, the property will not meet the investor's needs.

The analysis conducted above assumed zero vacancy and inflation rates, fixed lease rates, a static required rate of return and market cap rate, and a 100 percent equity purchase. A simple relaxation of the hurdle rate of return or any other assumption would be sufficient to generate a series of scenarios for purchase price and rate of return.

As mentioned before, accurate assessment of expenses is difficult at best in many property valuations. A large subjective element enters into the determination of the likely resale value of the property at the end of the assumed holding period. An approach suggested by James W. Hoag attempts to resolve this problem, at least in part, by using a regression approach that is in a sense a synthesis of the market value and income approaches to valuation.[3] He suggests regressing the prices at which properties trade against fundamental characteristics of value such as income and expenses in the year of purchase, net leases, capital improvements and so forth, national economic measures such as business inventories and volume of sales of industrial properties, and regional measures of locational and temporal value. Such a regression model can be used to estimate

---

[3]James W. Hoag, "Towards Indices of Real Estate Value and Return," *Journal of Finance*, 35 (May 1980), pp. 569-80.

TABLE 5–2
Pro Forma Effect of Leverage
(year 1)

	No Leverage		8.5 Percent Mortgage	
	Best Case	Worst Case	Best Case	Worst Case
Equity	$1,690,000	$1,690,000	$ 338,000	$ 338,000
Debt	0	0	1,352,000	1,352,000
Gross potential income	1,690,000	(1,000)	169,000	(1,000)
Less: Interest on debt	0	0	11,900	11,900
Taxable income	169,000	(1,000)	157,100	(12,900)
Less: Taxes	64,220	(380)	59,698	(4,902)
Net operating income	$104,780	($620)	$97,402	($7,998)
Aftertax return to equity (NOI/equity)	6.20%	−0.04%	28.82%	−2.37%

the market value of a portfolio of real estate holdings even though the individual properties do not come to market.

The Effect of Leverage on Valuation. To this point, we have not considered the effect of leverage on valuation. Financing a property by a mortgage or other debt instrument increases the return to equity, not only because returns are thus concentrated in the hands of the equity holders but also because interest on the debt can be used to offset taxable income and thus reduce the amount of taxes paid. However, it does so at the cost of increasing the risk of the equity.

Consider the following simple illustration. Suppose, in the earlier example, the purchaser of the property decides to finance 80 percent of the $1,690,000 purchase with a $1,352,000 nonamortizing 8.5 percent mortgage. The purchaser faces a 38 percent tax on the income received and has other income to offset any losses. In Table 5–2 we consider a best-case scenario where all the lease space is taken and a worst-case scenario in which the lease space will remain vacant in the first year.

Where all leases are taken, the return on equity rises from 6.20 percent to 28.82 percent with leverage. The tax bill has been reduced by $4,522, partially offsetting payments to debt holders, and the resulting net operating income after interest and taxes is allocated to a smaller amount of equity. However, this scenario is the best case. In the worst-case scenario, leverage magnifies the potential loss in the return to equity holders. On average, return to equity increases with leverage; so does risk. Leverage increases the range of possible returns to equity. If the investor is at all risk averse, the required return to equity should also rise with leverage.

At this point, it is useful to draw a distinction between the value of a property and value of equity in a property. The property itself is no more or less risky as a result of the degree of leverage involved in financing the purchase of the property; the tax benefits are associated with the financing of the property and not with the property itself. A block of apartments and an industrial plant will have the same tax advantages from leverage if they can be purchased for the same price. Consequently properties should be valued as if they were to be financed by 100 percent equity; the appropriate amount of leverage should be determined by a separate calculation. In other words, in comparing properties, the NOI should be computed without regard either for mortgage and other debt payments or for the tax benefits associated with the interest component of those payments.

Treating the financing package separately simplifies the analysis of the financing of property. There has been a recent proliferation of forms of property ownership such as partnerships, syndications, real estate investment trusts (REITS), and mortgage-backed securities that have attributes of both debt and equity. They are properly thought of as claims contingent on the value of the underlying property (see Chapter Six). This development emphasizes the importance of a careful analysis of financing alternatives.

Return. Real estate investments typically have been associated with large positive returns. In the period from 1947 to 1984 a dollar invested in real estate investments increased 20-fold, and (as can be seen from Table 5–3) returns were only exceeded by the returns on stock equity investments. Yet these investments appear to have very small risk. Note the low standard deviation of real estate returns and also the low correlation of such returns with those of other assets. It would appear that real estate can add significant diversification within a large portfolio of assets.

The apparent high return and low risk of real estate investments seems incongruous with the perception of risk associated with such investments, REITS in particular. These numbers tend to underestimate risk for two reasons. The valuation process on which these numbers are based tends to "smooth" returns, and these numbers do not reflect the leverage that is typical in most real estate financing. "Real Estate" numbers in Table 5–3

TABLE 5-3
Annual Returns for U.S. Real Estate and Other Investments, and Inflation, 1947–1984

	Real Estate	Stocks	Small Stocks	Corporate Bonds	Long-Term Government Bonds	Treasury Bills	Inflation
Mean and standard deviation of annual returns (percent)							
Arithmetic mean	8.30%	12.58%	17.81%	4.23%	3.56%	4.69%	4.33%
Geometric mean	8.24	11.27	14.78	3.88	3.24	4.64	4.27
Standard deviation	3.67	17.13	27.03	9.24	8.69	3.43	3.67
Correlations of annual returns							
Real estate	1.000						
Stocks	−0.062	1.000					
Small stocks	0.029	0.786	1.000				
Corporate bonds	−0.060	0.124	0.013	1.000			
Long-term governments	−0.077	−0.013	−0.101	0.949	1.000		
Treasury bills	0.403	−0.231	−0.011	0.200	0.237	1.000	
Inflation	0.849	−0.274	−0.080	−0.187	−0.152	0.650	1.000

refer to a value-weighted composite of unleveraged residential, farm, and business real estate investments.[4]

Property valuations tend to vary less than the prices at which properties actually change hands. One can interpret this result as: (1) the real estate markets are "too volatile" or (2) the valuation process is too conservative, taking stabilized income and expense items and estimates of highest and best use that increase only with inflation. The valuation process itself would imply the high correlation between measured returns on real estate and the inflation rate observed in Table 5–3. Regardless of which interpretation is correct it is the prices at which properties actually trade, rather than the current valuations, that are relevant for performance measurement and risk assessment. These numbers should be treated with care in portfolio analysis.

These numbers are also biased down to the extent that they do not reflect the effect of leverage on the return and risk of equity investments in real estate. As mentioned above, leverage increases expected return, not only by virtue of concentrating return in the hands of equity holders but also by virtue of the favorable tax treatment of payments to debt holders. The risk of real estate equity is also higher than the numbers in Table 5–3 would indicate. Assuming the debt has no risk, the standard deviation of equity returns on a property financed by an 80 percent mortgage would increase by a factor of five (five being the reciprocal of the percentage of equity finance, which in this instance is 20 percent). Thus the 3.67 percent standard deviation reported above for unleveraged real estate investment returns would imply a 21.35 percent standard deviation of equity returns, given an 80 percent mortgage.

Market Analysis

The example of the previous section presented a highly simplified version of project valuation. Most actual cases are far more complex, dealing with more tenants, differing lease terms and conditions, variable inflation rates, and variable market conditions. Market conditions as represented by a market vacancy rate affect the length of individual leases and the rental rates at lease renewal. Market conditions may be simulated and applied to the analysis of a project in which the tenants are not yet signed up or

---

[4]The numbers were derived from Gary P. Brinson and Roger G. Ibbotson, *Investment Markets: Gaining the Performance Advantage* (New York: McGraw-Hill, forthcoming); Ibbotson Associates, *Stocks, Bonds, Bills and Inflation: 1985 Yearbook* (Chicago: Ibbotson Associates, Capital Management Research Center, 1986).

existing tenants have lease expiration dates prior to the anticipated date of sale of a property. As will be demonstrated in the third section of this chapter, market conditions are also relevant to portfolio analysis.

The vacancy rate is a summary, or reduced form, statistic conveying information about the supply of and demand for various types of real estate in particular markets at particular times. The vacancy rate is calculated as total rentable space (in square feet) minus leased space, expressed as a percent of total rentable space. In theory all comparable space in a market should be individually measured and examined for occupancy in order to calculate the rate. In fact the rate is calculated by various groups and individuals for select markets and submarkets, structure types, and periods of time using varying degrees of rigor. The two best-known sources for vacancy data are Coldwell Banker and the Office Network. The former collects data on 31 cities for office and industrial space; the latter follows only office space in approximately 30 cities.

The vacancy rate, even in its reduced form, is able to provide useful information on current market conditions and the current market relative to its own norms, to the U.S. market as a whole, and to alternative investment locations.

Table 5–4 contains vacancy data for the nation and the cities of Atlanta and San Francisco. A rapid scan of the data reveals that Atlanta generally experiences high vacancy rates, San Francisco experiences low rates, and the U.S. moves between the two. The mean values support this observation as do the medians. The median for San Francisco is significantly below its mean, indicating a nonnormal distribution. The mode for San Francisco consists of the 0 to .9 percent range within which over half of the values fall. Three values each fall into the ranges of 5.0 percent to 5.9 percent and 6.0 percent to 6.9 percent, making this distribution somewhat bimodal. The San Francisco distribution is also characterized by a high standard deviation relative to its mean. An examination of the plot of San Francisco office market vacancies over time (see Figure 5–1) establishes that while there are no outliers, there has been an apparent shift in the behavior of the market. Vacancy rates have tended to increase over time in both the national and regional markets.

The Atlanta data present a more consistent portrait. The mean, mode, and median are quite similar. There are no outliers, and the standard deviation reflects variation around the mean over time rather than a major market shift.

The mean and standard deviation calculations indicate that normally (95 percent of the time) the national vacancy rate varies between a theo-

TABLE 5–4
Office Market Vacancy Rates, June 1978 to
March 1985
(quarterly)

	National	Atlanta	San Francisco
1978			
June	6.9	17.8	0.9
September	6.2	14.2	0.7
December	5.6	13.3	0.4
1979			
March	5.2	12.5	0.5
June	4.8	10.0	1.6
September	4.2	12.0	0.2
December	3.6	11.6	0.4
1980			
March	3.4	11.9	0.2
June	3.4	12.5	0.2
September	3.9	13.1	0.1
December	4.1	13.9	0.1
1981			
March	3.8	12.1	0.1
June	4.1	11.6	0.1
September	4.4	12.3	0.3
December	4.8	17.7	0.4
1982			
March	5.5	15.4	0.8
June	7.1	15.2	3.4
September	8.9	20.1	3.6
December	10.3	19.4	5.7
1983			
March	10.8	19.9	5.9
June	11.7	18.4	6.1
September	11.7	16.3	6.4
December	12.4	16.0	5.9
1984			
March	13.1	14.7	6.9
June	13.5	14.5	8.6
September	14.2	14.1	9.0
December	14.7	15.5	10.1
1985			
March	15.3	15.8	10.9
Mean	7.8	14.7	3.2
Median	5.9	14.4	.85
Standard deviation	4.0	2.7	3.5

SOURCE: Coldwell Banker

FIGURE 5–1
Office Market Vacancy Rates:
National, Atlanta, San Francisco

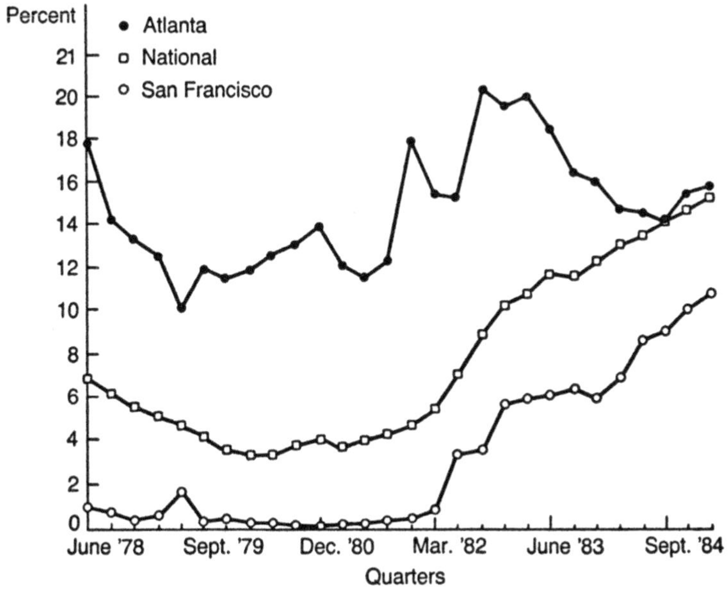

retical − .2 percent and a high of 15.8 percent. The March 1985 rate of 15.3 percent is therefore unusually high. This relationship between the "norm" and the current level may be a one-time market condition that may or may not continue into the future. The structure of the market would need to be analyzed to establish a behavioral cause and to assess the likely persistence of such behavior. Alternatively, current behavior does not represent a true aberration but rather a normal cyclical event that has not been captured by a time series that begins in the second quarter of 1978. A different statistic used for market analysis and discussed below would suggest the alternative explanation.

In sharp contrast, the Atlanta vacancy rate varies within a theoretical range of 9.3 percent to 20.1 percent, with a March 1985 value of 15.8 percent. The current value is not out of line with normal behavior. A review of the data plot in Figure 5–1 would even suggest that a full market cycle is captured within the time period for which the data are available.

TABLE 5–5
Correlation of National and Regional Vacancy Rates and Time
(second quarter 1978 through first quarter 1985)

	Vacancy Rate			
	National	Atlanta	San Francisco	Time
Vacancy rate				
National	1.000			
Atlanta	0.539	1.000		
San Francisco	0.979	0.461	1.000	
Time	0.843	0.465	0.874	1.000

The correlation matrix in Table 5–5 provides some information useful for comparative purposes. Vacancy rates have tended to rise from 1978 to 1985, as reflected in the positive correlation between vacancy rates and time. This is less true of the Atlanta market, for which the correlation is smaller. Again, before a firm inference about the future could be based on this statistic, one would want to be sure that the data are representative of the behavior of each market. In fact there is reason to doubt the steady rise in vacancies will persist at the national level; and as we shall see, these data are more indicative of longer-term cyclical movements in these rates. The correlation matrix also shows a very high correlation between national vacancy rates and those for San Francisco. Rather than indicating any causality, this correlation probably indicates similar responses to various market factors. Although the San Francisco vacancy rate is included as a part of the national rate, each city is a small enough portion of the national vacancy rate that independent behavior is possible. The correlation between the nation and Atlanta is low, indicating that similar market factors are probably not governing the two markets.

The high correlation between San Francisco and the nation allows the employment of a useful modeling or forecasting procedure. It is possible to model (for analytical or forecasting applications) the national vacancy rate in as careful and detailed a fashion as possible and then to estimate a very simple equation for San Francisco, using national data. The estimated coefficients of such a relationship will capture differences in the responsiveness of San Francisco and the nation to an identical set of market factors.

Table 5–6 illustrates the result of a simple regression of the national vacancy rate on the San Francisco vacancy rate. The regression statistics

TABLE 5–6
Regression of San Francisco Vacancy Rates on
National Rates
(second quarter 1978 through first quarter 1985)

	Coefficient	Standard Error	t-Value
Intercept	−3.47907	0.3058	−11.38
National vacancy rate	0.85898	0.0350	24.57

Residual standard error = 0.7429.
Multiple R-square = 0.9587.
N = 28.
F-value = 603.739 on 1, 26 degrees of freedom.
Durbin-Watson statistic = 0.8851.

confirm the strength of the relationship between the nation and San Francisco. The R^2 (.9587) is high, the t-statistic (24.57) on national is very strong, and the residual standard error is very low (.7429). However, the fact that the Durbin-Watson statistic is so low is disturbing:[5] the autocorrelation of the residuals is .49. Such a low Durbin-Watson statistic is a good indication that the regression model is misspecified: an explanatory variable has been left out of the analysis.

It would seem reasonable that a good predictor of next month's vacancy rate is this month's rate. Including the lagged vacancy rate as an explanatory variable yields the results reported in Table 5–7. The Durbin-Watson statistic is no longer significant, and the autocorrelation of the residuals is −.004.

With time-oriented data it is sometimes useful to include an additional variable (here called time) in a regression equation. The correlation analysis presented in Table 5–5 would seem to indicate that such a variable would have significant explanatory power.

Table 5–8 presents the results of the regression including time. The additional variable is in fact not significant. Using the vacancy rate of the previous month as an explanatory variable appears to capture the fact that vacancy rates tend to move with time. Rather than indicating that San Francisco rates are merely trending upwards over time, these data seem

---

[5]The Durbin-Watson statistic of .8851 is less than the critical value of 1.10 (1 percent significance level). This indicates that the positive serial correlation of .49 is statistically significant.

TABLE 5–7

Regression of San Francisco Vacancy Rates on National
Rates and Rates for Previous Quarter
(third quarter 1978 through first quarter 1985)

	Coefficient	Standard Error	t-Value
Intercept	−2.11747	0.5797	−3.65
National vacancy rate	0.54001	0.1312	4.12
Previous-quarter rate	0.40703	0.1647	2.47

Residual standard error = 0.6277.
Multiple R-square = 0.9724.
N = 27.
F-value = 422.189 on 2, 24 degrees of freedom.
Durbin-Watson statistic = 1.8838.

TABLE 5–8

Regression of San Francisco Vacancy Rates on National
Rates, Rates for Previous Quarter, and Time
(third quarter 1978 through first quarter 1985)

	Coefficient	Standard Error	t-Value
Intercept	−2.25254	0.5718	−3.94
National vacancy rate	0.47081	0.1358	3.46
Previous-quarter rate	0.39368	0.1606	2.45
Time	0.04759	0.0315	1.51

Residual standard error = 0.6115.
Multiple R-square = 0.9749.
N = 27.
F-value = 297.29 on 3, 23 degrees of freedom.
Durbin-Watson statistic = 2.0254.

---

more indicative of a cyclical pattern of movements in vacancy rates. A good predictor of next month's vacancy rate is this month's rate. However, 28 quarters of data cannot be conclusive here. With a more comprehensive data base, a more explicit time-series model of the data would be called for.

The stage is now set for the modeling and forecasting of the national office vacancy rate. These results would then be used in the San Francisco model to generate a forecast of the city's office market. At this point, unfortunately, the problems with vacancy rate data emerge. The fact that the rate is a summary statistic means that modeling will be difficult.

The vacancy rate summarizes the relationship between the supply of and demand for space. Since these two components are separately motivated, it is preferable to analyze each separately and then form a vacancy rate or a proxy. A methodology that builds the vacancy rate (or a proxy) in this fashion has been developed and is in use. (This author constructs a statistic entitled the Real Estate Market Index—REMI; others call it a vacancy rate. The basic techniques are similar.)

Essentially the REMI and its counterparts are constructed by first calculating construction contract awards in square footage on the demand side. The difference between square feet constructed and square feet demanded is then expressed as a percentage of square feet constructed. The data used by the various groups calculating this statistic vary, but generally F. W. Dodge–McGraw-Hill contract awards and Commerce Department construction permits dominate the supply side, while the demand side is dominated by standard employment data generated via government administrative programs at the Bureau of Labor Statistics. The primary advantage of the data is that they are available on a reasonably consistent basis over time, at great geographic detail, and for many structure types.

The historical supply-side data are generated by taking construction contract awards or permits issued and projecting them forward to a "put in place" concept. Thus the flow of new square footage available for lease is known. Clearly, a contract awarded today will become a building in the future, so the raw data provide an implicit short-run forecast. This flow series may be converted to a total-stock-of-space series only with difficulty or a set of assumptions. It is the author's practice to generate a five-year moving sum to create a stock series for space up to five years old.

The nature of the raw data provides a year or two of virtually known additions to stock. Projecting stock (or additions) beyond this is more difficult. What turns out to be useful is simply to rely on the historic mean as a "most likely" future scenario and then to develop high and low straight line projections around that mean. The standard deviation of the put-in-place series provides some guidance in setting the high and low construction scenarios. Again, to develop the most realistic bands, it is critical to analyze the put-in-place series as the vacancy series were analyzed earlier. In addition, contemporary knowledge of the market being analyzed is critical in order to anticipate shifts in market behavior.

The demand side requires a series on the population using the space in question. For example, office demand may arise from employment in nonmanufacturing sectors or from white-collar workers or from workers earning particular salary levels. The key here is not so much which cut is made of the universe of the work force but rather how the selected subset

TABLE 5–9
Regression of National Vacancy Rates on the Real
Estate Market Index
(second quarter 1978 through first quarter 1985)

	Coefficient	Standard Error	t-Value
Intercept	12.17044	0.3519	34.58
Real Estate Market Index	4.18101	0.2520	16.59

Residual standard error = 1.2244.
Multiple R-square = 0.9136.
N = 28.
F-value = 275.26 on 1, 26 degrees of freedom.
Durbin-Watson statistic = 0.1355.

is translated into square-footage terms. Once the subset of the work force has been selected it must be modeled and forecast. National employment forecasts are available through nearly every major Wall Street economist's office, and subnational forecasts are available from a variety of economic consulting firms. Alternatively one can construct an employment demand model on a personal computer and can manage the forecast to meet one's own beliefs and theories. The employment data must be translated into square-footage terms with a square-foot-per-worker scalar or series. This author calculates the change in the selected employment level and multiplies it by a square-foot-per-worker number developed by analyzing the historic relationship between space and use. Thus a periodic new demand for space series is generated. This series is made equivalent to the supply series by calculating a five-year moving sum.

The supply and demand series have thus been created independently, and each has significant simulation capability. What-if scenarios may be created by manipulating the demand and/or the supply sides and *then* seeing the magnitude of effect on the reduced form vacancy, or a proxy, statistic.

Since the national vacancy rate is not easy to model and forecast from a conceptual perspective, the REMI may be employed here as a forecasting tool for the vacancy rate. Table 5–9 contains a regression analysis relating the national vacancy rate to the constructed Real Estate Market Index series. The statistics confirm that the fit of the model appears to be acceptable, but the Durbin-Watson statistic of .1355 indicates that the positive serial correlation of .9282 in the residuals is even more significant

TABLE 5–10
Regression of National Vacancy Rates on the Real Estate Market
Index, Current and Lagged One Quarter, and the National Rates
Lagged One Quarter and One Year
(third quarter 1979 through first quarter 1985)

	Coefficient	Standard Error	t-Value
Intercept	5.18411	1.9264	2.69
Real Estate Market Index	4.18829	0.8631	4.85
Lagged market index	−3.25101	1.0255	−3.17
Lagged national rate	0.65215	0.1448	4.50
National rate lagged one year	1.12589	0.4467	2.52

Residual standard error = 0.3199.
Multiple R-square = 0.9956.
N = 23.
F-value = 1030.825 on 4, 18 degrees of freedom.
Durbin-Watson statistic = 1.9041.

than before. The data at the national level appear to be far more cyclical than the data at the regional level. In addition, there appears to be a significant seasonal component. Table 5–10 presents the results of regression analysis that indicate the significance of the national vacancy rate last quarter and last year as predictors of this quarter's vacancy rate. However, the market index remains a significant explanatory variable and its coefficient, 4.18829, is virtually unchanged from the results reported in Table 5–9. Clearly, the importance of the market index has not diminished with the inclusion of other explanatory variables in the regression.

The careful analysis of subnational market conditions over time is possible using these tools. The addition of the REMI or its equivalent permits both the forecasting of vacancy rates (where available) and the independent analysis and forecasting of the REMI.

The Phoenix, Arizona, REMI is used below to model and forecast the Coldwell Banker office vacancy rate for Phoenix. These two series are constructed for the Maricopa County area so they are comparably based, with a correlation of .824.

Table 5–11 presents results regressing the vacancy rate on the REMI and the vacancy rate measured for the previous year. The brief historic time series available obviously renders the equation less statistically reliable, but this data dilemma tends to occur with some frequency. In all of the analysis presented in this chapter, the role of the analyst looms large.

TABLE 5–11
Regression of Annual Phoenix Vacancy Rates on the Phoenix Real
Estate Market Index and Rates for Previous Year
(1979 through 1985)

	Coefficient	Standard Error	t-Value
Intercept	7.88833	5.8487	1.35
Phoenix Real Estate Market Index	3.01289	1.7915	1.68
Lagged Phoenix vacancy rate	0.77404	0.3765	2.06

Residual standard error = 3.1827.
Multiple R-square = 0.8522.
$N = 7$.
F-value = 11.53524 on 2, 4 degrees of freedom.
Durbin-Watson statistic = 1.9113.

Clearly, there is more than enough room for the application of experienced judgment.

Table 5–12 provides historical and forecast data generated by the preceding regression. The Real Estate Market Index for Phoenix was constructed using an employment (or demand) forecast in conjunction with

---

TABLE 5–12
Actual and Predicted Vacancy Rates for the
Phoenix Area

	Vacancy Rate	Market Index
Historical data		
1978	10.500	−1.097
1979	5.300	−2.036
1980	6.700	−2.654
1981	8.200	−2.104
1982	10.100	−0.913
1983	13.200	−0.342
1984	19.700	−0.198
1985	23.100	−0.371
Predictions		
1986	24.440	−0.441
1987	24.510	−0.762
1988	24.260	−0.863
1989	24.720	−0.646
1990	25.643	−0.458

---

the short-term projection of current construction contract awards and a longer-term, "most likely" projection of contract awards. The assumption underlying the demand forecast is that demand is likely to continue to be strong in the short run, trending slightly downwards to 1990. The supply side is expected to cool down slightly from current high levels under the pressure of the unusually high level of vacancy rates that are causing declining effective rental rates and increased construction lender caution.

Integration of Property and Market Analysis

In this example, the Phoenix vacancy rate analyzed above will be applied to the earlier property analysis. The market rental rate will be $17 per square foot, zero rent and expense inflation will be assumed, and expenses will be limited to the $.10 per square foot structural reserve. The building will now be cast as a speculative development with no signed tenants. The prospective investor must analyze the market and this project's relationship to the market to generate realistic leasing scenarios in order to determine value and offering price. Although our focus is on the impact on the internal rate of return (IRR), it is clear from the first part of this chapter that offering price, rate of return, and future value are directly related.

Table 5–13 presents two leased-up scenarios. Scenario I assumes that the building will be fully leased upon completion and will remain leased except for a 5 percent vacancy factor. This vacancy factor does not imply that 95 percent of the building is occupied at all times. Rather, it captures the effect of tenant mobility and the time required to refit space as each tenant leaves and is replaced by another. Scenario II hypothesizes that the building will perform similarly to the market. That is, in the first year of operation, occupancy of 79.5 percent could be anticipated; and by Year 5, occupancy would decline to 74.2 percent as the entire market softens. It is unlikely that any one building would perform exactly like the carefully defined aggregate market, but Scenario II provides a way to analyze the market's effect on the property and to contrast this with an optimistic (traditional in the real estate industry) view. While the point of this analysis is to be as accurate as possible, it is equally important to assess sensitivities so that risk may be fully understood.

Suppose the asking price of the building were set at $16,050,000, assuming a 5 percent vacancy factor. The IRR on Scenario I would be 10 percent and the IRR on Scenario II is 3.88 percent. Returns are quite sensitive to market conditions expressed as property vacancy rates.

TABLE 5–13

Property and Market Analysis Scenarios

	Year				
	1	2	3	4	5
Scenario I					
Gross potential income	$1,700,000	$1,700,000	$1,700,000	$1,700,000	$1,700,000
Less:					
Vacancy factor (5 percent)	85,000	85,000	85,000	85,000	85,000
$.10 reserve	10,000	10,000	10,000	10,000	10,000
Net operating income	1,605,000	1,605,000	1,605,000	1,605,000	1,605,000
Present value at 10 percent capitalization rate	$16,050,000				$16,050,000
Scenario II					
Gross income	$1,700,000	$1,700,000	$1,700,000	$1,700,000	$1,700,000
Less:					
Vacancy factor	24.4%	24.5%	24.3%	24.7%	25.6%
$.10 reserve	10,000	10,000	10,000	10,000	10,000
Net operating income	1,275,200	1,273,500	1,276,900	1,270,100	1,254,800
Present value at 10 percent capitalization rate	$12,609,054				$12,548,000

This example could be used to demonstrate the importance of rental and expense inflation assumptions and capitalization rate assumptions. Each component of this seemingly straightforward spreadsheet is subject to considerable underlying analytic effort. The value of the analytics is generated both in the increased accuracy of the pro forma statement and in the heightened appreciation of the sensitivity of the key statistics to the assumptions driving the analysis.

PORTFOLIO ANALYSIS

Market analysis has a role in interproject or portfolio analysis as well as in project analysis. Essentially, the objective of portfolio analysis is to design a portfolio of real estate holdings that achieve an overall return commensurate with the level of risk selected by the portfolio manager. The optimal way to discharge this assignment would be to collect a long time series on each of the universe of properties' rates of return. These returns would then be used in a mathematical model designed to identify through the analysis of covariance a series of unique, efficient portfolios (each paired with a risk level) from which the manager could select a preferred portfolio.

The implementation of this ideal process is a fairly simple matter for common stocks. In real estate, as usual, the data are difficult to come by. Time series on returns that would permit the analysis of risk are not available for specific properties. The closest that one can come to time series on returns for various market segments is the index that records the performance of properties managed by members of the National Council of Real Estate Investment Fiduciaries, known as the FRC Property Index. The time series is quarterly, beginning in December 1977. One catch is that because the commingled funds involved cover only around 850 properties, the data can only be meaningfully disaggregated into five structure categories *or* four geographic categories. In addition the data are not representative of the universe of commercial properties. This lack of representation and degree of aggregation renders the data useless for any meaningful portfolio optimization exercise. Of greater concern, though, is the fact that the time series is based on appraised values rather than transaction prices. As noted earlier in this chapter, appraisals can smooth the true volatility by about a factor of five.

The other sources of real estate return data (notably Evaluation Associates Inc.) report on the performance of particular funds. The composition of these funds changes over time; so while this data might be of use in the performance evaluation of portfolio managers, it is of limited use in optimization efforts. It also suffers from the problems associated with dependence on appraisals.

A more recent approach to portfolio design begins with an intuitively plausible but impossible to verify assumption: vacancy rates and real estate returns are behaviorally related. Improvements in market vacancy rates are very likely to translate into rising market and property rental rates. As rents rise, net operating income should rise, and capitalized or discounted cash flows should follow. As vacancy rates rise, the reverse chain of events ought to occur. This approach is able to take advantage of the readily available vacancy rate data and constructed data such as the REMI. The virtue of data like the REMI and its counterparts is that the universe of real estate may be included in the optimizer and the analysis may be conducted by very disaggregated geographic and structure-type markets. While an individual property within a market might not behave precisely as indicated by the relevant REMI or vacancy rate, it is highly likely that the two will be closely related.

CONCLUSION

Quantitative methods are gradually emerging as a valuable tool in real estate analysis. Progress has been relatively slow, however, because high-quality data are scarce. Properties are infrequently turned over and deals are usually negotiated privately. This forces analysts to rely on estimated values such as appraisals in their application of quantitative methods. The securitization of real estate in the form of REITS and mortgage-backed securities may yield some useful data for quantitative analysis. Moreover, quantitative methods may be used to improve the quality of the raw data as suggested by the development of a real estate market index.

REFERENCES

Brinson, G. P., and R. G. Ibbotson. *Investment Markets: Gaining the Performance Advantage*. New York: McGraw-Hill, 1987.

Hoag, J. W. "Towards Indices of Real Estate Value and Return." *Journal of Finance*, 35 (May 1980), pp. 569–80.

Ibbotson Associates. *Stocks, Bonds, Bills and Inflation: 1985 Yearbook*. Chicago: Ibbotson Associates, Capital Management Research Center, 1986.

Wendt, P. F., and A. R. Cerf. *Real Estate Investment Analysis and Taxation*. New York: McGraw-Hill, 1979.

CHAPTER SIX

Quantitative Methods in Derivative Security Analysis

Christopher B. Barry and Andrew H. Chen

INTRODUCTION

Derivative securities have values and cash flows determined by the behavior of other securities, called the *underlying securities*. For example a common stock call option gives the owner of the option the right to buy a given number of shares of stock at a specified price within a specified time period. The value of the option depends on the value of its underlying asset, the common stock. Similarly a Treasury bill (T-bill) futures contract obliges the owner to purchase T-bills at a fixed price on a particular date. The value of the futures contract is derived from the value of the under-lying asset, the T-bills. Derivative securities, then, are securities that allow the buyer or seller of the securities to arrange payoffs "contingent" on the values of other securities. As a result, derivative securities enlarge the opportunity set of payoffs that can be obtained by investors.

This chapter will introduce the basic concepts and results of applying quantitative methods to the analysis of derivative securities. Call option securities are emphasized in particular, since the state of the field is well advanced in the analysis of those securities. The chapter begins with a discussion of basic properties of options and of some useful boundaries on their values. Next follows a discussion of simple option portfolio strategies that illustrates how their cash flows and the probability distributions of their cash flows relate to the underlying assets. Then arbitrage concepts are presented that are important in valuing derivative securities and analyzing strategies, followed by a development of two well-known models for option valuation. A brief empirical section presents results from the literature regarding the returns to put and call option portfolios and indicating how well the theoretical models work in practice. Finally, the applicability of option pricing principles to a variety of other types of securities will be discussed.

BASIC PROPERTIES OF OPTION VALUES

Option contracts that are traded on the major options exchanges are of two primary types: calls and puts. A *call option* gives the owner of the contract the right to buy a fixed number of shares of the underlying security at a fixed price, called the exercise or strike price, within a fixed time period. A *put option* gives the owner of the contract the right to sell a fixed number of shares of the underlying security at a fixed price within a fixed time period.

Since an option is the right to buy or sell a given number of shares of the underlying stock at a given price on or before a specified date, options derive their values from the prices of the underlying assets and from the terms in the option contract. Since a call option is a right (rather than an obligation) to buy the underlying stock at the exercise price, only if the stock price at expiration is greater than the option exercise price will the holder of a call exercise the option and receive the difference between the stock price and the exercise price; if the stock price is equal to or less than the exercise price, the holder of the call will let the option expire rather than exercise it. Thus, at the expiration date the call has zero value if the exercise price is greater than the underlying stock price. Hence we can express the value of a call at the expiration date (T) of the option as the stock minus the exercise price (K), or zero, whichever is greater. This establishes the minimum value of a call. Since buying the underlying stock is obviously an alternative to buying a call on the stock, the maximum value of the call is the price of the stock itself.

Thus we can show the upper and lower boundaries of the price of a call as illustrated in Figure 6–1.

FIGURE 6–1
Boundaries of Call Price

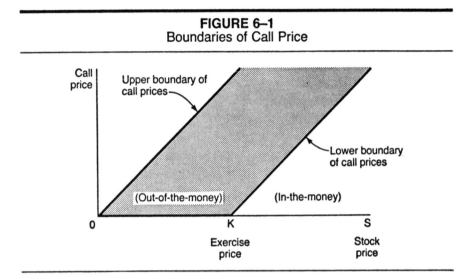

At expiration, a call has zero value if the stock price is equal to or less than the exercise price, and the call option price increases a dollar for each dollar increase in the stock price if the stock price is greater than the exercise price. Therefore the possible value of a call option at expiration may be represented by a kinked line consisting of a horizontal line segment from the origin to the exercise price, K, and the upward-sloping line from the exercise price of a call. If a call option expires worthless at maturity, the call is said to expire *out of the money*. If it has a positive value at maturity, the call will be exercised and not allowed to expire, and the call is said to be *in the money*. These descriptions of the relationship between exercise price and underlying stock price at expiration are often loosely used during the life of the option. A call option is said to be traded in the money, at the money, or out of the money whenever the current price of the underlying stock is greater than, close to, or less than the exercise price of the call, respectively.

The value of a call at expiration is referred to as its *intrinsic value*. At any time prior to expiration the call option should be worth at least its intrinsic value, otherwise investors who own the stock would sell stock and buy the call instead, profiting by the difference between the exercise price and the stock minus the call price. To the extent that the option may be further in the money at expiration than it currently is, it may be worth even more than its intrinsic value. However, it will not be worth more

---

FIGURE 6–2
Boundaries of Put Prices

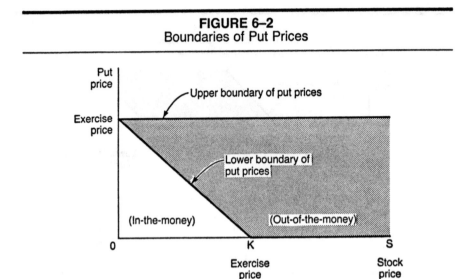

---

than the stock, since then the investors would sell the call and buy the stock. As we shall see, these *arbitrage* arguments are essential to an understanding of what it is that determines option values.

Similarly a put option is a right and not an obligation to sell a given number of shares of the underlying stock at the exercise price. The value of a put at expiration is equal to either the exercise price minus the stock price at expiration or zero, whichever is greater. This gives the minimum value of a put price. Also note that the value of a put cannot exceed the exercise price, even if the stock price drops to zero. Thus we present the upper and the lower boundaries of the put price as in Figure 6–2. A put is said to be traded in the money, at the money, or out of the money if the current stock price is less than, close to, or greater than the exercise price, respectively.

SIMPLE OPTIONS STRATEGIES

There are many options strategies that can be employed by investors in their portfolio management decisions. For instance an investor can purchase or sell short either a call option or a put option alone (*naked strategy*), trade the options with the underlying stocks at the same time

FIGURE 6–3
Profit/Loss for Call Buyer (solid line) and Call Writer (dotted line)

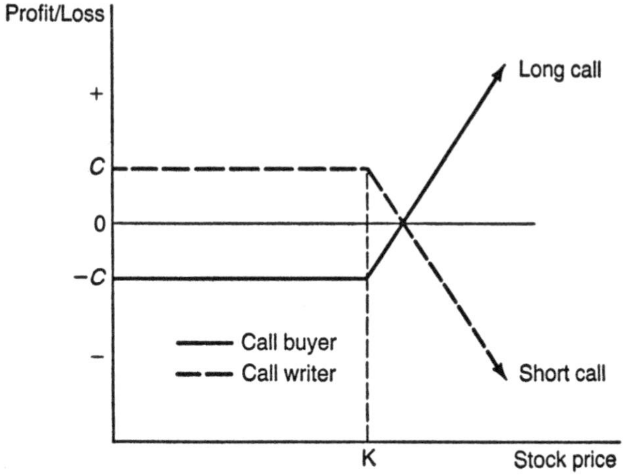

(*hedging strategies*), trade calls or puts with different exercise prices or different expiration dates (*spreading strategies*), or combine calls and puts in one transaction (*combination strategies*). We shall describe only a few simple naked and hedging strategies.

Long or Short Call Option

A call option is the right to buy the stock at the option exercise price. The price that an investor has to pay to acquire the right to buy the stock is referred to as the *call premium* or *call price*. If an investor pays a call premium of C dollars today to obtain a call option, his profit or loss at the expiration date from buying the call can be easily determined. If the stock price is below the exercise price of K at expiration, the investor will let the option expire worthless and incur the loss of the initial investment, the call premium C. If the stock price at expiration is above the exercise price, then the investor gains the difference between the cost of buying the stock and the market price at which the stock can be sold. The profit/loss diagrams for the call buyer and call option writer are illustrated in Figure 6–3. The profit or loss to the call writer at expiration is just the opposite of that for the call buyer.

FIGURE 6–4
Profit/Loss for Put Buyer (solid line) and Put Writer (dotted line)

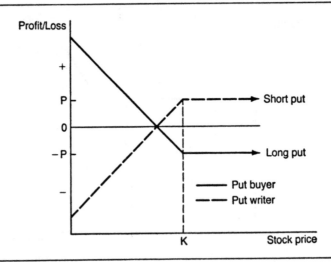

Long or Short Put Option

A put option is the right to sell the stock at the exercise price. If an investor pays put premium P today for the put option, his profit or loss at expiration can be determined easily. If the stock price at expiration is less than the exercise price, the investor can gain an amount equal to the exercise price minus the stock price; if the stock price is above the exercise price, the investor will let the option expire and incur a loss of the initial investment, which is equal to the put premium.

The profit/loss at expiration for a put buyer and put writer is illustrated in Figure 6–4. For the writer of a put, the profit at expiration will be the put premium received if the stock price is greater than the exercise price and the option is allowed to expire worthless. However, if the stock price at expiration is less than the exercise price, the net payoff to a put writer will be $P - (K - S)$.

Buying a Protective Put

A hedging strategy for buying stock and buying a put option is similar to buying insurance against unfavorable stock outcomes. The protective put avoids the downside risk faced by the investor. This strategy is referred to

FIGURE 6–5
Profit/Loss for Protective Put

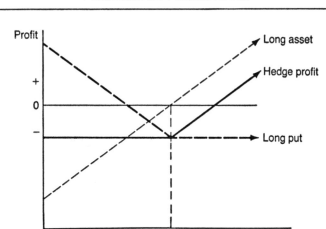

as buying a protective put. Figure 6–5 shows the profit/loss diagram for the strategy of buying a protective put. For simplicity we assume that the option was traded at the money and the put premium was P when the strategy was established. As illustrated in the figure, if the stock price at expiration is greater than the exercise price, the put has no value and the value of the hedged portfolio will be equal to the stock price minus the put premium. On the other hand, if the stock price at expiration is less than the exercise price, the investor can exercise the option and deliver the stock to the put writer for the payment of K (same as the stock purchase price) and thus incur a loss of P. Therefore, with a protective put the maximum loss that an investor can incur is limited.

The protective put can also be illustrated using probability distributions that account for the probabilities of various outcomes. Suppose that a stock portfolio of $80,000 has a six-month distribution of returns that is normal with a mean return of .075 (7.5 percent) and a standard deviation of .30 (30 percent). Then the expected value of the portfolio in six months is also normal, and it has a mean of $86,000 (computed as $80,000 × 1.075) and a standard deviation of 24,000 (computed as 80,000 × .3).

The distribution of payoffs is illustrated in Figure 6–6. Since the distribution is normal in Panel A, it is symmetric around its mean value of $86,000. Panel B depicts the distribution of payoffs when a protective put is bought. Assume that the put costs $5,000 (or $3.125 × 1,600 shares). Its purchase shifts all portfolio values that were more than $80,000 down by $5,000. However, the put protects the portfolio from all stock price declines. Any stock price that would have led to a portfolio value of $80,000 or less now leads to a portfolio value of exactly $75,000. $75,000 then has a probability equal to the probability of all stock prices less than or equal to $50, and that probability can be shown to be .3235. The probability at $75,000 is known as a probability mass in contrast to the probability densities for payoffs above $75,000.

This example illustrates how an investor can change the opportunity set by combining options with other securities in a portfolio. Examining Figure 6–6, the protective put transforms a symmetric, normal probability distribution into one in which the lower tail is removed, or *truncated*. The resulting distribution is skewed to the right (that is, has positive skewness) and has a lower standard deviation. Whether its mean is lower or higher than the mean using only stock depends on the size of the total premium paid, but that effect may be offset by the truncation effect.

Writing a Covered Call

A strategy of writing a covered call involves buying the stock and shorting the call option. If the stock price at expiration is equal to or less than the exercise price, the call expires worthless, and the investor keeps the call premium (which will improve the value of the portfolio). On the other hand, if the stock price at expiration is greater than the exercise price, the investor can deliver the stock and receive the payment of K when the call option is exercised. The profit/loss diagram of writing a covered call is illustrated in Figure 6–7.

As in the case of the protective put, the effect of the covered call on the distribution of portfolio value can be obtained as illustrated in Figure 6–8. Assume that the call options sell for a premium of $3.75 for a total call premium income of $6,000 ($3.75 x 1,600 shares) and that the call has an exercise price of $50 per share. If the stock price declines, the call option premium income helps to offset the losses on the stock. However, if the stock price rises above $50, you cannot share in that increase because you are obligated to deliver the stock at $50. Nevertheless, in such cases the portfolio is worth $86,000. The premium income shifts the probability distribution of portfolio value to the right until $86,000 is reached. Since for all stock prices above $50 you receive a portfolio value of $86,000, the probability that the portfolio will be worth exactly $86,000 is the same as the probability that the stock price will exceed $50, which

FIGURE 6–6
Distribution of Payoffs

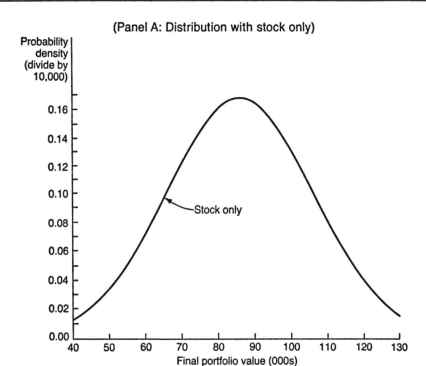

(Panel A: Distribution with stock only)

Probability density (divide by 10,000)

0.16
0.14
0.12
0.10
0.08 — Stock only
0.06
0.04
0.02
0.00

40   50   60   70   80   90   100   110   120   130
Final portfolio value (000s)

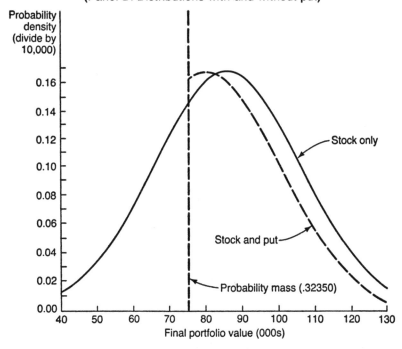

(Panel B: Distributions with and without put)

Probability density (divide by 10,000)

0.16
0.14
0.12   Stock only
0.10
0.08
0.06   Stock and put
0.04
0.02   Probability mass (.32350)
0.00

40   50   60   70   80   90   100   110   120   130
Final portfolio value (000s)

FIGURE 6–7
Profit/Loss for Writing Covered Call

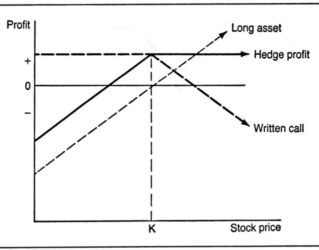

is .5987. In this case the probability distribution of payoffs has a higher mode than in the case of the protective put, and it has a somewhat lower standard deviation (and semiinterquartile range). But the distribution is left-skewed.

It should be apparent from these examples that skewness is an important factor in assessing option strategies. Skewness is generally less important in assessing common stock portfolios, since stock return distributions generally appear to be at least approximately symmetric. Option strategies generally impart skewness to a portfolio's distribution of returns.

Option Margins and Holding Period Returns

When an option is bought or sold or used in the context of a portfolio, it may be difficult to determine the holding period return. For example, if the strategy is simply to write a naked call, the option seller receives a payment of C per option transacted. But since the option writer is subject to the risk of having to deliver stock, a margin is required as well. The minimum margin requirement is:

$$M = \text{Maximum of } [(1.3 \times S) - K, 2.50]$$

and the price of the option can cover a portion of the margin. As an

FIGURE 6–8
Distribution of Portfolio Value

(Panel A: Distribution with stock only)

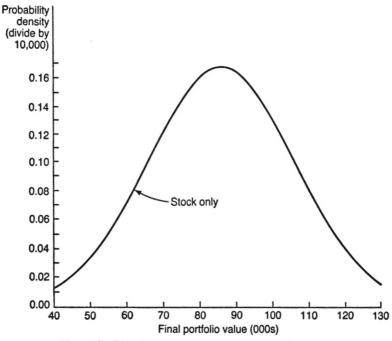

(Panel B: Distribution with and without written call)

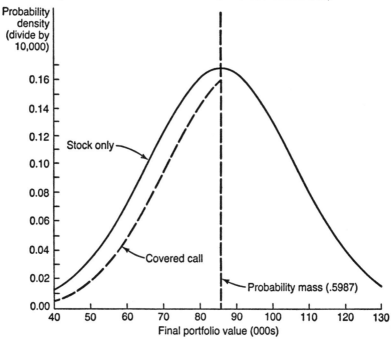

example, if the stock price is $40, the exercise price is $50, and the price of the call is $4, then the investor must put up a margin of:

$$\text{Maximum of } [52 - 50, 2.50]$$

which is $2.50. The margin is entirely covered by the price of the call itself, and rate of return for the position taken by itself is meaningless.

On the other hand, a covered call position has a more complex set of requirements. If the call is out of the money, then margin is required on the stock but no additional margin is required on the option. If the call is in the money, then an additional margin is required; but again, the margin for the entire position is reduced by the price of the call itself.

It follows that options introduce some complexities to the task of finding the holding period return in a portfolio. Margin rules now in existence allow the investor to identify combinations of securities that minimize the overall margin requirement. J. Cox and M. Rubinstein provide details on the margin requirements for a variety of option positions and provide an algorithm for identifying the pairings of options and stocks that minimize margin requirements.[1]

ARBITRAGE AND OPTION VALUATION

Suppose the price of a stock is currently $60 and you could buy a call option on it with an exercise price of $50. If the call sold for, say, $5, then you could buy the call and immediately exercise it for a $10 gain, netting you $5 with no risk whatsoever. As noted before, this opportunity illustrates pure arbitrage: the gaining of certain profits at no net investment.

Since active traders follow market prices closely, constantly seeking opportunities for easy rewards, it is unlikely that significant arbitrage opportunities of this kind could persist for long. As a result, economists have developed many results to describe the relationships among the prices of various securities, and those results often depend on the absence of arbitrage.

The above example can be used by economists to argue that the price of an option must always equal or exceed the exercise value of the option—that is, the amount that could be earned by exercising the option.

---

[1] J. Cox and M. Rubinstein, *Option Markets,* Englewood Cliffs, N.J.: Prentice-Hall, 1985.

For put and call options, if the exercise price is K and the stock price is S, then the values of puts and calls must satisfy

$$C \geq S - K$$

and

$$P \geq K - S$$

where C and P denote the call price and put price, respectively. Also, an option gives the holder a right, not an obligation. The option holder can, in the worst case, merely throw the option away or ignore it, so the option would never have a negative value. Thus the option must have a value at least as large as zero or the exercise value, whichever is larger:

$$\text{Call value} \geq \text{Maximum of } [0, S - K]$$

and

$$\text{Put value} \geq \text{Maximum of } [0, K - S]$$

An additional result is that an investor with "perfect access" to the markets can create a portfolio consisting of a put, the stock, and a loan that has the same payoffs for all ending stock prices as the call has. By perfect access, we mean that the investor pays no transaction costs and can borrow at the lowest rate available in the market, the riskless rate. The following two positions will have the same payoffs at all possible stock prices:

> Position A: Buy one share of stock.
> Buy one put option (exercisable at K).
> Borrow $PV(K)$.
> Position B: Buy one call option (exercisable at K).

In Position A, $PV(K)$ denotes the present value of the exercise price. Thus the position includes borrowing an amount that will require repayment of the amount K at the expiration date of the options.

Now consider the cash flows that will occur at the expiration of the two options, as shown in Table 6–1. As the results indicate, the portfolio (Position A) has exactly the payoffs of the call regardless of the final value of the stock. In essence, the purchase of stock along with a put contract and borrowing the present value of the exercise price of the option create an *equivalent* position to the call option. The position so obtained (Position A) is referred to as a *synthetic call.*

TABLE 6–1
Cash Flows to a Portfolio and to a Call

	Ending Price of Stock	
	$ST \leq K$	$ST > K$
Position A		
Stock is worth	ST	ST
Put is worth	$K - ST$	0
Pay off loan	$-K$	$-K$
Total cash flow	0	$ST - K$
Position B		
Call is worth	0	$ST - K$

Position A and Position B have the same cash flows at the expiration date of the option. Unless the two positions cost the same amount to enter, there is an arbitrage opportunity. For example, if the call costs more than the synthetic call, then one could sell the call and carry out the transactions in the synthetic call. The result would be a positive cash flow now (that is, income) and no net cash flows later. On the other hand, if the call was "underpriced" relative to the synthetic call, then one could buy the call and reverse the transactions in the synthetic call. Again the result would be positive income now with no net cash flows later. The existence of active arbitrageurs in the market will prevent any such mispricing from persisting in the market.

The "no arbitrage" condition implied by the equivalence of the call to the synthetic call leads to the following relationship that must hold among the various securities:

$$\text{Call value} = S + \text{Put value} - PV(K)$$

The expression is usually rearranged to define a condition on the value of the put in terms of the call and written as:

$$\text{Put value} = \text{Call value} - S + PV(K)$$

This relationship is known as *put-call parity*. It is the absence of perfect parity that gives rise to arbitrage opportunities in the market for options.

In using relationships such as put-call parity to look for possible mispricing of options, it is important to keep in mind that they may appear at times to be mispriced when in fact there is no mispricing. For example, the relationship requires that all prices are observed *contemporaneously*. Suppose we observe prices in the *The Wall Street Journal* for three such securities, and parity does not hold. If the prices are all closing prices, they might reflect final trades at different times during the day, with the later price reflecting new information that came to the market. Then the earlier price might not be a price at which a trade could now be made. For example, the put might not have traded since 11 A.M., while the call and the stock both traded at 3 P.M. Then the observed put price might not be a price at which a trade could have been executed at 3 P.M. There are powerful market forces acting to take advantage of arbitrage opportunities and hence to eliminate mispricing, so one should not hastily conclude that the markets have missed something.

Dividends on the underlying stock also affect the parity relationship. If during the life of the put and call option contracts there will be dividends paid on the stock, the prices of the put and call will be affected. In fact the call may not be held to expiration if dividends are to be paid (that is, it may be optimal to exercise the call prematurely), and an American put may be exercised prematurely even if there are no dividends to be paid. The put-call parity relationship can be adjusted in an approximate way to accommodate dividends. If $PV(D)$ represents the present value of dividends to be paid during the life of the options, then the relationship can be approximated by:

$$\text{Put value} = \text{Call value} - S + PV(K) - PV(D)$$

The no-arbitrage conditions illustrated in this section have been extended in the finance literature so that the value of an option can be computed under general conditions. Those extensions generally involve the use of options and stock to create a riskless hedge. Then, imposing the condition that a riskless investment must earn the riskless rate available in the market on alternative investments, a pricing relationship is obtained to value the option. Two models that apply this logic and that are important in practice are developed in the next section.

OPTION PRICING MODELS

Based on general arbitrage arguments, we have shown in previous sections that option values must lie within certain boundaries and that the following relationship between the option values and those of the underlying assets will hold only on the expiration dates (T) of the options:

$$\text{Call value at } T = \text{Maximum of } [S_T - K, 0]$$
$$\text{Put value at } T = \text{Maximum of } [K - S_T, 0]$$

At any time other than the expiration date the value of an option will be different from that given above. This section develops expressions that value the option at any time during its life.

On what variables do the values of options depend? How do those variables influence the values of the options? Answers to these questions can be given in broad terms without resorting to mathematical models. Values of call options are influenced by these variables: exercise price of the option, current price of the stock, time to maturity of the option, volatility of the underlying stock, and the level of interest rates over the life of the option. In addition many other variables (including dividends, taxes, transactions costs, and others) can influence option values, but we will confine our discussion to the above five key variables, taken one at a time.

The effects of the five variables on option values are intuitive. For example, the exercise price is the price at which the owner of the option can buy the stock. The lower the exercise price, the more profitable the option will be at exercise as long as the stock price exceeds the exercise price. Thus the value of a call option is always greater, the lower the exercise price. (Similarly a put option is always worth more, the greater the exercise price.)

The effect of the current stock price is the reverse of the effect of the exercise price. All else being equal, the option is more valuable, the greater the current stock price. For one thing, the lower bound on the option's value is increased by raising S. Also, the likelihood that the option will be exercised profitably (or sold at a profit) is greater, the larger the current stock price. Increasing the stock price merely moves the probability distribution of gains to the right; positive gains are thus more likely, and the probability of larger gains is increased. (The opposite is true for puts).

Time to maturity has several effects on the option value. First, because it delays the date of exercise, $PV(K)$ is reduced, raising the lower bound of the option's value. Also, an option with a long life has all of the features of an option with a shorter life except one: the owner is not forced to exercise at the earlier date if it is not advantageous to do so. Finally, by giving the share more time in which to experience a share price rise (or fall), there is more dispersion in the final share price. Thus the probability of larger gains is increased. In sum, the longer its time to maturity, the more valuable an option will be.[2]

The variance or volatility in the return of the stock is another important determinant of the value of an option. The higher the dispersion of the stock's returns, the greater the probability of larger gains from owning the option contract. Recall the probability distributions shown in Figures 6–6A and 6–8A. An increase in variance, all other things being equal, "flattens" the distribution of share prices, making both extremely small and extremely large stock prices more probable. On the downside there is no effect on the option buyer; as long as the stock price is below the striking price, the option expires worthless. Making the stock price even lower does not reduce the value of the option below zero. However, on the upside, the option holder is more likely to have larger gains as the variance rate increases; the option holder gains on the upside and is unaffected on the downside. The net effect is that an option is worth more the greater the volatility of the stock.

The final term to be considered is the riskless rate. Here it is important to reemphasize that we are examining these effects one at a time. If the riskless rate rises, the present value of the exercise price declines. As a result the lower bound of the option value rises, and in fact the option value also rises. An increase in interest rates may also have a negative effect on share prices (making S smaller), but here we are examining the effect of r while holding S constant. (The opposite is true for puts.)

The effects of each of these five variables will be made more explicit in this section by developing models of option prices. In those models the effects of the variables can be observed directly. For the models to be regarded as reasonable they should agree with our intuition about the determinants of option values. Indeed they do.

The Black-Scholes Option Pricing Model

As shown earlier, the value of an option at expiration is the larger of zero or the exercise value, and at any time prior to maturity the value is bounded below by the larger of zero or the stock price less the present

---

[2]This effect can be ambiguous for put options that may be exercised only at maturity, so-called *European* puts. Reduction in PV(K) reduces put value, but the dispersion increases value. However, for so-called *American* puts that can be exercised prior to maturity, the effect is unambiguous since such options can be exercised early. For the American puts and calls that trade on United States exchanges, value increases with time to maturity.

value of the exercise price. Consider the two values S and $PV(K)$. S is the value of the stock now, and $PV(K)$ is the value now of the exercise price to be paid later. Intuitively it seems reasonable to think that the option value would be some weighted combination of S and $PV(K)$. In other words, it is intuitive to postulate that there are weights ws and wk such that the option value is:

$$\text{Call value} = S \times ws - PV(K) \times wk$$

What weights might be reasonable? At expiration, either it is profitable to exercise or it is not profitable to exercise. If it is profitable, then the weights would both be one (1), that is:

$$\text{Call value} = S - K$$

and if not, the weights would both be zero, giving:

$$\text{Call value} = 0$$

So one might postulate that the weights ws and wk have something to do with the probability that exercise is profitable. The Black-Scholes option pricing model (BSOPM) gives exact values to those weights. After developing the model below we will interpret it in terms of these weights ws and wk.

The Black-Scholes model was derived by Fischer Black and Myron Scholes in an article published in 1973.[3] The publication of the paper coincided with the opening of the Chicago Board Options Exchange, so that trading in options was stimulated simultaneously by the start-up of a new system for trading options and a new theory for valuing them.

Black and Scholes assumed that the continuously compounded (one plus) rate of return of the stock over some time interval T has a log normal distribution with a variance of V times T. Other assumptions of the model include:

1. No taxes or transactions costs.
2. No dividends are paid on the stock over the life of the option.
3. No short sales restrictions.
4. Riskless borrowing and lending available at the continuous rate r.
5. The portfolio may be adjusted instantaneously.
6. The option can be exercised only at maturity.

---

[3]Fischer Black and Myron Scholes, "The Pricing of Options and Corporate Liabilities," *Journal of Political Economy* 81 (May 1973), pp. 637–54.

With these assumptions, Black and Scholes derived their famous call option pricing equation:

$$\text{Call value} = S \times N(D1) - \{K \times e^{-rT}\} \times N(D2)$$

where

S = Current stock price.

K = Exercise price of option.

T = Time to maturity of the option.

$N(.)$ = Standard normal distribution function.

$$D1 = \frac{\text{natural } \log\left(\dfrac{S}{K}\right) + \left(r + \dfrac{V}{2}\right) \times T}{(V \times T)^{.5}}$$

$$D2 = D1 - (V \times T)^{.5}$$

V = Variance of return of the stock.

e = Exponential constant, 2.71828 (See Chapter 2, p. 18)

While the Black-Scholes formula appears to be formidable, its components can be interpreted in terms of the probability model we proposed at the start of this section, with weights ws and wk. The model as shown above is of the general form discussed earlier, that is:

$$S \times ws - PV(K) \times wk$$

The weight ws is given by $N(D1)$. The term $\{K \times e^{-rT}\}$ is nothing more than the present value of the exercise price, $PV(K)$ at the continuously compounded rate, r. Thus the weight wk is given by $N(D2)$ which has the interpretation of being the probability of exercise at expiration. Thus:

$$\{K \times e^{-rT}\} \times N(D2)$$

can be interpreted as the expected present value of the outlay for exercising the option. Thus the BSOPM is the weighted sum of the stock price and present value of exercise price.

To illustrate the computations used in the model, suppose the input data are as follows:

S = 45.

K = 50.

T = .75 (nine months).

V = $.4^2$ = .16.

r = .08 (annual rate).

Then,

$$D1 = \frac{\text{natural log } (45/50) + [(.08 + .16/2) \times .75]}{(.16 \times .75)^{.5}}$$

$$= \frac{\text{natural log } (45/50) + .12}{.3466} = \frac{-.10544 + .12}{.3466}$$

$$= .0423$$

$$D2 = D1 - (.16 \times .75)^{.5}$$

$$= .0423 - .3464 = -.3041$$

$$N(D1) = .51687$$

$$N(D2) = .38053$$

Finally,

$$C = (45 \times .51687) - \{50 \times 2.71828^{-.08 \times .75}\} \times .38053$$

$$= 23.26 - 17.92 = \$5.34$$

The calculations illustrate the use of the model, given that the inputs are known. A later example will illustrate how to obtain the inputs from a set of historical security prices.

Properties of the BSOPM. The BSOPM serves as a basis for understanding how the key determinants of option values affect the value of the option. The value of the option predicted by the model is related to the other variables as follows:

Variable	Effect on Option Value
Stock price (S)	Positive
Exercise price (K)	Negative
Time to maturity (T)	Positive
Stock risk (V)	Positive
Riskless rate(r)	Positive

These effects are in agreement with intuition, which is the first test of a mathematical model and which was discussed at the beginning of this section.

Use of the Model with Real Data. To apply the BSOPM, a number of input values must be estimated. The stock price itself is easily observed, and the exercise price and time to maturity of the option are known. Two inputs must be estimated: the riskless rate over the life of the option and the variance of the stock's rate of return. The riskless rate is obtained from the yield on Treasury bills with a maturity close to that of the option, and the stock's variance is most easily estimated from a series of historical prices of the stock.

We will apply the model to the valuation of Datapoint options. Datapoint is a stock that had never paid a cash dividend as of the date of the data, so the assumption was made that no dividends would be paid during the life of the option. The following data were obtained from March 19, 1982, trading:

Date: March 19, 1982.
Expiration: May 22, 1982.
T: $^{64}\!/_{365}$ days $=$ .17534.
Stock price: 23.125.

In order to estimate the riskless rate, Treasury bill quotations were obtained from *The Wall Street Journal,* as shown in Table 6–2. The yield figure reported in the *Journal* is not appropriate for our purposes; it is a simple (that is, not compounded) yield figure based on the asked discount (although in fact it will generally be a reasonable approximation to the yield figure we will obtain). Our objective is to find the continuously compounded annual return on the T-bills.

To obtain the yield, the average of the bid and asked discounts are applied. (In some cases the bid discount itself will be appropriate; in others the ask discount will be appropriate.) The average discount is 11.20. That figure is converted into a yield:

$$\text{T-bill life} = 65 \text{ days}$$
$$\text{65-day discount} = \frac{11.2 \times 65}{360} = 2.0222 \text{ percent}$$
$$\text{65-day return} = \frac{2.0222}{100 - 2.0222} = 2.064 \text{ percent}$$
$$\text{Annual return} = 1.02064^{(365/65)} - 1 = 12.15 \text{ percent}$$

The annual return figure can be converted into a continuously compounded annual equivalent:

$$\text{Continuous } r = \text{Natural log } (1 + \text{return})$$
$$= \ln(1.1215) = .11467 = 11.467 \text{ percent}$$

TABLE 6–2
U.S. Treasury Bills

Maturity Date	Discount		Yield
	Bid	Asked	
5–24–84	11.24	11.16	11.55

As mentioned previously, the 11.55 percent yield figure reported in *The Wall Street Journal* is a bit off the mark.

The variance of the stock's continuous rate of return must also be estimated. This estimation can be done in a variety of ways, including a subjective assessment by the analyst, but the most common approach is to use historical stock prices for the stock in question. While daily data over perhaps a six-month time interval are most commonly used, the ideas are well illustrated by using a few months of monthly data. On March 19 the historical data shown in Table 6–3 were observed. Those prices were used to calculate a variance estimate as illustrated by the table, resulting in an annualized variance estimate of .44044. With logarithmic returns as used here, a monthly variance is converted into an annual one merely by multiplying it by 12. This variance corresponds to an annual standard deviation of .66366, which is relatively high among common stocks.

The rate of return, time to expiration, and variance must all be expressed in *equivalent time units*. What this means is simply that if the time to expiration is in years, the return measure should be an annualized return and the variance should also be annualized. If time is in months, then the rate of return and variance should correspond. The choice of time units is irrelevant as long as it is consistent for all three inputs. The figures above are all in annualized units since those are most familiar.

To compute the value of the option, the model is applied as in the previous numerical example. The inputs are:

$S = 23.12500.$
$K = 25.00000.$
$T = 0.17534.$
$r = 0.11467.$
$V = 0.44044.$

TABLE 6–3
Variance Calculations for Datapoint
(monthly data)

Month	End Price	Price Relative* (PR)	Natural log (PR)	Squared Error
1	54.750	NA	NA	NA
2	60.750	1.10959	0.10399	0.02946
3	65.500	1.07819	0.07528	0.02043
4	57.500	0.87786	-0.13027	0.00392
5	53.375	0.92826	-0.07444	0.00005
6	46.125	0.86417	-0.14599	0.00614
7	46.750	1.01355	0.01346	0.00658
8	48.250	1.03209	0.03158	0.00985
9	48.750	1.01036	0.01031	0.00608
10	51.250	1.05128	0.05001	0.01385
11	51.000	1.04615	0.04512	0.01272
12	28.125	0.55147	-0.59517	0.27827
13	23.125	0.82222	-0.19574	0.01641

Average return† = -0.06765.
Monthly variance‡ = 0.03670.
Annualized variance§ = 0.44044.
Annualized standard deviation = 0.66366.

*The price relative is the month's price divided by the previous month's price. The natural log of the price relative, then, gives the (continuous) return over the month. The squared difference between the month's return and the average return is shown in the last column.
†Average return is computed as the mean of the 12 log price relatives.
‡Monthly variance is the sum of squared differences divided by 11, which is the number of returns minus one.
§Annualized variance is monthly variance times 12.

Those inputs lead to an estimated option value as shown in these calculations:

$$D1 = \frac{\text{natural log } (23.125/25) + \left(.11467 + \dfrac{.44044}{2}\right) \times .17534}{(.44044 \times .17534)^{.5}}$$

$$= -0.06924$$
$$D2 = D1 - (.44044 \times .17534)^{.5} = -0.34713$$
$$N(D1) = 0.47240$$
$$N(D2) = 0.36485$$

These values lead to a price estimate of 1.99930, which corresponds to an option closing price of exactly $2.

The numbers above were not contrived to give a result so close to the observed option value—they represent the actual data available for the estimation. The results are sensitive to the estimated inputs, however. For the example above, the estimate was also computed using the prior 13 weeks of data; and as it turned out, the estimated price exceeded $3. This illustrates the point that the results are sensitive to the inputs. In the Datapoint example the three-month period prior to March 19, 1982, was an unusually turbulent (high-volatility) time. In pricing the option at $2 the market seemed to convey the conviction that the volatile period was not indicative of the subsequent period of the life of the option.

One particularly interesting approach to estimating the option's variance is to let the Black-Scholes model determine the variance. That is, given the price of the option and given all other inputs except the option's variance, there will be a unique variance (called the *implied variance*) such that the model price agrees with the observed price. Thus the option itself can provide evidence of the stock's underlying variability.

Given the sensitivity of the BSOPM price of the option to its inputs, caution must be used in interpreting the results of a price calculation. For example, in the case of the Datapoint option, a researcher using the mentioned weekly data might have concluded that the option's value was $3 and the option was therefore "underpriced" at $2. Such conclusions should only be reached with great care and attention to the inputs.

Sensitivity to Assumptions. As indicated in previous chapters, all quantitative methods depend on sets of assumptions. The results from using such methods to ascertain value can best be thought of as approximations, the quality of which depend on the extent to which these assumptions approach reality. As indicated earlier, the BSOPM depends on a rather formidable-appearing set of assumptions. Fortunately there are only two that are really crucial to the analysis.

The most serious assumption would appear to be the assumption that the option can be exercised only at expiration. Such options are referred to as *European options*. Options trading in the United States can be exercised prior to maturity. These are called *American options*.[4] While such options *may* be exercised prior to maturity, it turns out that American options *will not* be exercised prior to maturity. However, this is not the case for options on stocks that pay dividends.

---

[4]This terminology is somewhat misleading. Most options trading on European exchanges can be exercised prior to maturity.

Early exercise is not optimal for stocks that do not pay dividends, because of economic arguments that show the option is always worth more than its exercise value $(S - K)$ prior to maturity. Those arguments are not valid for all options on dividend-paying stocks because the value of the stock declines on the ex-dividend date by the amount of the dividend. That price decline causes the ex-dividend value of the option to be the value based on the old stock price less the dividend, which can cause a discrete decline in the price of the option. In some cases the exercise value of the option prior to dividend payment may be greater than the market value of the option on the ex-dividend stock price. Thus the BSOPM must be adjusted for the possibility of premature exercise.

There are various ways of adjusting for dividends. One simple way is to assume the option can be exercised only on each of the various ex-dividend dates and to obtain values associated with each of the dates. For example imagine an option with one ex-dividend date prior to the maturity of the option. Compute the value of the option and compare the value so obtained to the value assuming the option is held to maturity (but using a stock price equal to the current price less the present value of the expected dividend payment). The larger of the two values would give the value of the option, assuming an "optimal exercise" strategy is followed. However, this approach tends to understate the value of the option.

Cox and Rubinstein[5] refer to the value obtained by the procedure above as the "pseudo-American" call value, since the procedure derives an anticipated optimal exercise date. In reality the optimal exercise date will depend on the path the stock price takes after the computations are made. The stock price may subsequently fall, so that early exercise is no longer optimal, or rise, so that early exercise becomes optimal. Cox and Rubinstein demonstrate a procedure for determining call prices that fully accounts for the prospect of early exercise and recognizes that exercise policy is dynamic.

The BSOPM and Put Valuation. Earlier a parity between put and call prices was illustrated. If the parity relationship fails to hold, there will be opportunities for arbitrageurs to act and earn arbitrage profits, so market forces tend to maintain the put-call parity relationship.

Put-call parity was shown to imply

$$\text{Put value} = \text{Call value} - S + PV(K)$$

Substituting the BSOPM call value into the parity relationship, we can derive the value of a put assuming both that the put is European (no early

---

[5]Cox and Rubinstein, *Option Markets*. (Englewood Cliffs, NJ: 1985) Prentice-Hall.

exercise) and that the underlying stock pays no dividends. It turns out that American puts may be exercised prematurely even if the underlying security pays no dividends, so the BSOPM value tends to understate the value of American puts even on nondividend-paying stocks.

There are no closed-form solutions for the valuation of American puts. Michael Parkinson, a physicist, has developed numerical techniques for their valuation,[6] and Cox and Rubinstein present methods for such puts as well (with and without dividends). Such methods are available in computer software packages.

Two-State Option Pricing Model

The Black-Scholes model is an elegant model that has been important in the literature and in practice. A simpler approach called the *binomial option pricing model* (BOPM) is identical to the BSOPM under certain limiting conditions. The BOPM assumes that only two things can happen to the stock: it can go up or it can go down (it cannot, however, remain unchanged). The BOPM is rather intuitive, as will be evident in this discussion, and can be applied somewhat more generally than can the Black-Scholes model.

One-Period Model.   A numerical example will be used to illustrate how a riskless hedged portfolio can be constructed and the value of a call option with one period to expiration can be derived under the assumption that the stock prices follow simple two-state movements.

Example: Suppose the current price of a stock is $S = \$100$, and at the end of a period the price will either be up to $S_1 = \$110$ with a probability of 80 percent or be down to $S_1 = \$90$ with a probability of 20 percent. A call on the stock is available with an exercise price of $K = \$100$, expiring at the end of the period. The risk-free rate of interest at which one can lend or borrow is assumed to be 5 percent. The question is "What should the value of this call be so that there will be no risk-free arbitrage opportunity?" Consider forming the following strategy of writing covered calls:

1. Buy one share of the stock at $100.
2. Write two calls.

---

[6]M. Parkinson, "Option Pricing: The American Put," *Journal of Business* 50 (January 1977), pp. 21–36.

TABLE 6–4
Payoffs for Covered Call Strategy

Current Position	State	End-of-Period Position Stock	Call	Hedged Position
Long one share	Up	100	−20	90
Write two calls	Down	90	0	90

The initial investment for this strategy of writing covered calls is the price paid for a share of the stock minus the proceeds received from shorting two calls ($100 - 2C$). Table 6–4 below gives the payoffs to this strategy for each possible outcome for the stock price at expiration.

As shown in Table 6–4, the strategy described above is a riskless strategy; that is, the payoff is always the same regardless of the state. Thus, to prevent a profitable riskless arbitrage the cost of establishing the strategy of writing covered calls must be such that:

$$(100 - 2C)(1 + .05) = 90$$

That is, the final certain payoff of $90 must reflect a riskless rate of return on the initial investment. Therefore the value of the call that assures no riskless arbitrage opportunity must be:

$$\text{Call value} = \frac{100 - 85.71}{2} = \$7.14$$

If the call is not priced at $7.14, a sure arbitrage profit would be possible. For example, if $C = \$8$, the cost of establishing a riskless strategy of writing covered calls will be $84. Thus one can borrow $85.71 at 5 percent and promise to pay $90 back for the loan at the end of the period. Using $84 of the borrowed money to establish the writing-covered-calls strategy that will always result in a payoff of $90 for the repayment of the loan, the person has realized a sure profit of $1.71 at the beginning of the period.

This example might seem a little too neat. How general is this example? If the stock can only go up or down in price by certain, specified amounts, it is *always* possible to construct the riskless hedge. Intuitively, the *hedge ratio*, the number of stocks that have to be purchased to cover each call that is written, depends on how far the call price can move relative to the potential stock price move. Relatively straightforward algebra will verify that the hedge ratio (h) in this example will be given by:

$$\text{Hedge ratio, } h = \frac{C_u - C_d}{uS - dS} = \frac{10 - 0}{110 - 90} = \frac{1}{2}$$

where

C_u = the value of the call in an "up" state

C_d = the value of the call in the "down" state

u = one plus the return on the stock in the "up" state

d = one plus the return on the stock in the "down" state

Therefore a riskless strategy of writing a covered call is to buy one share of the stock and to short two calls, as we have shown in Table 6–4. The above application of the formula for the risk-neutral hedge ratio indicates that the ratio is determined by the range of the call values and the stock prices at the end of the period.

Since we know that two options can be written for every stock held to establish a riskless hedge, we can use the above arithmetic to conclude that the option value is $7.14. In order to simplify the arithmetic, it is possible to use a little algebra to substitute the expression for the riskless hedge into the call value formula and solve for the call value *directly*.[7] If we define

$$p = \frac{(1 + r) - d}{u - d}$$

as an *implied probability* (where r is the riskless rate of interest), which is a function of the range of stock price movements and the risk-free rate of interest, then the expression for the value of a call can be simplified to:

$$C = \frac{pC_u + (1 - p)C_d}{1 + r}$$

Thus the value of a call is simply the expected value of the call at the end of the period, weighted by the implied probabilities and discounted at the risk-free rate of interest.

This equation can be employed directly to obtain the values of the call in the example:

---

[7]For details see John Cox and Mark Rubinstein, *Options Markets* (Englewood Cliffs, NJ: 1985) Prentice-Hall, pp. 172–73.

$$p = \frac{1.05 - .90}{1.10 - .90} = \frac{3}{4}$$

$$C = \frac{(3/4)10 + (1/4)0}{1.05} = \$7.14$$

Two-Period Model. Using the same arguments as in the one-period case, we can extend the analysis to a two-period case and obtain the value of a call with two periods to expiration.

Example: Given the same assumptions used in the earlier example except that the call has two periods to expiration, the question is how much the call should be worth today to prevent a riskless arbitrage opportunity, given that the current stock price is $100 and that it will go up or down 10 percent at the end of each period. Thus the stock price at the time when the call option has one period left will be $110 or $90, and at the expiration date of the option, the stock price will be one of the following:

$$uuS = 100(1.1)(1.1) = \$121$$
$$udS = 100(1.1)(.9) = \$99$$
$$ddS = 100(.9)(.9) = \$81$$

The following diagram shows the movements of the stock price:

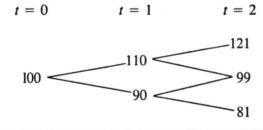

Since the call option at the expiration date must be the positive value of the stock price at expiration date minus the exercise price of $100, we know that the value of a call after two up movements, $C_{uu} = 121 - 100 = 21$, and the values after an up-down and a down-up movement C_{ud} and C_{du} are both zero. Working backwards we can use the one-period option pricing formula to obtain the value of the call at time $t = 1$. If the stock price is at $uS = \$110$ with one period left, then the value of the call at expiration will be $C_{uu} = 21$ or $C_{ud} = 0$. We know from the one-period example that:

$$C_u = \frac{(3/4)21 + (1/4)0}{1.05} = \$15.00$$

If the stock price is $dS = \$90$ with one period left, then the value of the call at expiration will be $C_{du} = 0$ or $C_{dd} = 0$. So we know that $C_d = 0$; that is, the call has no value.

Working backwards for one more period the current stock price is $100 with two periods left before the call option expires. Since the value of the call one period from now is either $C_u = \$15.00$ or $C_d = \$0$, we can obtain the value of the call today:

$$C = \frac{(3/4)15.00 + (1/4)0}{1.05} = \$10.71$$

The following diagram shows the values of the call at different points in time:

Comparing the value of the call in the single-period example with the value of the call in the current example, which has two periods to expiration, we know that the longer the life of a call, other things being equal, the greater the value of the call will be.

The general two-state option pricing formula for the two-period case can also be obtained directly. After some algebra, it can be shown that the value of the call with two periods remaining is

$$C = \frac{p^2 C_{uu} + 2p(1 - p)C_{ud} + (1 - p)^2 C_{dd}}{(1 + r)^2}$$

The value of the call in the numerical example, with two periods before its expiration, can therefore be obtained:

$$C = \frac{(3/4)^2 21 + 2(3/4)(1/4)0 + (1/4)^2 0}{(1.05)^2} = \$10.71$$

Applying the same procedure that has been used to extend from the one-period case to the two-period case, we can extend from the two-period case to the three-period and the many-period cases. While the computational procedures in the three- and the many-period cases are complicated, the basic arbitrage argument in deriving the value of a call option is the same. John Cox and Mark Rubinstein[8] and R. Jarrow and A. Rudd[9] include derivations of the BOPM for any number of time periods.

The two-period model is only a very crude model; to approximate the continuous-time case would seem to require many time periods. Yet even the two-period model can approximate the Black-Scholes value of an option (albeit in many cases not very well). Consider the earlier example in which the BSOPM was applied to an option with this data:

$S = 45$
$K = 50$
$T = .75$
$V = .16$
$r = .08$

The terms u, d, and p can all be approximated in order to use the two-period BOPM for evaluating the option. Following the suggestions of Jarrow and Rudd in the context of a slightly different formulation of the model, we can approximate the parameters as follows:

$$u = 1 + \left[\left(r - \frac{V}{2} \right) \times T/2 \right] + \sqrt{V \times \frac{T}{2}}$$

$$d = 1 + \left[\left(r - \frac{V}{2} \right) \times T/2 \right] - \sqrt{V \times \frac{T}{2}}$$

These values give a value of the option of

$$C = \$5.86$$

The BSOPM value was $5.34. Although the two values differ appreciably, the two-state model has done a good job, considering only two trading periods were assumed for an option with nine months' life remaining.

---

[8]John Cox and Mark Rubinstein, *Option Markets* (Englewood Cliffs, NJ: 1985) Prentice-Hall, Chapter 5.

[9]R. Jarrow and A. Rudd, *Options Pricing,* (Homewood, Ill: 1983) Richard D. Irwin.

The error of approximation diminishes very considerably with the number of periods assumed. As the number of periods increases and the time interval (and u and d) between periods decreases, the result will lead to the many-period BOPM. In the limit, the model becomes the continuous-time Black-Scholes option pricing model. However, the value of this approach to valuing options does not lie in the extent to which option values do or do not approximate the Black-Scholes values. Rather, the value is to be found in situations where Black-Scholes is either inappropriate or difficult to apply. Cox and Rubinstein[10] show that it provides a relatively straightforward way of analyzing warrants, convertible and callable bonds, different compound options, and options on futures and other instruments. In each case the rule is to trace out the cash flows to be received in each state, and work backwards to obtain the value today of the option under study.

EMPIRICAL ANALYSIS OF OPTIONS

There are no data bases of option prices available that are as rich and extensive as those available to describe the behavior of common stocks, bonds, and other securities. To the extent that security return patterns vary over time, then, we may be less confident of the behavior of option returns than we are about stock returns. However, since the opening of the options exchanges in 1973, data bases have been available that cover all transactions in common stock options, so we do have some knowledge of the historical pattern of returns from option strategies. This section will describe some of that available experience in two parts: historical returns to option strategies and the historical performance of option pricing models.

Historical Returns

It should be apparent from the probability distributions displayed in Figures 6–6 and 6–8 that skewness is an important attribute of the returns to buying or selling put or call options. In the empirical analysis of common stocks it was apparent that mean (or central tendency) and standard deviation (or dispersion) tell a large part of the story in describing the returns to common stocks. Options, however, display a great deal of skewness. Thus, in judging the risk measures and expected returns of option strate-

---

[10]John Cox and Mark Rubinstein, *Options Markets*, (Englewood Cliffs, NJ: 1985) Prentice-Hall, Chapter 7.

gies, conclusions must be drawn with special attention to the effects of skewness. Recalling the definition of skewness in Chapter Two, it should be apparent that a long position in a call or put has positive skewness (tails of the distribution to the right) and that a short position in a call or put has negative skewness (tails of the distribution to the left). To the extent that right skewness is desirable, then, one might expect to observe such "oddities" as negative mean returns from strategies of buying options. However, options are typically not used in isolation; they are used in conjunction with other securities. For example, the put buyer who also holds the stock is holding a "protective put" that eliminates downside risk. The call writer's prospects depend both on the call and on other positions held; the call position may be naked or covered. In short, the motives of option buyers and sellers are not easily inferred from their option positions alone, and our understanding of option returns must be tempered with that realization.

Only a relatively limited number of empirical studies are available depicting the historical return properties of option strategies. In studies of stock and bond returns, actual prices of the securities are used. Because of the relative paucity of data on options, however, authors in some of the best-known options studies have not used actual option prices but have computed returns assuming that the BSOPM or other theoretical models actually hold. Since empirical research has failed to confirm the validity of any specific model, returns computed "as if" the models held leave something to be desired. On the other hand, studies using actual option prices are limited by short data series, and they too leave something to be desired.

Gary Trennepohl and William Dukes[11] studied returns from call option buying and from covered call writing strategies. They assumed that the price of the call in call buying had to be put up as an initial payment and that the investor's net initial investment in covered call writing was the price of the stock less the price of the call. The options were calls listed on the Chicago Board Options Exchange in the period 1973 through 1976. The authors reached these general conclusions: Covered call writing had a positive weekly mean return, a relatively small standard deviation, and negative skewness. Call buying had negative mean returns, relatively high standard deviations (on the order of 25 percent per week), and right skewness.

---

[11]G. L. Trennepohl and W. P. Dukes, "Return and Risk from Listed Option Investments," *Journal of Financial Research* 2 (Spring 1979), pp. 37–49.

Michael Gambola, Rodney Roenfeldt, and Philip Cooley[12] examined returns from various option spreading strategies. The strategies were either calendar (time) spreads or vertical (price) spreads. The time period examined was again 1973 through 1976. Spreads involve simultaneous transactions in options that have differing expiration dates (calendar spreads) or exercise prices (vertical spreads).

The idea is to take a long position in one option and a short position in another in order to profit from the relative movement of prices of the options. The BSOPM gives an indication of which of the two options would be affected more by price changes. In-the-money options tend to increase more in price than do out-of-the-money options for a given change in stock price. Similarly options tend to be more sensitive to stock price changes the longer the time to maturity of the option.

Given these results, one can construct "bullish" and "bearish" spreads (that is, spreads that increase in value as the stock price rises or falls, respectively). A bullish calendar spread would involve buying a long call and selling a short call. A bullish vertical spread would involve buying a call with a low exercise price and selling a call with a high exercise price.

Gambola, Roenfeldt, and Cooley[13] found that bullish spreads had favorable risk-return characteristics relative to single-option strategies. Calendar spreads in particular did well during periods in which stock prices moved favorably, and the calendar spreads produced only small losses during unfavorable periods. After adjusting for the considerably higher commissions from spread transactions, however, it turned out that spreads compared unfavorably with option buying and writing strategies.

Empirical Analyses of Option Pricing Models

It is one matter to develop models of option pricing that are satisfactory on theoretical grounds; it is quite another to find models that predict actual market behavior. A large number of studies have examined the empirical validity of various option pricing models. The tests have generally shown that there were some limitations in the validity of the models; in some cases the tests have led to the development of models that attempt to depict

---

[12]M. J. Gambola, R. L. Roenfeldt, and P. L. Cooley, "Spreading Strategies in CBOE Options: Evidence on Market Performance," *Journal of Financial Research* 1 (Winter 1978), pp. 35–44.

[13]Gambola, Roenfeldt, and Cooley, "Spreading Strategies in CBOE Options: Evidence on Market Performance," *Journal of Financial Research* 1 (Winter 1978), pp. 35–44.

reality more accurately. Dan Galai[14] has recently surveyed many of the tests of option pricing models. In his paper, he concludes that:

1. The Black-Scholes model performs relatively well, especially for at-the-money options. Deviations from model prices are consistently observed for deep in-the-money and deep out-of-the-money options.
2. No alternative model consistently offers better predictions than the B–S model.
3. The major problem faced by the B–S model, or any other model suggested so far, is the nonstationarity of the risk estimator of the underlying stock.
4. No one model accounts for transaction costs and taxes, which may affect the prices of traded options.

Galai's survey summarizes a large body of empirical research that continues to evolve. Theoreticians continue to work toward better models to describe the option pricing process, and empiricists continue to examine those models. At some point we will have perhaps developed the ideal model that captures all that is relevant to the option pricing process. That point has not yet been reached. Meanwhile the BSOPM, one of the earliest models of option pricing, has stood the test of time and remains a reasonable alternative.

OPTION PRICING THEORY APPLIED TO OTHER ASSETS

The concepts of option pricing theory are more generally concepts for the valuation of contingent claims. Such claims arise in a variety of seemingly unrelated contexts, including risky debt, convertibility options on debt, call provisions on debt, government insurance of bank and S&L deposits, government insurance of pension benefits, and others. Even the common stock of a firm may be viewed as an option on the assets of the firm: the shareholders (due to limited liability) have a claim worth zero if the value of the firm is less than the value of its debt, but it is worth the difference between the firm's value and the value of debt if the firm is worth more than the debt claim. In addition there are call and put options on many

---

[14]Dan Galai, "A Survey of Empirical Tests of Option Pricing Models" (Working paper no. 2–83, Graduate School of Management, University of California at Los Angeles, 1983.)

kinds of assets other than common stock, including options on stock indexes, commodities, debt securities (private and public), futures contracts, and others. Furthermore, options and option-like portfolio investments can be used to insure the values of certain portfolios against loss below a certain level.

One simple example is the warrant on stocks. A warrant gives its holder the right to buy stock at a fixed price within a specified time period; in short it is a call option. Warrants are not written with the same standardized terms that apply to listed call options, but they are in other respects simply specialized options. All that has been said about the valuation of calls thus applies directly to warrants as well.

Option pricing analysis is far more widely applicable than the examples in the earlier sections indicate. Some additional applications will be considered in this section.

Valuing Risky Debt and Valuing the Firm

Imagine a firm financed entirely from equity and a simple debt contract. The debt must be paid off at the end of one period, and the amount due will be D. If the firm is not worth D at the end of the period, the equity holders can forfeit the firm—in essence, *put* the firm—to the debt holders in exchange for cancellation of the debt. The equity holders then face a set of payoffs:

$$\text{Payoff} = 0 \qquad \text{if value} \le D$$
$$= V - D \quad \text{if value} > D$$

where V is the value of the firm's assets at the end of the period. In this case the risky variable is V. The stock then has the same type of payoff patterns as a call option on the assets of the firm, with a striking price equal to the total debt obligation (principal and interest).

From the standpoint of the debt holders the payoff is D if the value of the firm exceeds D, and it is V if the value of the firm is less than D:

$$\text{Payoff} = D \text{ if value} \ge D$$
$$= V \text{ if value} < D$$

Their position is like that of a covered call writer who writes a call on the firm with an exercise price of D. The value of risky debt is thus the value of the firm less the value of a call option on the assets of the firm.

Other Debt Features

Two other debt features, convertibility and callability, can also be evaluated from the standpoint of option pricing theory. A convertible bond is one that can be exchanged for stock at a predetermined exchange rate, which implies an exercise price in terms of the bond price. The holder of the convertible bond then holds a call option on the stock of the firm. The debt holder's desire to avoid risk is then changed since the value of the debt holder's option is increased when the firm increases its stock price variability. The option pricing feature—an option is more valuable the greater the variability in return to the underlying asset—has a direct application to this case.

The callability feature gives the firm a call option on the debt. If the level of interest rates declines, for example, the value of the debt rises, and the firm could finance the same level of debt at a lower interest cost. The call feature gives the firm the right to call the bond at a schedule of prices, with the price generally declining as the date at which the call is exercised increases. In essence the call feature is similar to having a series of call options, with the later options being available only if the earlier calls have not been exercised. Again it follows that as the uncertainty in future interest rates increases, the value of the call feature increases and as a result the value of the bond is reduced.

Insurance Contracts: Deposit and ERISA

The Federal Deposit Insurance Corporation and the Federal Savings and Loan Insurance Corporation insure deposit accounts in member institutions. For a fixed premium—that curiously does not vary with the risk of the institution—the agency guarantees the deposits made in the institutions. From the standpoint of depositors it is as though they held a protective put on their deposits. The value of the put is obviously an increasing function of the risk associated with the deposit's value in the institution. Since a failing institution effectively "puts" the deposits to the insuring agency, the insurance contract actually gives the institution an incentive to bear greater risks than it might otherwise bear. The agency's failure to charge premiums that recognize the risk of fluctuations in deposit value—failure, in essence, to value the put, recognizing that the value increases with the risk of the underlying asset—creates an incentive perverse to the aims of the agency.

A virtually identical situation exists in the Pension Benefit Guarantee Corporation's insurance of pension accounts under the Employee Retirement Income Security Act. The corporation pays a premium for pension fund insurance, and the value of that insurance (or put option) increases as the risk of the pension fund increases. Since the PBGC does not discriminate on the basis of risk, it implicitly provides incentives to take on added risk. In insurance, such effects are termed *moral hazards*.

Performance Fees

Portfolio managers can be compensated under a variety of schemes. One approach is to pay the manager a fixed fee or a fixed proportion of the value of the assets under management. Such an approach leaves management indifferent to the level of risk in the portfolio (ignoring issues such as the fear of losing the account altogether). An alternative is to reward the manager under a scheme in which the manager participates in the gains beyond some threshold level but does not share the risk on the downside. From the standpoint of option pricing theory, this approach gives the manager a call option. The call option is valuable at maturity—the end of the evaluation period—if the value of the portfolio exceeds the threshold level. See Chapter Eight for a more detailed discussion of this application.

Options on Other Assets

Competition in new-product development in securities has led to a bewildering array of new instruments in recent years. Many of them involve creating derivative securities such that the underlying asset is itself a derivative security. For example, consider an option to buy a futures contract for U.S. Treasury issues. From the standpoint of valuing the option, the underlying asset is the futures contract. To value the option, one needs to know the variability in the time series of futures prices, the level of interest rates *during the life of the option,* the life of the option itself, current futures prices, and the striking price. Finding the inputs may be more difficult than in the case of common stock options, but the principles are the same.

Recently options on stock market indexes have been introduced. These options allow the investor to alter the *market risk* component of a portfolio in fundamental ways. In this case the underlying asset is the portfolio against which the option is written. For example, one may purchase a call option on the Value Line Stock Index or on other major stock indexes.

CONCLUSION

In this chapter, we have examined put and call options as examples of a general class of securities known as derivative securities. It should be clear that analysis of derivative securities depends importantly on the application of quantitative methods. Without quantitative tools it is virtually impossible to value these securities; and without a sound understanding of quantitative principles the impact of derivative securities on a portfolio's performance can be seriously misunderstood. Finally, the quantitative principles that underlie analysis of derivative securities can be extended to a wide variety of investment applications.

REFERENCES

Black, F., and M. Scholes. "The Pricing of Options and Corporate Liabilities." *Journal of Political Economy* 81 (May 1973), pp. 637–54.

Cox, J., and M. Rubinstein. *Option Markets*. Englewood Cliffs, N.J.: Prentice-Hall, 1985.

Galai, D. "A Survey of Empirical Tests of Option Pricing Models." Working paper #2–83, Graduate School of Management, University of California at Los Angeles, 1983.

Gambola, M. J.; R. L. Roenfeldt; and P. L. Cooley. "Spreading Strategies in CBOE Options: Evidence on Market Performance." *Journal of Financial Research* 1 (Winter 1978), pp. 35–44.

Jarrow, R., and A. Rudd, *Option Pricing*. Homewood, Ill.: Richard D. Irwin, 1983.

Parkinson, M. "Option Pricing: The American Put." *Journal of Business* 50 (January 1977), pp. 21–36.

Trennepohl, G. L., and W. P. Dukes. "Return and Risk from Listed Option Investments." *Journal of Financial Research* 2 (Spring 1979), pp. 37–49.

CHAPTER SEVEN

Quantitative Methods in Asset Allocation

Stephen J. Brown and Mark P. Kritzman

INTRODUCTION

This chapter demonstrates the application of quantitative methods to asset allocation. It begins with a discussion of the calculation of expected return and standard deviation for a combination of assets and proceeds with a review of the estimating issues involved in asset allocation. The next section describes how an optimal portfolio can be identified from the efficient set, and the final section addresses dynamic hedging strategies, whereby the quantitative framework of option pricing theory is applied to determine a portfolio's asset allocation.

The application of quantitative methods to asset allocation is well established within the investment industry. With the recent advances in dynamic hedging strategies, it appears that quantitative methods will continue as an integral part of the asset allocation process.

EXPECTED RETURN AND RISK

The expected return of a combination of asset classes is simply the weighted average of the expected returns of the component assets. If common stocks were expected to return 12 percent and long-term corporate bonds were expected to return 5.1 percent per year, a portfolio that consists of 60 percent common stocks and 40 percent bonds would have an expected return of 9.24 percent. To see this, note that 60 cents invested in stocks would be expected to grow to 67.2 cents [67.2 = 60 × (1 + .12)] and 40 cents invested in bonds would be expected to grow to 42.04 cents; a dollar in the portfolio would be expected to grow to $1.0924 in one year, an expected return of 9.24 percent. In other words:

$$\text{Expected return} = (.6 \times 12) + (.4 \times 5.1) = 9.24$$

and in general:

$$\text{Expected return} = (w_1 \times ER_1) + (w_2 \times ER_2) + (w_3 \times ER_3) + \cdots$$

where

w_1, w_2, w_3 = Proportion of the portfolio invested in assets 1, 2, and 3.

ER_1, ER_2, ER_3 = Expected return on assets 1, 2, and 3.

The weights w_1, w_2, and w_3 are referred to as *portfolio weights* and are measured as of the beginning of the period in question.

The formula for the standard deviation of portfolio returns reflects the fact that returns can offset one another. Suppose the expected return of XYZ common is 20 percent and that of Hedge Securities Inc. is only 2 percent per year, while the standard deviation of each investment is about 20 percent. Hedge Securities appears an unattractive investment because it has low return and high risk. However, suppose that for every percentage point of return under expectation that XYZ earns, Hedge earns an equal amount over expectation. The returns of the two securities are said to have a perfect negative correlation. A portfolio with 50 percent invested in XYZ and 50 percent invested in Hedge will have a return of 11 percent per year regardless of what happens to XYZ; the expected return is 11 percent [11 = (.5 × 20) + (.5 × 2)], and the standard deviation of the portfolio return is zero. This example explains why it is that positions in options and futures contracts that are considered high-risk investments can actually eliminate risk when held in a portfolio along with the assets on which those contracts are based.

In the other extreme, the assets in question have a perfect positive correlation. Such a situation can arise where the portfolio consists of two classes of common stock issued by the same corporation under similar terms or, in the case of a pension fund, where the fund assets are allocated between two money managers with identical investment philosophies. In such an extreme case the standard deviation of the overall portfolio return is simply the portfolio weighted average of the standard deviations of the assets that comprise the portfolio. In this case the formula for the standard deviation of portfolio returns is analogous to the above formula for the expected return.

In a typical case where the portfolio assets are less than perfectly correlated the standard deviation of the portfolio returns will be somewhat less than the weighted average of the component security standard deviations. This reflects the fact that security returns are less than perfectly correlated. The fact that the investor can reduce risk simply by holding securities within a larger portfolio is said to represent the *gains from diversification*. The magnitude of these potential gains will depend on the extent to which the security returns are correlated. The relationship between the portfolio standard deviation and correlations of component securities is given by the square root of the portfolio variance:

$$
\text{Portfolio variance} = \underbrace{w_1^2 s_1^2}_{\text{1 asset}} + 2w_1 w_2 r_{12} s_1 s_2 + 2w_1 w_3 r_{13} s_1 s_3 + \cdots
$$

$$
\underbrace{+ w_2^2 s_2^2}_{\text{2 assets}} + 2w_2 w_3 r_{23} s_2 s_3 + \cdots
$$

$$
\underbrace{+ w_3^2 s_3^2}_{\text{3 assets}} + \cdots
$$

$$
\underbrace{}_{\text{More than 3 assets}} + \cdots
$$

where

w_1, w_2, and w_3 = Proportion of the portfolio invested in assets 1, 2, 3.

s_1, s_2, and s_3 = Standard deviations of returns on assets 1, 2, 3.

r_{12}, r_{13}, and r_{23} = Correlations between returns on assets 1 and 2, 1 and 3, and 2 and 3, respectively.

To see how this formula works, consider that the portfolio invested 60 percent in common stocks and 40 percent in long-term corporate bonds. As mentioned before, such a portfolio will have an expected return of 9.24 percent. If the standard deviation of bond returns is 8.3 percent and the standard deviation of common stock returns is 21.2 percent, then the standard deviation of the portfolio returns can be calculated using the first two

TABLE 7–1
Expected Return and Standard Deviation of Portfolios
of Stocks and Bonds

Portfolio	Stock Portfolio Weight	Bond Portfolio Weight	Expected Return	Standard Deviation $(r = .18)$	Standard Deviation $(r = +1.00)$	Standard Deviation $(r = -1.00)$
0	0.00	1.00	5.10%	8.30%	8.30%	8.30%
1	0.05	0.95	5.45	8.14	8.95	6.83
2	0.10	0.90	5.79	8.12	9.59	5.35
3	0.15	0.85	6.14	8.24	10.24	3.88
4	0.20	0.80	6.48	8.50	10.88	2.40
5	0.25	0.75	6.83	8.87	11.53	0.93
6	0.28	0.72	7.04	9.16	11.93	.00
7	0.30	0.70	7.17	9.35	12.17	0.55
8	0.35	0.65	7.52	9.93	12.82	2.03
9	0.40	0.60	7.86	10.58	13.46	3.50
10	0.45	0.55	8.21	11.29	14.11	4.98
11	0.50	0.50	8.55	12.06	14.75	6.45
12	0.55	0.45	8.90	12.87	15.40	7.93
13	0.60	0.40	9.24	13.71	16.04	9.40
14	0.65	0.35	9.59	14.59	16.69	10.88
15	0.70	0.30	9.93	15.48	17.33	12.35
16	0.75	0.25	10.28	16.40	17.98	13.83
17	0.80	0.20	10.62	17.34	18.62	15.30
18	0.85	0.15	10.97	18.29	19.27	16.78
19	0.90	0.10	11.31	19.25	19.91	18.25
20	0.95	0.05	11.66	20.22	20.56	19.73
21	1.00	0.00	12.00	21.20	21.20	21.20

columns of the variance formula above. If the correlation between stock and bond returns is .18[1], the standard deviation (SD) is 13.71 percent, computed as:

$$SD = \sqrt{(.6^2 \times 21.2^2) + (2 \times .6 \times .4 \times .18 \times 21.2 \times 8.3) + (.4^2 \times 8.3^2)}$$
$$= 13.71$$

To gain some further insight the expected return and standard deviation of returns for a variety of portfolios is given in Table 7–1. There Portfolios 0 and 21 correspond to all-bond and all-stock portfolios, re-

---

[1]These and other numbers in this section are derived from Ibbotson Associates. *Stocks, Bonds, Bills and Inflation: 1985 Yearbook.* Chicago: Ibbotson Associates, Capital Management Research Center, 1986.

spectively. The all-bond portfolio has an expected return of 5.10 percent and a standard deviation of 8.30 percent, and the all-stock portfolio has an expected return of 12.0 percent and standard deviation of 21.2 percent. A portfolio consisting of 60 percent stocks and 40 percent bonds would have an expected return of 9.24 percent and a standard deviation of 13.71 percent if the correlation between bond and stock returns is 18 percent ($r = .18$). If bond and stock returns were perfectly correlated ($r = 1.00$), then the expected return would be the same but the standard deviation would be 60 percent of the distance between the bond standard deviation and the higher stock return standard deviation, or 16.04 percent. The fact that bond and stock returns are not perfectly correlated implies a reduction in the standard deviation of portfolio returns. If the bonds represented a perfect hedge to the stock investment or, in other words, were perfectly *negatively* correlated ($r = -1.00$), the standard deviation would be only 9.40 percent. In that case, in fact, there exists a portfolio consisting of 28 percent stocks and 72 percent bonds (Portfolio 6) that has a zero standard deviation of returns. Such a portfolio would return 7.04 percent with certainty.

It is common to plot expected return against standard deviation in a figure similar to that presented as Figure 7–1. The center line gives the set of choices between portfolios that are completely invested in bonds and those that are completely invested in stocks if the correlation between returns on the two asset classes is .18. The other lines give the set of choices if the assets were perfectly correlated, as well as if they were perfectly negatively correlated in their returns. Such a figure can be drawn where there are more than two asset classes; each point on the line then has the interpretation of being the standard deviation and expected return of a portfolio chosen to minimize standard deviation for that level of expected return given the correlations and other parameter values input to the analysis. Thus it is referred to as the *minimum standard deviation* (or *variance*) frontier.

From this figure it is apparent that an all-bond portfolio does not have desirable risk and return attributes; portfolios exist that have the same or lower risk, as measured by the standard deviation of returns, but a higher expected return. Portfolio 3 in Table 7–1 has an expected return of 6.14 percent but a standard deviation of only 8.24 percent, dominating the all-bond portfolio. The extent of this gain would be even higher if the two asset returns were less correlated. However, it is not possible to rule out an all-stock portfolio on this basis.

FIGURE 7–1
Mean and Standard Deviation of Risky Portfolios

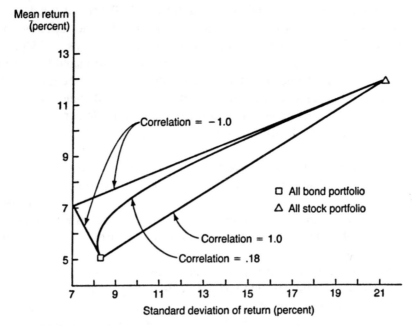

ESTIMATION ISSUES

Asset allocation procedures generally assume a limited number of asset classes because of the great demands such procedures make on data that is limited in both quality and availability.

To estimate the variance of portfolio returns, the analyst needs to know the values of many correlation parameters. Asset allocation procedures require estimates of all such correlations as well as estimates of standard deviations and expected returns. Moreover these parameter values are assumed to be known with certainty. If the portfolio manager recommends a particular portfolio of assets based on parameter inputs that are estimated, the fact that such estimates can differ from the true underlying parameters subjects the portfolio to *estimation risk*. There are at least three approaches to this particular problem. The first and most obvious approach is to use the highest-quality transactions data for returns to estimate the various parameters. This will minimize but not eliminate the problem.

The second approach is to account for estimation risk explicitly in the asset allocation process as just another source of risk. The third approach is to simplify the problem in order to reduce the number of parameter values that need to be estimated.

With sufficient high-quality data and using the formulas given in Chapter Two, one should be able to estimate the value of relevent parameter inputs with such precision that estimation risk is not an issue. Unfortunately the parameter values tend to change over extended periods of data; there is a finite limit to the amount of useful data. For the purpose of portfolio analysis, returns should be measured on the basis of transaction prices.

The use of appraisal data is unsatisfactory for at least two reasons. Even where these data provide a satisfactory measure of expected return, the appraisal process artificially smooths prices, leading to low estimates of the standard deviation of return. Measured real estate returns have a much lower standard deviation than do returns to REIT securities backed by real estate assets (even after accounting for the leverage associated with such securities). Real estate is one area where appraisal values are virtually all the analyst has to work with. In addition, real estate returns have an artificially low correlation with other assets whose returns are based on transactions data. This illustrates another problem: both the quality and quantity of data can vary across asset classes.

Even where data is readily available and is of high quality, as is usually the case with equity portfolios, there is a practical limit to the number of assets that can be studied. Suppose the portfolio under study is large and well diversified, comprising over 500 equities. If the very large correlation matrix is estimated on the basis of less than 500 periods of returns, a portfolio can always be found that appears to have a standard deviation of zero. The data corresponds to a maximum of only 500 scenarios of returns; a portfolio can be constructed out of the 500 securities to match exactly every historical scenario. The correlation matrix estimated on the basis of fewer periods of data than there are securities is said to be *singular*. Obviously, the results of such analysis are misleading; with 500 assets, the number of possible return scenarios is far in excess of that number.

This example illustrates that the acquisition of high-quality data is alone not sufficient to eliminate the effects of estimation risk. One approach is to account for this risk directly. Suppose the standard deviations and correlations are known values, but expected returns are estimated on the basis of T periods of returns. The uncertainty facing the investor arises not only from the variance of returns but also from uncertainty that results from using estimates of expected returns. Thus the standard deviations should be augmented by a factor equal to the square root of the sum $1 + 1/T$, where the $1/T$ factor accounts for the fact that expected returns are not known with certainty. Where the standard deviations and correlations also have to be estimated and historical data represent the sole source of information for the analyst, a similar form of reasoning follows,[2] and estimates of the standard deviation parameters should be augmented by a factor equal to

$$\sqrt{(T + 1)(T - 1)/T(T - n - 2)}$$

where n represents the number of securities under study. This formula assumes that there are at least three more periods of returns than there are securities under study $(T > n + 2)$.

Fortunately the available data does not necessarily represent the sole source of information for the analyst. Returns on assets within specific asset classes and within particular industries tend to move together in systematic ways. This suggests that simple one-factor and multifactor models of a type discussed in Chapter Two and Chapter Three might lead to simplified models with fewer parameters to be estimated. Recall that in such models asset returns were correlated with each other only to the extent that they were correlated to factors of uncertainty common across all assets. In the case of a single-factor model:

$$R_i = a_i + (b_i \times R_m) + e_i$$

where

R_i and R_m represent the return on asset i and on the market factor.

e_i represents the return idiosyncratic to security i.

The correlation between the return on security i and security j, r_{ij}, is given by:

$$r_{ij} = b_i \times b_j \times \frac{\text{variance of } R_m}{s_i \times s_j}$$

where s_i and s_j represent the standard deviation of returns on assets i and j, respectively.

This leads to a substantial reduction in the number of parameters to be estimated. In the case of 100 assets, the number of parameters falls

---

[2]For the development of this concept, see V. S. Bawa, S. J. Brown and R. W. Klein *Estimation Risk and Optimal Portfolio Choice* (Amsterdam: 1979).

from 100 expected returns, 100 standard deviations, and 4,950 (100 × 99/2) correlations—a total of 5,150 parameters—to only 100 expected returns, 100 standard deviations, 100 betas (b_is) and one factor variance parameter, a total of 301 parameters all told.

However, this reduction in the number of parameters to be estimated comes at the cost of assuming that the single-factor model is in fact correct. The restrictiveness of this model can be relaxed by assuming that a multifactor model explains security returns. If so, then a somewhat more complicated formula applies,[3] although it is still true that the number of parameters to be estimated is substantially reduced. Another approach is to estimate the correlation coefficients directly through use of the single or multifactor models and average the coefficients so obtained over industry groups.[4] This procedure assumes that the underlying or true correlation coefficients are in fact the same within industry groups; returns within broad industry categories tend to move in similar ways. The fact that individual correlation coefficients differ within such categories may be just a manifestation of the random error associated with trying to estimate these numbers precisely. As a consequence the average correlation coefficient may be a better estimate of the underlying correlation between the returns of the assets in question than the individual correlation estimates.

These simple models are a response to the difficulties associated with estimating the large number of correlations required as inputs to any asset allocation problem of reasonable scale. To the extent that they are useful they introduce information above and beyond what is available in the return data themselves. This information may not be exactly and literally

---

[3]In the case where the common factors of variation are themselves uncorrelated (the assumption of factor analysis) the formula is given by

$$r_{ij} = \frac{b_{1i}b_{1j}s_{f1}^2 + 2b_{1i}b_{2j}s_{f1}s_{f2} + 2b_{1i}b_{3i}s_{f1}s_{f3} + \cdots}{s_i \times s_j}$$

$$+ b_{2i}b_{2j}s_{f2}^2 \qquad + 2b_{2i}b_{3j}s_{f2}s_{f3} + \cdots$$

$$+ b_{3i}b_{3j}s_{f3}^2 \qquad +$$

where

b_{1i}, b_{2i}, and b_{3i} = Factor exposures of security i to factors 1, 2, and 3.

b_{1j}, b_{2j}, and b_{3j} = Factor exposures of security j to factors 1, 2, and 3.

s_{f1}, s_{f2} and s_{f3} = Standard deviations of factors 1, 2, and 3.

[4]This approach was suggested by E. Elton and M. Gruber "Estimating the Dependence Structure of Share Price—Implications for Portfolio Selection," *Journal of Finance* 28 (December 1973), pp. 1265–1273.

correct; approximations are involved. There is thus a necessary trade-off. The correctly specified model that estimates every correlation directly from the sample data of rates of return implies an estimation risk that may be unacceptable to the analyst. The model that is easier to estimate precisely but is slightly misspecified may be the more acceptable choice.

THE OPTIMAL PORTFOLIO

Figure 7–1 illustrates that asset classes can be combined to produce portfolios that offer the highest expected return for a given level of risk. They also minimize risk for every level of expected return. Portfolios that accomplish these objectives are termed *efficient,* and the set of all such portfolios is referred to as the *efficient frontier.* A hypothetical efficient frontier is shown in Figure 7–2. Portfolios 1, 2, and 3 represent efficient asset mixes whereas Portfolio 4 represents an inefficient asset mix. At the risk level associated with Portfolio 4, a higher expected return is available from Portfolio 2; and given its expected return, risk can be reduced by selecting Portfolio 1.

Based on the long-term historical performance of the capital markets, Portfolio 1 might reflect a heavy commitment to short-term securities, while Portfolio 3 would probably include a substantial position in common stocks.

Although the efficient frontier isolates those portfolios that offer the highest expected return for a given level of risk, it does not by itself indicate which of these portfolios is most appropriate for the client. A conservative client, for example, would be willing to sacrifice high expected return in exchange for a greater degree of certainty in the outcome whereas an aggressive client would be more willing to incur uncertainty in exchange for a higher expected return. In theory, an investor's willingness to exchange expected return for risk reduction is called an investor preference curve or a utility function.

If a utility function were plotted with expected return on the vertical axis and standard deviation on the horizontal axis (as in Figure 7–3), it would typically be convex. That is, at low levels of expected return, an investor is more willing to incur risk in exchange for additional units of expected return than he is at high levels of expected return. The point along the utility function that is tangent to the efficient frontier represents the optimal trade-off between expected return and risk for the investor, given that he or she is limited to portfolios along the efficient frontier.

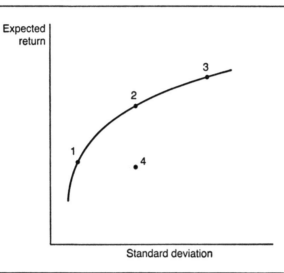

FIGURE 7–2
Hypothetical Efficient Frontier

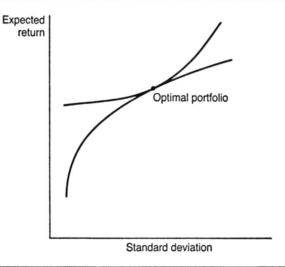

FIGURE 7–3
The Optimal Portfolio

Those portfolios below the efficient frontier are undesirable and those above the frontier are unobtainable, given the assumptions about each asset class's expected return, standard deviation, and correlation with the other asset classes.

William Sharpe suggests that an appropriate measure of utility for an asset mix is expected return less a *risk penalty,* and he defines risk penalty as risk squared divided by risk tolerance.[5] This definition is consistent with the notion that risk aversion is convex. For example, if an asset mix has a 10.5 percent standard deviation and the investor has a risk tolerance of 50, then the appropriate risk penalty is 110.25 percent divided by 50, which equals 2.2 percent. If the portfolio has an expected return of 12 percent, its utility equals 12 percent minus 2.2 percent, which is 9.8 percent. This utility is then compared to the utility of other asset mixes to determine which one has the highest utility, given the investor's risk tolerance. The asset mix with the highest utility is the investor's optimal asset mix.

The chief obstacle to implementation of this approach is that risk-return trade-offs defined in these terms are unintuitive to most investors.

An alternative approach is to restate a portfolio's expected return and standard deviation in terms of such a portfolio's likelihood of achieving some objective. On this basis an investor may feel more comfortable in choosing among portfolios with different asset mixes. For example, a conservative investor may be very sensitive to negative returns. Given a choice between a portfolio with an expected return of 8 percent with a standard deviation of 4 percent versus a portfolio with an expected return of 15 percent with a standard deviation of 15 percent, he can base his selection on the likelihood each portfolio has of exceeding a 0 percent return. Since 0 percent is two standard deviations below the expected return of the conservative portfolio (expected return = 8 percent, standard deviation = 4 percent), there is a 98 percent chance that the portfolio will generate a positive return.

Zero percent is only one standard deviation below the expected return of the more aggressive portfolio; hence we have less confidence (84 percent) that the portfolio will produce a positive return.

In general we can estimate a portfolio's probability of exceeding a target in terms of the number of standard deviations of return the expected return is away from the target. This number of standard deviations (z) is given by the formula

---

[5]W. Sharpe, *Asset Allocation Tools* (Palo Alto, Calif.: Scientific Press, 1985), p. 74.

$$\text{Number of Standard Deviation} = \frac{x - ER}{s} = z$$

where

x = Target return.
ER = Expected return.
s = Standard deviation.

In the case of the conservative asset mix, the mean is 8 percent and the standard deviation is 4 percent. If the target were 12 percent it would be one standard deviation above mean return, or

$$z = \frac{12 - 8}{4} = 1$$

For the aggressive mix, the mean and standard deviation equal 15, and the target is now .2 standard deviations below the mean:

$$z = \frac{12 - 15}{15} = -.2$$

These numbers can be translated into the probability of meeting a target, using the standard normal distribution function available in most elementary statistics textbooks:

$$\text{Probability of meeting target} = 1 - N[z]$$

where $N[z]$ is the probability that returns are more than z standard deviations below the mean return. In the conservative asset mix case:

$$\begin{aligned}\text{Probability of meeting 12 percent target} &= 1 - N[1]\\ &= 1 - .84\\ &= 16 \text{ percent}\end{aligned}$$

In the aggressive asset mix case:

$$\begin{aligned}\text{Probability of meeting 12 percent target} &= 1 - N[-.2]\\ &= 1 - .42\\ &= 58 \text{ percent}\end{aligned}$$

This analysis would argue in favor of the aggressive mix, given the 12 percent target.

If our investment horizon were four years rather than one year and we assume that our annual assumptions about risk and return were valid for the entire four years, then we could estimate the probability of achieving a return on average over the four-year horizon for the aggressive asset mix as 66 percent:

$$z = \frac{12 - 15}{\dfrac{15}{\sqrt{4}}} = -.4$$

Probability of meeting target $= 1 - N[-.4]$
$$= 1 - .33 = 66 \text{ percent}$$

In general, if we assume that our annual risk and return assumptions apply over T years, we can estimate the probability of achieving a result on average over T years, using:

$$z = \frac{x - ER}{\dfrac{s}{\sqrt{T}}}$$

This approach is an approximation that loses accuracy as T increases, because it does not account for the compounding of returns.[6]

The probability of achieving a return on average that is lower than the expected return increases as the number of years in the investment horizon increases, because returns are smoothed over time (low returns in certain years are offset by high returns in other years). Specifically, if returns from year to year are independent the annualized variance of returns decreases roughly with time, and the annualized standard deviation therefore decreases approximately with the square root of time.

What if we had a multiple-year investment horizon and we were concerned about never experiencing a year in which the portfolio generated a negative return? If our investment horizon was five years our objective would be to achieve a positive return in five consecutive years. If an asset mix has only a 1 in 10 chance of producing a negative return in any one year, it has a 90 percent chance of producing a positive return in any one year. Again, if we assume that returns are serially independent, then the probability of this asset mix achieving a positive return in two consecutive years is $.90^2$, or 81 percent. The probability of experiencing a positive return in five consecutive years is $.90^5$, which equals 59 percent. Thus, although this asset mix has only a 1 in 10 chance of generating a negative return in any one year, its chance of generating a negative return in one or more of the next five years is 41 percent (1.0 - .59).

---

[6]An alternative is to recast the analysis, substituting for the rate of return R the *logarithm* of $(1 + R)$. This automatically accounts for the compounding effect.

As shown above, it is fairly easy to restate expected return and standard deviation in terms of the probability of achieving a particular objective, thus rendering comparison among alternative asset mixes reasonably intuitive.

Selection of the appropriate return objective is also an important issue, and it sometimes can be dealt with through quantitative techniques. Consider, for example, a pension fund with an objective of funding current and future benefits. A reasonable objective may be to achieve an asset value in the pension fund equal to the future value of the pension liabilities, thus ensuring benefit security for the plan participants.

If we can anticipate contributions and disbursements to and from the pension fund and if we can project the growth in liabilities, then by using the present value formula we can solve for the rate of return required on the pension assets to achieve full funding of liabilities within a given time frame.

Assume an initial asset value of $100 million for the pension fund, a present value of $115 million growing at 5 percent annually for the liabilities, and the following contributions and disbursements:

Year	Contributions ($ millions)	Disbursements ($ millions)
1	6	3
2	6	4
3	5	5
4	5	6
5	4	6

We can solve for the internal rate of return required to achieve full funding within five years as follows:

$$100 = \frac{(-6 + 3)}{(1 + r)} + \frac{(-6 + 4)}{(1 + r)^2} + \frac{(-5 + 5)}{(1 + r)^3}$$
$$+ \frac{(-5 + 6)}{(1 + r)^4} + \frac{(-5 + 6) + 115(1 + .05)^5}{(1 + r)^5}$$

$$r = .073$$

The contributions can be thought of as negative payments from the pension fund; hence their negative sign.

The next step, of course, would be to estimate the likelihood of each asset mix achieving an average annual rate of return of 7.32 percent over the next five years[7] and to weigh these results with the probability estimates of other objectives.

This example oversimplifies asset/liability analysis, but it does demonstrate (conceptually at least) the applicability of the present value formula.

DYNAMIC HEDGING

Thus far in our discussion of asset allocation we have assumed implicitly that the asset positions were bought and held. As an alternative to a buy/hold asset allocation strategy, dynamic strategies are often employed. For example, some investors continually rebalance a portfolio to maintain its initial asset mix, thus shifting funds from the asset class with favorable relative performance to the asset class with unfavorable relative performance.

Absolute Protection: Risky versus Riskless Assets

Another popular dynamic strategy is portfolio insurance. This strategy calls for the continual rebalancing of a portfolio between a risky and a riskless component so as to ensure that the total fund's terminal value will not fall below a prespecified minimum level. This protection is accomplished by gradually shifting funds from the risky to the riskless component as the portfolio value decreases and from the riskless to the risky component as the portfolio value increases. This type of dynamic strategy produces essentially the same result as purchasing a protective put option on a portfolio. However, it does not require investment in options; it simply requires the continual rebalancing of a portfolio between a risky and a riskless component.

A put option on a risky asset can be replicated by selling the risky asset short and lending at the risk-free rate.[8] The amount to sell short and to lend can be determined from the binomial model or the Black-Scholes model, both of which are described in Chapter Six.

For example, suppose we wish to replicate a put option with an exercise price of $95 on a risky asset that is currently valued at $100. Assume

---

[7]To be precise, a 7.32 percent return is required each year, not just an average over the five years.

[8]For a demonstration of this strategy, see Mark Rubinstein and Hayne Leland, "Replicating Options with Positions in Stock and Cash," *Financial Analysts Journal*, 37 (July–August 1981), pp. 63–72.

that the asset will either increase to $110 or decrease to $90 one year from now as shown below and that it pays no dividend.

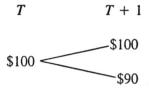

$$T \qquad\qquad T + 1$$

$$\$100 \begin{array}{c} \diagup \$100 \\ \diagdown \$90 \end{array}$$

If the asset increases to $110 the put option will expire worthless; if it decreases to $90 the put option will be worth $5 (that is, 95 − 90). With these two possible values for the put option and with the risk-free rate, we can solve for the amount to sell short and the amount to lend in order to replicate the put option:

Put option value = $100 \times D - (1 + r) \times B = 0$ for increase
Put option value = $90 \times D - (1 + r) \times B = 5$ for decrease

where

D = Amount of the asset to sell short.
r = Risk-free rate of return.
B = Amount to borrow (if as in this case it is a negative value, it represents the amount to lend).

If we assume that the risk-free rate equals 8 percent, then by solving the above equations simultaneously we find that D equals $-.25$ and B equals -25.46. Therefore, by selling short $25 of the risky asset and lending $25.46, we will replicate a put option with an exercise price of $95 on a $100 risky asset that will either increase or decrease 10 percent. Moreover, this put option will be worth $.46:

$$(100 \times -.25) + 25.46 = .46$$

To see this equivalence, consider the return of selling short and lending if the risky asset increases 10 percent. A $25 short position would lose $2.50, which would be partially offset by the interest of $2.04 (25.46 × .08). The difference, $-\$.46$, is the same return we would receive by paying $.46 for a put option that expires worthless. If the risky asset decreases 10 percent the $25 short position would return $2.50, which when added to the $2.04 generated from the $25.46 lent at 8 percent gives a total return of $4.54. This amount exactly equals the return from a put option that costs $.46 to purchase and is worth $5 at expiration.

As shown earlier, we can replicate a put option by selling short and lending. To replicate a *protective put strategy,* we need only to combine the above strategy with investment in the risky asset we are seeking to protect; that is, we would invest $75 of a $100 portfolio (100 − 25) in the risky asset, and the balance plus the $.46 for the put option in the risk-free asset.

The values derived above assume only two possible outcomes for the risky asset. Hence these values are approximations that in the limit approach the true theoretical values given by the Black-Scholes model. Since a call option has the same payoff as a protective put strategy, the Black-Scholes model's term N(D1), which is called delta, gives the amount to invest in the risky asset in order to replicate a protective put strategy.

For example, assume we wish to invest $100 so as to ensure that we will have at least $95 one year hence with participation in the S&P 500, if it performs favorably. This strategy is equivalent to investment in the S&P with a protective put option. Further assume that the S&P is currently valued at $100. To replicate this option strategy, we can use the Black-Scholes model to determine N(D1), the percentage to invest in the S&P 500, by setting the exercise price equal to $95.

Recall from Chapter Six that the value of a call option equals:

$$C = S \times N(D1) - \{K \times e^{-rT}\} \times N(D2)$$

where
- S = Current stock price.
- K = Exercise price of the option.
- r = Risk-free rate of interest.
- T = Time to maturity of the option.
- $N(.)$ = Standard normal distribution function.
- $D1 = \dfrac{\text{natural log } (S/K) + (r + V/2) \times T}{(V \times T)^{.5}}$
- $D2 = D1 - (V \times T)^{.5}$
- V = Variance of the return of the stock.
- e = Exponential constant, 2.71828 (see Chapter 2, p. 18)

If we assume that the S&P 500 has a standard deviation of 20 percent and that the risk-free return is 8 percent, N(D1) equals .775, as shown below:

$$D1 = \frac{\text{natural log } (100/95) + (.08 + .04/2) \times 1}{(.04 \times 1)^{.5}} = .7565$$

$$N(D1) = .775$$

Furthermore, the value of the call equals \$15.17, as shown below:

$$D2 = .7565 - (.04 \times 1)^{.5} = .5565$$
$$N(D2) = .711$$
$$C = 100 \times .7753 - \{95 \times 2.71828^{-.08}\} \times .7111$$
$$C = 15.17$$

From put-call parity (see Chapter Six) the value of a corresponding put option on the S&P 500 equals \$2.87. Since we only have \$100 to invest we cannot afford to buy \$100 of the S&P and a put option valued at \$2.87. Therefore $N(D1)$ is not exactly the percentage to invest in the S&P 500 in order to replicate the protective put strategy. We must repeat the valuation by iteratively changing the amount of the S&P we can afford to protect, such that this amount together with the value of the put exactly equals \$100. $N(D1)$ times this amount of the S&P then gives us the fraction of the \$100 to be invested in the S&P, with the balance to be invested in the risk-free asset.

If we were to proceed in this fashion, we would find that we could protect \$96.15 invested in the S&P with a put option valued at \$3.85, which exactly sums to the \$100 we have available. At these values, $N(D1)$ equals .712. Therefore, we would allocate \$68.48 (.7122 x \$96.15) to the S&P and \$31.52 to a risk-free asset. Moreover, as the S&P's value changes throughout the horizon and as we approach expiration, we must adjust these allocations in accordance with the changing value for $N(D1)$. If we pursue this strategy continuously under perfect market conditions (that is, no frictions such as transaction costs) we will be assured of a minimum terminal value of \$95. Furthermore, if the S&P produces a higher return than the risk-free return, we should expect a terminal value equal to 96.15 percent of the S&P's terminal value (again assuming an initial value for the S&P of \$100).

Relative Protection: Assets versus Liabilities

In the above analysis, we have assumed that we can only choose between a risky and a riskless asset. What if we are not as concerned with the absolute value of our portfolio at some future date as we are with its relative value? For example, it may make sense to protect a pension fund's value in relation to the value of the pension liabilities. It is possible to adapt the portfolio insurance methodology described above to ensure that a prespecified ratio of pension assets to pension liabilities will be met or exceeded. To accomplish this type of protection, we need to replace the riskless component with a portfolio that mimics the changes in value of the pension liabilities. With this substitution we need to modify the Black-Scholes formula by redefining risk and return as *net* risk and *net* return. Therefore net variance is calculated as:

$$V_N = V_A + V_L - 2 \times r_{AL} \times V_A^{.5} \times V_L^{.5}$$

where

V_N = Net variance of the pension assets and liabilities.

V_A = Variance of the assets.

V_L = Variance of the liabilities.

r_{AL} = Correlation between the pension assets and liabilities.

Within this context, the risk-free return equals 0 percent since it represents the *net* return of the portfolio that mimics the liabilities relative to the return of the liabilities. With these two modifications we can rewrite the Black-Scholes formula:

$$C = A \times N(D1) - L \times N(D2)$$

where

C = Value of an option to exchange one risky asset for another.

A = Value of the pension assets.

L = Value of the pension liabilities.

$N(.)$ = Standard normal distribution function.

$$D1 = \frac{\text{natural log } (A/L) + (V_N/2) \times T}{(V \times T)^{.5}}$$

$D2 = D1 - (V \times T)^{.5}$

V_N = Net variance, as defined earlier.

T = Investment horizon.

This formula is identical to W. Margrabe's model of an option to exchange one asset for another.[9] It can be used just as the Black-Scholes model was used earlier to replicate a protective put strategy. In this application, we are replicating a protective put strategy whereby the put has a variable exercise price that is indexed to the value of the pension liabilities and whereby the strategy calls for continually rebalancing a portfolio between a risky component and a liability-mimicking component.

---

[9]W. Margrabe, "The Value of an Option to Exchange One Asset for Another," *Journal of Finance*, 33 (March 1978), pp. 117–86.

CONCLUSION

As this chapter demonstrates, quantitative methods are widely applied in support of asset allocation decisions. In fact, the level of complexity of the quantitative techniques used in asset allocation is relatively advanced and increasing at a rapid pace. To compete effectively in this arena the serious financial analyst should be conversant with the quantitative techniques described in this chapter.

REFERENCES

Bawa, V. S., S. J. Brown, and R. W. Klein. *Estimation Risk and Optimal Portfolio Choice* (Amsterdam: 1979), North Holland.

Elton, E., and M. Gruber. "Estimating the Dependence Structure of Share Prices—Implications for Portfolio Selection," *Journal of Finance* 28, (December 1973), pp. 1265–1273.

Ibbotson Associates. *Stocks, Bonds, Bills and Inflation: 1985 Yearbook.* (Chicago: 1986), Ibbotson Associates, Capital Management Research Center.

Margrabe, W. "The Value of an Option to Exchange One Asset for Another." *Journal of Finance* 33 (March 1978), pp. 117–86.

Rubinstein, M. and H. Leland. "Replicating Options with Positions in Stock and Cash." *Financial Analysts Journal* 37 (July–August 1981), pp. 63–72.

Sharpe, W. *Asset Allocation Tools* (Palo Alto, Calif.: 1985), Scientific Press.

CHAPTER EIGHT

Quantitative Methods in Performance Measurement

Mark P. Kritzman

INTRODUCTION

The five preceding chapters demonstrate how the quantitative principles described in Chapter Two can be applied to improve the investment process. This chapter extends the same quantitative principles to investment performance measurement.

The purpose of performance measurement is neither to reward nor to penalize managers for past performance but rather to identify managers who are likely to add value to a portfolio going forward. Hence past performance is relevant only to the extent it reveals something about a manager's likelihood of future success. Unfortunately, past performance is influenced heavily by the randomness of security returns. Thus such performance by itself may tell us little about the likelihood of future success. Within this context performance measurement should be viewed as a means of uncovering evidence of manager conduct. This evidence should be used in conjunction with one's qualitative appraisal of the manager to determine if the manager is indeed likely to add value to the portfolio.

This chapter begins with a discussion of rates of return and proceeds with a review of the conventional techniques for ranking returns and risk-adjusting returns. This review is followed by a discussion of some important limitations to performance measurement, such as benchmark error and the ambiguity between skill and chance. Next are introduced some more-advanced techniques designed to overcome these limitations, including performance attribution, normal portfolios, and nonparametric performance measurement. The next section demonstrates how the quantitative framework of option pricing theory can be applied to analyze performance-based fees. The chapter concludes with a discussion of how managers adapt their behavior in order to circumvent various performance measurement techniques.

As will become apparent, performance measurement is highly dependent upon the application of quantitative tools. The limitation of quantitative tools, though, is also very apparent when applied to performance measurement.

RATE OF RETURN

Rate of return is a straightforward concept. It is equal to the income generated by an investment plus or minus the investment's change in price during the measurement period, all divided by the beginning price, controlling for contributions and disbursements.

For *common stock,* therefore:

$$\text{Rate of return} = \frac{\text{Dividends} + (\text{Ending price} - \text{Beginning price})}{\text{Beginning price}}$$

For *bonds* we simply substitute coupons for dividends:

$$\text{Rate of return} = \frac{\text{Coupons} + (\text{Ending price} - \text{Beginning price})}{\text{Beginning price}}$$

For *real estate* the income component is net operating income:

$$\text{Rate of return} = \frac{\text{Net operating income} + (\text{Ending price} - \text{Beginning price})}{\text{Beginning price}}$$

Although rate of return is conceptually simple, it is sometimes obscured by measurement problems. For example, real estate prices are often not readily available, since properties are turned over infrequently. Values based on appraisals are used instead of actual transaction-based prices, and an appraised value can differ significantly from the price at which a property could be sold.

The rate of return on discount instruments such as Treasury bills can also be potentially misleading. These instruments are purchased at a discount from their redemption price. A Treasury bill, for example, may be purchased for $9,500 and redeemed 26 weeks later for $10,000. Its rate of return, therefore, is not 5 percent but rather $500 divided by $9,500, which equals 5.26 percent for one-half year.

So, although the concept of rate of return is simple, one should apply it carefully, recognizing the unique features of the various investment media.

TIME–WEIGHTED AND DOLLAR–WEIGHTED RATES OF RETURN

As indicated in Chapter Two, the time-weighted rate of return is the standard by which investment performance is measured. It is used as the basis of comparison with competing portfolio managers and with benchmarks such as the S&P 500 Stock Index. Although the dollar-weighted rate of return measures the actual internal growth rate of the portfolio, it does not measure a portfolio manager's performance accurately. It is influenced by portfolio contributions and disbursements that are beyond the control of the portfolio manager.

Example: An investment management firm, Brownian Management, is given $10 million to invest on January 1, 1981. It is given additional contributions of $2 million on January 1, 1982, $4 million on January 1, 1983, and $6 million on January 1, 1984. On January 1, 1985, the company is required to disburse $5 million from the portfolio. By December 31, 1985, the portfolio grows to $34 million. What rate of return should be used to measure Brownian Management's performance?

The dollar-weighted rate of return of the portfolio, or its internal growth rate, is simply the rate of return that discounts the final market value of $34 million and the interim cash flows back to the initial market value of $10 million. It is derived directly from the present value formula described on page 7.

$$PV = \frac{-2}{1 + r} + \frac{-4}{(1 + r)^2} + \frac{-6}{(1 + r)^3} + \frac{5}{(1 + r)^4} + \frac{34}{(1 + r)^5} = 10$$

$$r = .167$$

Thus the dollar-weighted rate of return equals 16.7 percent.

The actual returns generated by Brownian Management on the assets under their management were -7.9 percent in 1981, 24.3 percent in 1982, 25.6 percent in 1983, 8.5 percent in 1984, and 31.0 percent in 1985. The $34 million figure represents the future value of contributions less disbursements given these returns. If we link the returns, we find that the cumulative return over the entire period was 104.4 percent:

$$r = (1 - .079)(1 + .243)(1 + .256)(1 + .085)(1 + .310) - 1 = 1.044$$

Thus the time-weighted rate of return equals 104.4 percent.

This result, however, is a five-year cumulative return. Certainly it is not comparable with the dollar-weighted rate of return in the above example which is an annualized value. Therefore, when the measurement period extends beyond one year, it is useful to annualize the time-weighted rate of return in order to establish a common frame of reference. It is misleading to annualize returns over periods that are shorter than one year; the implication that a quarterly or semiannual return will persist for the balance of the year is unwarranted.

To annualize the five-year cumulative return of 104.4 percent, we simply add 1, raise this value to the 1/5 power, and subtract 1. Hence the annualized return equals 15.4 percent:

$$(1 + 1.044)^{\frac{1}{5}} - 1 = .154$$

In general the formula for annualizing a return (whether it is less than or greater than one year) is:

$$AR = (1 + R)^{1/n} - 1$$

where

AR = Annualized return.
R = Return over entire measurement period.
n = Number of years in measurement period.

If the client had switched the timing of the $5 million disbursement with the $6 million contribution, the ending market value would have been $32.8 million rather than $34 million, given the same returns on funds invested. The dollar-weighted rate of return would have been 17.5 percent instead of 16.7 percent:

$$PV = \frac{-2}{1 + r} + \frac{-4}{(1 + r)^2} + \frac{5}{(1 + r)^3} + \frac{-6}{(1 + r)^4} + \frac{32.8}{(1 + r)^5} = 10$$
$$r = .175$$

Nonetheless the return generated by Brownian Management on the assets under its control each year would not have changed. Clearly, therefore, the time-weighted rate of return controls for the impact that contributions and disbursements have on the portfolio and isolates the return due to investment management.

The time-weighted rate of return, although different from the dollar-weighted rate of return over a measurement period with cash flows, can be reconciled quite easily with the present value framework. It is equivalent to the linked dollar-weighted rates of return between cash flows.

Again consider the example. Although the dollar-weighted rate of return over the entire five years is 16.7 percent, the dollar-weighted rate of return for each individual year is different.

In 1981, the dollar-weighted rate of return can be found by discounting the market value at the end of the year back to the initial market value:

$$\frac{9.21}{1 + r} = 10$$
$$r = -.079$$

The same procedure can be used to find the dollar-weighted rate of return in the second year. That is, the market value at the end of the second year is discounted back to the market value at the beginning of the second year. Note that the market value at the beginning of the second year includes the $2 million contribution made on January 1, 1982.

$$\frac{13.93}{1 + r} = 11.21$$
$$r = .243$$

If we repeat this procedure for years 1983 through 1985, we find that the dollar-weighted rates of return are 25.6 percent, 8.5 percent, and 31 percent, respectively.

These annual dollar-weighted rates of return are exactly equivalent to the returns generated by Brownian Management each year. Hence the present value framework described in Chapter Two can be applied to measure investment performance, given the simple modification of discounting the market value before each cash flow back to the market value subsequent to each prior cash flow and linking these returns. This procedure will yield the portfolio's time-weighted rate of return over the entire measurement period, which can easily be annualized if appropriate.

Universe Comparisons

In the foregoing example Brownian Management generated an annualized time-weighted rate of return of 15.4 percent for the five years ending in 1985. How good is this result?

One way to answer this question is to compare its rate of return to the returns achieved by other portfolio managers with whom it competes. In fact, universe comparisons are the most common approach for evaluating portfolio managers. The procedure is quite simple. The returns of a representative sample of portfolio managers are collected and assembled into a universe. The universe is then segmented into percentile groupings, and each manager is evaluated by the grouping in which he or she appears. For example, if 100 managers are included in the universe and only 10 of them have a return equal to or greater than 15.4 percent, then a manager whose return exceeds 15.4 percent is a top-decile performer for the five years ending in 1985. If 25 managers produced returns equal to or in excess of 15.4 percent, then a manager with a 15.4 percent return or greater would rank within the top quartile.

The universe comparison approach simply ranks each participant's return and divides the absolute ranking by the number of managers in the sample to determine the percentile ranking.

A typical universe comparison exhibit is shown in Figure 8–1, which ranks managers over four periods: one quarter, one year, three years, and five years ending on December 31, 1985. The bars for each period span the returns ranging from the 95th to the 5th percentile of the universe. The plots within the bars show the percentile ranking of Brownian Management as well as a relevant benchmark. Although performance during four periods is shown, these periods all end on the same date; they overlap each other. Therefore, a manager's ranking in all of the periods can be largely affected by the manager's performance in the most recent quarter. By using overlapping periods to compare managers, relative performance may appear to be more consistent than it really is.

Figure 8–2 shows the percentile ranking of Brownian Management over five independent quarters. It is more apparent from this exhibit that Brownian Management's percentile rankings are rather unstable from quarter to quarter. The use of discrete measurement periods is a more reliable indicator of consistency.

The appeal of the universe comparison approach is its simplicity. Nonetheless it has several limitations. First, there should be uniformity of style across managers within a given universe or the ranking may be spe-

FIGURE 8–1
Universe Comparison: Overlapping Periods

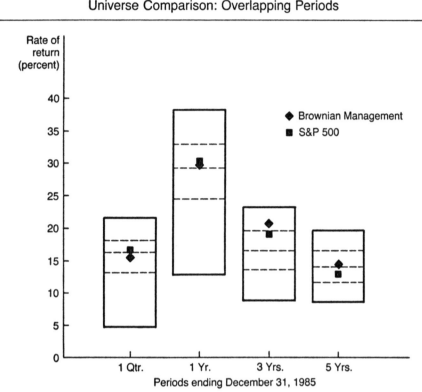

cious. For example, it would not be very informative to include equity and fixed-income managers in the same universe since their performance will be influenced largely by the performance of the markets in which they operate. More subtle variations of this problem can also jeopardize the integrity of a universe comparison. Some equity managers concentrate their selection of securities among large companies, while other managers focus on small companies. This difference in style will affect the results so that the ranking may reflect not the managers' discretionary investment judgments but rather their investment style. This issue is addressed in some depth later in this chapter.

Another shortcoming of universe comparisons is that most empirical evidence suggests there is no correlation between a manager's ranking in one period and his ranking in the subsequent period.

FIGURE 8–2
Universe Comparison: Discrete Periods

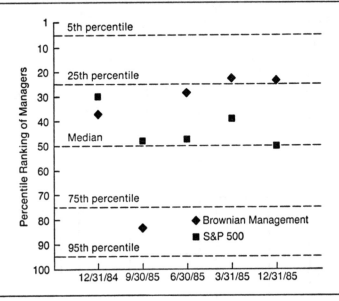

The implicit expectation of those who rely on universe comparisons to evaluate money managers is that relative performance will persist from period to period, that it is serially correlated. Regression analysis allows us to test this belief. For example, the percentile rankings of a group of managers over a particular measurement period can be regressed on their percentile rankings over the previous measurement period. In the extreme, if relative performance in the first period corresponded perfectly with relative performance in the subsequent period, the scatter plot would form a straight line emanating from the origin at 45 degrees, as shown in Figure 8–3. The intercept of the line would be zero while its slope would be one. The R-squared of such a relationship would also be 1. This relationship would indicate that a manager's percentile ranking in one period is repeated exactly in the next period.

Obviously it is quite unlikely that relative performance among portfolio managers is perfectly correlated from period to period. Nonetheless, most members of the investment industry harbor the belief that past relative performance foretells something about subsequent relative performance. For example, a common view is that top-quartile managers are

FIGURE 8–3
Perfect Positive Relationship

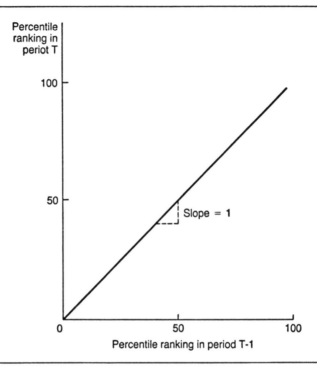

more likely to generate superior results in the next period than are bottom-quartile managers.

A study of the Bell System managers covering the period 1972 through 1981 showed that virtually no relationship existed between relative performance in the first five-year period and the second five-year period.[1] A perfect serial relationship would have produced an intercept of zero, a slope of one, and an R-squared of one. If relative performance were perfectly uncorrelated the intercept would equal 50 (the 50th percentile would be the best guess for next period's ranking), while the slope and R-squared

---

[1]See Mark Kritzman, "Can Bond Managers Perform Consistently?" *Journal of Portfolio Management*, Summer 1983, pp. 54–56. The equity results are from an unpublished portion of the same study.

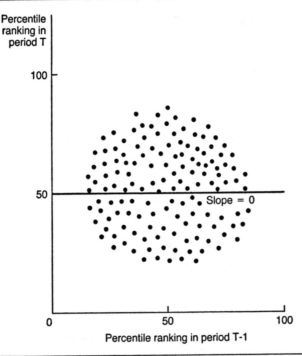

FIGURE 8–4
No Relationship

would both equal zero (see Figure 8–4). The actual results of the Bell System study are:

	Intercept	Slope	R–Squared
Equity managers	51	−0.05	0.00
Fixed-income managers	46	.10	0.00

These results show that relative performance is almost perfectly independent from period to period and that regardless of whether a manager appears in the top or bottom quartile in one period the best guess of the manager's ranking in the future is the 50th percentile!

RISK ADJUSTMENT

A fundamental principle of finance is that investors require compensation for bearing risk; hence riskier assets have higher expected returns than less risky assets. Moreover historical precedent has demonstrated that investors' expectations have been realized over most extended time periods. Figure 2–3 in Chapter Two shows that over the period 1926–1984, small stocks provided higher returns and higher variability of returns than large stocks and that the same relationship is true between large stocks and bonds. A portfolio manager, without exerting any skill whatsoever, could therefore increase a portfolio's expected return and, over most extended horizons, its realized return simply by increasing the portfolio's risk. Thus it is argued that portfolio managers should be evaluated according to their risk-adjusted returns, not their total returns.

As a first approximation for portfolio risk, one might consider the standard deviation of returns. The Sharpe measure[2] adjusts returns by dividing a portfolio's excess return (portfolio return less Treasury bill return) by the standard deviation of total return. This measure implicitly assumes that there is only one manager for the entire portfolio; hence total risk is relevant.

The Capital Asset Pricing Model (CAPM) assumes that there are two separate sources of portfolio risk: systemwide influences and company-specific influences. Since the risk associated with company-specific influences can be eliminated by diversification, investors are not compensated for bearing specific risk. They are compensated only for bearing systematic risk that cannot be diversified away.

The Treynor measure[3] relates return to systematic risk only and therefore can be applied to a situation where there are multiple managers. It is calculated by dividing a portfolio's excess return by its beta. Beta can be estimated by regressing the portfolio excess returns on the excess returns of the market portfolio over some representative time period. The coefficient from such a regression is beta. It measures the portfolio's expected change in excess return, given a one unit change in the market's excess return. For example, if Brownian Management had a beta of 1.25, they would be expected to generate 5.0 percent excess return when the market portfolio generates a 4.0 percent excess return.

---

[2]See William Sharpe "Mutual Fund Performance," *Journal of Business* 39 (January 1966), pp. 119–38.

[3]See Jack Treynor "How to Rate Management of Investment Funds," *Harvard Business Review* 44 (January–February 1965), pp. 63–75.

The intercept from a regression of the portfolio excess return on the market's excess return is referred to as alpha, and it measures the value added by the portfolio manager, given the level of risk (beta) chosen for the portfolio. For example, since Brownian Management generated a 4.8 percent excess return with a 1.25 beta while the market's excess return was 4.0 percent, their alpha (value added) was −0.2 percent:

Alpha = (Portfolio return − Risk-free return)
  − [Beta × (Market return − Risk-free return)]
  = (15.4 − 10.6) − [1.25 × (14.6 − 10.6)] = − 0.2 percent

Thus, although Brownian Management generated a higher return than the market, their value added was slightly negative after accounting for the risk they incurred.

Alpha is also referred to as the Jensen measure[4], and it too is suitable for a multiple-manager situation since it is based on systematic risk rather than total risk.

BENCHMARK ERROR

Performance measurement techniques that are based on the CAPM or that compare performance to the market assume implicitly that the market is observable. Of course, if we acknowledge that the market includes the entire wealth of the world, it cannot be observed, so indexes such as the S&P 500 Stock Index are used as a surrogate for the market and as a benchmark for performance.

The substitution of an index such as the S&P 500 for the market leads to theoretical as well as practical problems. For example, the CAPM assumption that the market is observable is obviously false. Therefore some argue that the validity of the CAPM cannot be tested—that any proposed test of the CAPM is in effect a joint test of the CAPM and the appropriateness of the particular benchmark chosen to represent the market. Therefore we have no way of judging whether or not performance measurement techniques based on the CAPM are theoretically sound.

Of a more practical nature is the problem that a manager's risk-adjusted performance is partly determined by the benchmark chosen for risk adjustment. Richard Roll demonstrated that manager rankings based on the CAPM are inconclusive except when alpha is negative, because the

---

[4]See Michael Jensen "The Performance of Mutual Funds in the Period 1945–1964," *Journal of Finance* 23 (May 1968), pp. 389–416.

benchmark may not be an optimal portfolio.[5] When alpha is negative, switching to an optimal benchmark will only make alpha more negative. When alpha is positive, however, it is not clear whether it represents superior performance or measurement error resulting from the application of a suboptimal benchmark. Moreover, Roll demonstrated that manager rankings can be exactly reversed simply by choosing a different benchmark to represent the market. Therefore what we perceive as superior manager performance may be nothing more than benchmark error.

Philip Dybvig and Stephen Ross argue further that even a negative alpha is inconclusive,[6] asserting that a manager with superior information can produce a negative alpha if the manager's information set differs from the information set of the evaluator. Therefore a negative alpha produced within the context of a particular information set might actually be a positive alpha within the context of a different information set.

These problems can be ameliorated to a large extent by using normal portfolios to measure performance, an approach discussed in some detail later in this chapter.

AMBIGUITY BETWEEN SKILL AND CHANCE

Perhaps a more serious problem with performance measurement is the ambiguity between skill and chance. This arises because investment returns over a short time period, even if they are risk adjusted, are mostly random. Therefore it is extremely difficult to infer skill or lack of skill from a summary statistic such as total return or risk-adjusted return.

The uncertainty about whether or not a portfolio's performance reflects manager conduct can be addressed using the same methodology described in the section on hypothesis testing in Chapter Two. In this particular situation the null hypothesis is that the value added by the manager does not differ significantly from zero.[7] The alternative hypothesis is that the manager has added significant value. If we divide the estimate of

---

[5]Richard Roll, "Performance Evaluation and Benchmark Errors," *Journal of Portfolio Management*, Summer 1980, pp. 5–12.

[6]P. Dybvig and S. Ross, "Differential Information and Performance Measurement Using a Security Market Line," *The Journal of Finance*, June 1985, pp. 383–99.

[7]Value added can be thought of as that part of the return caused by a manager's investment decisions. In the context of the CAPM it would be alpha. In the context of a normal portfolio it would equal the return differential between the managed portfolio and the normal portfolio.

mean value added by the standard error of the estimate,[8] we can compute a t-statistic to measure the significance of the value added by the manager.

For example, if the value added in a particular year equaled 4 percent and the standard error was 3 percent, the t-statistic would equal $4 \div 3$, or 1.33.[9] Therefore we would accept the null hypothesis that the value added by the manager does not differ significantly from zero.

If the manager's performance persisted for five years on average, we would compute the t-statistic as $4 \div (3 \div \sqrt{5})$. In this case the t-statistic equals 2.98; hence we would reject the null hypothesis and instead assert that value added is significantly different from zero or, more prosaically, that the manager is skillful rather than lucky.

By rearranging terms in the t-statistic computation, we can estimate how long a result must persist on average in order to assert confidently that it was caused by a manager's investment skill. Since:

$$t = \frac{\text{Value added} \times \text{Time}}{\text{Risk} \times \sqrt{\text{Time}}}$$

therefore:

$$\text{Time} = \text{Risk}^2 \times t^2 \times (\text{Value added})^{-2}$$

For example, if we want to be 95 percent confident that the value added by the manager is significantly greater than zero, we would require a t-statistic of 1.65. In the above example, where the manager's mean value added was 4 percent with a standard error of 3 percent, the result would have to persist on average for 1.53 years:

$$\text{Time} = 3^2 \times 1.65^2 \times 4^{-2} = 1.53$$

Table 8–1 shows the number of years required to distinguish a result from chance with 95 percent confidence, given various combinations of value added and the standard error of value added. It should be clear from this table that unless the mean value added is fairly large relative to its standard error, a very long measurement period is required to reject the null hypothesis that it does not differ significantly from zero.

---

[8]Recall from Chapter Two that the standard error is given by the standard deviation (in this case, of value added) divided by the square root of the number of observations used to estimate the sample mean.

[9]As is typical in this type of application involving a one-tailed test, we are assuming that a t-statistic of 1.65 is required for significance.

TABLE 8–1
Years Required for 95 Percent
Confidence that Result Reflects Skill and
Not Chance Return

	Return (percent)				
Risk	.5	.75	1.0	2.0	5.0
2%	44	19	11	3	0
3	98	44	25	6	1
4	174	77	44	11	2
6	392	174	98	25	4
8	697	310	174	44	7

PERFORMANCE ATTRIBUTION

An insignificant t-statistic does not necessarily imply an absence of skill. It simply indicates that skill is not apparent from the summary statistics used to describe the manager's performance.

It may be true for some managers, even given a low t-statistic, that skill exists at a particular type of decision. For example, a manager may be skillful in forecasting the relative performance of industries, yet he incurs risk in his market timing decisions, where he has no skill. Or a manager may possess insight about the behavior of a particular economic factor or security attribute that is associated with differences in return, yet risk incurred from other portfolio exposures may obscure his insights. Performance attribution partitions a portfolio's return and attributes it to the various decisions made by the portfolio manager or to the portfolio's factor exposures incurred either intentionally or unintentionally.

Regression analysis enables us to test whether or not an attribute is correlated with return by regressing differences in the attribute's value across securities with differences in return across securities. This type of regression is referred to as a cross-sectional regression and is displayed below:

$$R_i = \text{Constant} + g_i \times b_{1i} + g_2 \times b_{2i} + \ldots + e_i$$

where

R_i = Return to asset i.

$b_1, b_2, \ldots$ = Observed exposure of security i to attributes 1, 2, $\ldots$

$g_1, g_2, \ldots$ = Marginal returns to attributes 1, 2, ... that are to be estimated using the cross section of security returns.

e_i = Idiosyncratic component of returns.

This cross-sectional regression analysis is repeated for as many periods (usually months) as data is available in order to generate a history of attribute returns.

The t-statistic can be used to determine if differences in return are significantly correlated with differences in attribute value. If we establish 95 percent as our significance threshold, which is typical, then we expect to observe a t-statistic of greater than 1.96 in more than 5 percent of the regressions. If such is the case, then we can assert with 95 percent confidence that differences in the attribute value help to explain differences in return across our sample of securities.

William Sharpe has followed roughly this approach to identify security attributes that correspond with security returns.[10] A different approach for identifying a portfolio's sources of return employs an input-output model of the economy to measure the sensitivity of a company's earnings to shifts in fundamental economic factors.[11]

Although performance attribution provides greater detail about portfolio performance, this refinement may actually lead to even less reliable results than a summary measure of performance. Both factors and a company's sensitivity to factors shift over time, such that attempts to measure them with statistical tools may result in more noise than information.

NORMAL PORTFOLIO

Since the measurement of return and risk is determined in part by the chosen benchmark, it is important to choose a benchmark that isolates the return and risk due to discretionary investment management decisions. For example, a manager should not be evaluated according to the return and risk that is attributable to the manager's style, since almost any style can be mimicked mechanically. The choice of a style is the responsibility of the client who selects the manager.

A normal portfolio is designed to control for management style and to provide a benchmark against which the manager's discretionary investment

---

[10]See William Sharpe, "Factors in New York Stock Exchange Security Returns—1931–1979," *The Journal of Portfolio Management*, Summer 1982.

[11]Tony Estep, Nick Hanson, and Cal Johnson, "Sources of Value and Risk in Common Stocks," *Journal of Portfolio Management*, Summer 1983, pp. 5–13.

decisions can be evaluated. It can be viewed as a default portfolio or those securities a manager would hold in the absence of any information or judgment about their relative attractiveness.

The first step in constructing a normal portfolio is the same initial step required in performance attribution, which is to identify relevant attributes. As shown above, relevant attributes can be identified by regressing differences in return across a sample of securities with differences in various attributes among those securities. To determine if the hypothesized attributes are indeed relevant in explaining differences in return, each attribute's t-statistic should exceed 1.96 in more than 5 percent of the regressions. It is important to observe the t-statistics in a multiple regression context, since the attributes are likely to be partly correlated with each other.[12] In such a case their t-statistic would be overstated if they were derived independently from a series of simple regressions.

The next step in constructing a normal portfolio is to distinguish those attributes that reflect management style from those that reflect discretionary investment decisions. This task can be accomplished by examining the historical attribute exposures of the portfolio under consideration.

If the exposure of a portfolio to a particular attribute is fairly stable over time, the exposure probably reflects a manager's style. If the exposure to a particular attribute is highly variable over time, the changes in exposure probably reflect discretionary investment judgments. Whether a portfolio's attribute exposure is stable or variable can be determined by the ratio of the mean attribute exposure to the standard deviation of exposures.

Again we can perform a significance test. In this application the null hypothesis is that the average exposure to the attribute is zero; hence exposure to the attribute is part of the manager's discretionary investment decision. The alternative hypothesis is that exposure to the attribute differs significantly from zero and therefore reflects the manager's style. If the ratio exceeds 1.96 we reject the null hypothesis and explain the attribute exposure by management style.

The final step in the normal portfolio construction process is to identify the security holdings that comprise the normal portfolio. The names in the normal portfolio should be capitalization weighted so that passive investment in this portfolio would not require frequent rebalancing and the names in aggregate should exhibit approximately the same attributes as those identified with the manager's style.

---

[12]This phenomenon is called multicollinearity.

The process described above normalizes a portfolio so as to isolate a manager's selection decisions. It may also be desirable to normalize a portfolio to isolate a manager's timing decisions. The impact of timing can be measured simply by applying the managed portfolio's ongoing asset mix to representative benchmark (normal) portfolios for each asset class. The return of this hypothetical portfolio can then be compared to an alternative hypothetical portfolio invested in the normal portfolios in accordance with the manager's normal asset mix. This approach controls for that part of return due to investment decisions within each asset class.

NONPARAMETRIC PERFORMANCE MEASUREMENT

The performance measurement procedures described thus far depend on the estimation of parameters such as mean and variance and, in the more elaborate procedures, the validity of a model such as the CAPM or a particular multiple-factor model. The principal advantage of these procedures is that they provide a specific quantitative measure of value added. Nonetheless they have several important disadvantages:

- They usually require extensive data.
- They often depend on complex statistical techniques.
- The parameters are estimated with error.
- They depend on models that cannot be tested adequately.

Hence the resultant measure of value added, although specific, is not always correct.

The application of nonparametric techniques to measure performance circumvents the aforementioned problems because these techniques do not involve parameters nor do they depend on the validity of a particular asset pricing model. Moreover, nonparametric techniques are relatively simple. They do suffer from a serious limitation, however; nonparametric performance measurement does not yield a precise quantification of value added.

To illustrate the advantages and disadvantages of using nonparametric procedures to measure performance, suppose we wish to evaluate a portfolio manager's ability to time the market. A straightforward approach would be to observe when the manager favored equities over short-term securities and when he favored short-term securities over equities. We could then compare these decisions to the subsequent performance of equities and short-term securities and compute the percentage of times he was correct in assessing their relative attractiveness.

If we define P_e as the percentage of times that the manager favors equities when they subsequently outperform short-term securities and P_{st} as the percentage of times that the manager favors short-term securities when they subsequently outperform equities, then $P_e + P_{st}$ provides a measure of a manager's forecasting ability, as demonstrated by Robert Merton.[13]

Moreover, Merton shows that if we limit predictive ability to correct forecasts, then a manager has timing skill if $P_e + P_{st}$ is greater than one, because for his timing skill to be of value to others, his beliefs about the relative attractiveness of equities and short-term securities must not be commonly known or this information would be redundant. For example, if it is commonly known that stocks outperform short-term securities more than half the time, it requires no skill to forecast that stocks will always outperform short-term securities, even though such a forecast would be correct more than half the time. It should also be apparent that $P_e + P_{st}$ will equal two if a market timer has perfect predictive ability.

The important limitation of this approach is that the forecasts are qualitative—they do not include information about the magnitude of the predicted differential in return. Therefore it is possible for a market timer with a score of one (no timing ability) to generate a higher return through his timing decisions than, for example, a market timer with a score of 1.5. This result could occur if the market timer with no skill correctly favored equities when they outperformed short-term securities by a substantial margin while the market timer with significant skill favored equities when they only marginally outperformed short-term securities.

Hence, nonparametric techniques can yield useful insights about a portfolio manager's forecasting ability but not necessarily information sufficient to evaluate his investment skill.

INCENTIVE FEES

Quantitative methods can also be applied to evaluate compensation for managers whose fees are based on performance. Performance-based fees or incentive fees are typically structured with two components: a base component that is a flat percentage of assets under management and an

---

[13]Robert C. Merton, "On Market Timing and Investment Performance: 1. An Equilibrium Theory of Value for Market Forecasts," *Journal of Business* 54, no. 3 (1981), pp. 303–405.

FIGURE 8–5
Performance-Based Fee Arrangement

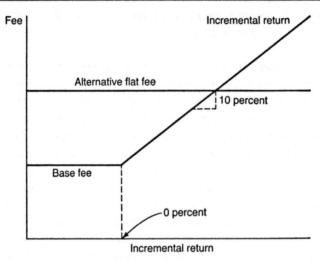

incentive component that is a percentage of the incremental return of the portfolio relative to the benchmark. This fee arrangement is illustrated in Figure 8–5.

If the portfolio returns less than or as much as the benchmark, such that incremental return is less than or equal to 0 percent, the manager collects a base fee that is equal to some constant percentage of assets under management. If the portfolio's return exceeds the return of the benchmark such that incremental return is positive, the manager collects the base fee plus some percentage of incremental return. Under an alternative flat-fee arrangement the fee would equal some constant percentage of assets regardless of the portfolio's incremental return.

The payoff diagram for an incentive fee is the same as the payoff diagram for a call option (see Chapter Six). With an incentive fee the manager in effect has a call option on superior performance. He can collect a fee indexed to his performance if it is favorable, or he can collect a flat fee if performance is unfavorable. Moreover he can arbitrage away his risk by taking opposite positions in his other clients' portfolios or in his own personal portfolio

Performance is defined in this context in terms of incremental return relative to a benchmark. Because performance is defined as a relative value the relevant measure of risk is net risk, or the uncertainty of incremental return. Net risk is affected by the covariance between the benchmark and the managed portfolio as well as by the individual risk of the two portfolios. It is equivalent to the standard deviation of a hypothetical portfolio consisting of a long position in the managed portfolio and a short position in the benchmark portfolio, and it is calculated as follows:

$$s = \sqrt{s_P{}^2 + s_B{}^2 - 2\,r_{PB}s_P s_B}$$

where

s = Net risk.

s_P = Portfolio standard deviation.

s_B = Benchmark standard deviation.

r_{PB} = Correlation coefficient.

Moreover the risk-free return in this context is 0 percent rather than the risk-free rate of interest, since the incremental return of the benchmark is 0 percent by definition.

With these two modifications, we can apply option theory to value an incentive fee. Recall from Chapter Six that the value of a call option equals:

$$\text{Call value} = S \times N(D1) - \{K \times e^{-rt}\} \times N(D2)$$

$$D1 = \frac{\text{natural log } (S/K) + (r + V/2) \times T}{(V \times T)^{.5}}$$

$$D2 = D1 - (V \times T)^{.5}$$

where

C = Call value.

S = Stock price.

K = Exercise price.

r = Risk-free interest rate.

T = Time to expiration.

V = Variance.

$N(.)$ = Normal cumulative density function.

Therefore the value of an incentive fee (a call option on superior performance) equals:[14]

---

[14]William Margrabe, "The Value of an Option to Exchange One Risky Asset for Another." *The Journal of Finance*, March 1978, pp. 177-186, shows that this formula is equivalent to the valuation of an option to exchange one risky asset for another.

$$V = d[P \times N(D1) - B \times N(D2)]$$

$$D1 = \frac{\text{natural log } (P/B) + \frac{1}{2}(s_P^2 + s_B^2 - 2r_{PB}s_Ps_B) \times T}{(s_P^2 + s_B^2 - 2r_{PB}s_Ps_B)^{.5} \times \sqrt{T}}$$

$$D2 = D1 - (s_P^2 + s_B^2 - 2r_{PB}s_Ps_B)^{.5} \times \sqrt{T}$$

where

V = Incentive fee value.
d = Participation in incremental return.
P = Portfolio price.
B = Benchmark price.
s_P = Portfolio standard deviation.
s_B = Benchmark standard deviation.
r_{PB} = Correlation.
T = Measurement period.
$N(.)$ = Normal cumulative density function.

The differences between the formula used to value an incentive fee and the standard Black-Scholes formula are:

- d is added to reflect the degree of participation in incremental return.
- The stock price is replaced by the price of the portfolio.
- The exercise price is replaced by the value of the benchmark portfolio.
- e^{-rt} drops out since r equals zero.
- The standard deviation of the stock return is replaced by the standard deviation of the portfolio's net return relative to the benchmark.

To demonstrate how this formula can be used to value an incentive fee, consider the following situation.

Assets under management: $10 million
Participation in incremental return: 10 percent
Portfolio standard deviation: 15 percent
Benchmark standard deviation: 15 percent
Correlation: 95 percent
Measurement period: 1 year

In this situation the incentive component is worth \$18,900 to the manager, as shown below:

$$D1 = \frac{\text{natural log } (10/10) + 1/2 (.15^2 + .15^2 - 2 \times .95 \times .15 \times .15) \, 1}{(.15^2 + .15^2 - 2 \times .95 \times .15 \times .15)^{1/2} \times 1}$$

$$= .0237$$

$$D2 = .0237 - .0474 = -.0237$$

$$N(D1) = .5094$$

$$N(D2) = .4905$$

$$V = .1(.5094 - .4905) (\$10 \text{ million}) = \$18,900$$

GAMING PERFORMANCE MEASUREMENT

Quantitative tools have certainly enhanced our ability to measure investment performance, but we are a long way from developing a foolproof, purely quantitative approach for identifying superior portfolio managers. Regardless of complexity, quantitative performance measurement techniques are inexact because they depend on noisy data. Moreover, performance measurement techniques can be gamed easily by those who are familiar with the statistical tools that are used or the asset pricing models upon which the techniques are based. In this section, we discuss three common ways managers can adapt their behavior in order to circumvent performance measurement techniques.

Closet Indexing

Perhaps the most common practice for gaming performance measurement is closet indexing. Index funds are portfolios designed to mimic a particular index, such as the S&P 500 Stock Index. They are constructed mechanically and involve no judgment about the investment merits of the component securities. The purpose of an index fund is to provide cost-effective diversification. Index funds are relatively inexpensive because they obviate the need for investment research and minimize transaction costs since securities are traded only to reinvest income or to rebalance the portfolio when there are contributions or disbursements.

Closet indexing refers to the practice of managing a portfolio such that its performance does not depart significantly from the performance of an index, yet charging clients active management fees for what is essentially passive management. The client may not perceive the similarity between the so-called actively managed portfolio and the index because the portfolio may hold many securities that are not in common with the index. Nonetheless, close tracking with the index is guaranteed because the securities in aggregate are highly correlated with the index. Portfolio managers might pursue such a strategy either intentionally or unintentionally because they do not wish to risk the chance of underperforming the index by a significant margin. Of course they also sacrifice the opportunity to outperform the index significantly. Managers who substantially underperform the index are highly vulnerable to termination. If they only marginally underperform the index, the clients may be inclined to tolerate another year or two of mediocre performance before taking action. The clients unfortunately end up paying active management fees and transaction costs for results that could be achieved mechanically at a substantially lower cost. A client with several active managers, all of whom overdiversify to track the index, is almost assured of underperforming an index fund after accounting for transaction costs and fees.

Skewness

Most performance measurement techniques assume implicitly that investment returns are approximately normally distributed. This assumption implies that the mean and variance of the return distribution are sufficient statistics to measure performance. Not all investment strategies, however, produce normal or even symmetric return distributions. By using derivative securities such as options or by using dynamic hedging strategies, it is possible to produce return distributions that are skewed. When only mean and variance are used to compute measures of performance for these strategies, the results can be misleading.

For example, alpha assumes that the returns of a portfolio are linearly related to the returns of the benchmark. A protective put option strategy, however, will produce a kinked relationship between the returns of a portfolio and the benchmark. The portfolio's return will be flat at the exercise price and linearly related to the benchmark returns above the exercise price. Beta will be estimated as the average of these two slopes, which *could* understate the true risk and thus overstate alpha.

This same result can be achieved without using options. A portfolio manager can replicate a protective put strategy by continually adjusting a portfolio's cash position in accordance with the hedge ratio from the option pricing formula. In general the portfolio manager would increase the cash position as the portfolio's price declined and decrease it as the portfolio's price increased. (See Chapter Seven for a more detailed description of this strategy, which is referred to as *dynamic hedging*.)

Strategies such as these produce kinked payoff patterns that result in asymmetric (skewed) return distributions (see Chapter Six). These strategies can be used to game the traditional performance measurement techniques, since these techniques ignore the effect of skewness.

Risk Modification

Incentive fees also can be gamed easily. Consider the incentive fee described earlier, where the manager received a base fee when underperforming the benchmark and a base fee plus an incentive component when outperforming the benchmark. It was shown earlier that this particular incentive structure is tantamount to granting the portfolio manager a call option that could be valued by using a variation of the Black-Scholes option pricing model.

Since the value of the incentive component is determined in part by the net risk of the benchmark and the managed portfolio, portfolio managers can increase the value of their incentive components and the expected value of their fee income merely by increasing the net risk between the benchmark and the managed portfolio. They can increase risk in three ways: they can increase the standard deviation of a managed portfolio if it is above the benchmark's standard deviation, decrease it if it is below, or reduce the managed portfolio's correlation with the benchmark. At the same time, they can hedge away their risk by taking opposite positions in their other clients' portfolios or in their personal portfolios.

The gaming situations described above are intended to illustrate the vulnerability of performance measurement techniques that depend strictly on quantitative tools. Obviously, there are many other ways by which performance measurement can be gamed; and even without gaming, performance measurement is a tenuous science at best.

CONCLUSION

Quantitative tools are a necessary component of performance measurement but by no means sufficient. The better we understand quantitative tools, including their limitations, the more effectively we will be able to apply them. Combined in proper balance with sound judgment, quantitative tools should enhance our ability to distinguish skillful managers from lucky managers.

REFERENCES

Dybvig, P., and S. Ross. "Differential Information and Performance Measurement Using a Security Market Line." *Journal of Finance,* June 1985, pp. 383–99.

Estep, P., N. Hanson, and C. Johnson. "Sources of Value and Risk in Common Stocks." *Journal of Portfolio Management,* Summer 1983, pp. 5-13.

Jensen, M. "The Performance of Mutual Funds in the Period 1945–1964." *Journal of Finance* 23 (May 1968), pp. 389–416.

Kritzman, M. "Can Bond Managers Perform Consistently?" *Journal of Portfolio Management,* Summer 1983, pp. 54–56.

Margrabe, W. "The Value of an Option to Exchange One Risky Asset for Another." *Journal of Finance,* March 1978, pp. 177–86.

Merton, R. C. "On Market Timing and Investment Performance: 1. An Equilibrium Theory of Value for Market Forecasts." *Journal of Business* 54, no. 3 (1981), pp. 363–405.

Roll, R. "Performance Evaluation and Benchmark Errors." *Journal of Portfolio Management,* Summer 1980, pp. 5–12.

Sharpe, W. "Factors in New York Stock Exchange Security returns—1931–1979". *The Journal of Portfolio Management,* Summer 1982.

Sharpe, W. "Mutual Fund Performance." *Journal of Business* 39 (January 1966), pp. 119–38.

Treynor, J. "How to Rate Management of Investment Funds." *Harvard Business Review* 44 (January-February 1965), pp. 63-75.

INDEX

A

ABC, 51–57
Accounting ratios, 65
Accrued interest, 80
Actual return, 83–84; *see also* Expected return
After-tax returns, 84
Alpha, 37
  of bonds, 96
  for performance measurement, 206
  and skewed return distributions, 218
Alternative hypothesis, 36; *see also* Hypothesis tests
American options, 156; *see also* European options
Annualization, 14
  of continuously compounded return, 18
Annuity, 81
  formula for, 11–12
Appraisals
  and expected return calculation, 179
  for property valuation, 114–17, 131
Arbitrage
  with call options, 135–36
  with covered calls, 159
  in money manager compensation, 214
  pricing theory for, 46
  pure, 144
  with synthetic calls, 146
Arbitrage profit, 6
Arithmetic rate of return, 13–14
  use of, 15 n
Asset classes, expected returns within, 180–82
Association, measures of, 28–34
Assumptions
  of Black-Scholes option pricing model, 156–57

Assumptions—*Cont.*
  of dividend discount model, 56–62
  sensitivity of quantitative methods to, 156–57
  simplifying, 8
Atlanta, vacancy rates in, 119–22

B

Barry, Christopher B., 133
Base fee, 214
Bayesian estimation, 63
Benchmark error, 206–7
Benchmarks
  and incentive compensation, 214
  normal portfolios as, 210–12
Beta, 33, 46–47
  of bonds, 96
  drift tendency of, 63–65
  factor coefficients as, 69
  and performance measurement, 205
  and skewed return distributions, 218
Bimodal data, 24
Binomial option pricing model, 158; *see also* Black-Scholes option pricing model
  many-period, 164
  one-period, 158–61
  two-period, 161–64
Black, Fischer, 150
Black-Scholes option pricing model, 149–52; *see also* Binomial option pricing model
  and incentive fee valuation, 216
  with net risk and net return, 192
  put valuation with, 157–58
  riskless rate estimation for, 152–53
  sensitivity to assumptions, 156–57
  success of, 167

Black-Scholes—*Cont.*
two-period binomial model to approximate, 163
variance estimation for, 154–56
Bond equivalent yields, 84
Bonds
actual return on, 83–84
aftertax return of, 84
callable; *see* Callable bonds
convertible; *see* Convertible bonds
correlation matrix for, 95
correlation with stocks, 31
current yields on, 84–85
dedication of, 104
default risk of, 90–91
discount yields on short-term, 84
duration of, 85–88
expected return of, 83
flat yield curves assumed for, 12
historical returns on, 93
horizon premiums and, 103
immunization of, 104–5
inflation and, 103
present value formula for, 81–82
rate of return formula for, 196
regression analysis for returns on, 94, 96
taxable status of, 91–92
terminology of, 79–80
types of, 80–81
yield curves for, 88–90
yield to maturity of, 16, 82–82
zero-coupon; *see* Zero-coupon bonds
Boxplot, 25–27
Brown, Stephen J., 1, 5, 173

C

Calendar spreads, 166
Callable bonds, 92
valuing, 169
Call options, 133; *see also* Options *and* Put options Black-Scholes pricing equation for, 151
covered; *see* Covered calls
hedge ratio for, 159–60
and incentive fees, 214
parity with puts, 146–47, 157–58
profitability of, 137
replicating hedges without, 190–91
synthetic, 145–46
two-period valuation of, 161–64

Call options—*Cont.*
value of, 135, 144–47
variables that determine value of, 148–49
Call premium, 137
Capital asset pricing model (CAPM), 45
discount rate estimation for, 60
portfolio risk in, 205
Capital Cities Communications, 57
Capital gains, 13
and bond yields, 91
Capitalization rate, 111
Capital risk, 104
Cash flows, 5–6
future value of, 8
increasing over time, 9–10
irregular, 18
level over time, 8–9
present value of, 7
Central tendency, measures of, 20–24
Chen, Andrew H., 133
Chicago Board Options Exchange, 150
Closet indexing, 217–18
Coldwell Banker, 119
Constant dollar costs, 39–40
Constant growth model, 53
Construction contract awards, 125
Continuously compounded return, 18–19
Convertible bonds, 92–93
valuing, 169
Convexity, 87
Cooley, P. L., 166
Correlation coefficient, 30–31
individual vs. average, 181
Correlation matrix, 31
for bond returns by category, 95
singular, 179
for vacancy rates, 122
Correlation parameters, 178
within asset classes, 180–81
Corwin, Margaret A., 79
Cost approach to property valuation, 110
Coupon bonds, 80
Coupon rate, 80
vs. duration, 86–87
Covariance, 30
Covered call, 140–42
payoffs for, 159
success of, 165
Cox, John, 144, 157, 158, 163, 164
Cragg, John, 66
Credit risk; *see* Default risk

Cross-sectional regression analysis, 50, 209–10
Current yield, 84–85

D

Data, improving, 63
Datapoint, 153–56
Debt
  long-term, 54–55
  term of, 80
  valuing risky, 168
Dedication of investments, 104
Default premium, 91
Default risk, 83, 90–91
  and historical returns, 93
Defense sensitivity, 75–76
Degrees of freedom, 37
Deposit insurance, 169
Derivative securities, 133; *see also* Options underlied by derivative securities, 170
Discount bonds; *see* Zero-coupon bonds
Discount factors, 82
  and bond duration, 87
  for Treasury securities, 99–100
Discount rate, 7
  in dividend discount model, 52, 60
  forecasting, 52–53
Discount yields, 84
Dispersion, measures of, 24–28
Diversification, 175
  with index funds, 217
Dividend discount model (DDM), 10, 51–57
  assumptions of, 12, 56–62
Dividend payout ratio, 52
Dividends
  forecasting, 52
  and option pricing, 156–57
  and put-call parity, 147
Dollar-weighted rate of return, 17, 197; *see also* Time-weighted rate of return
  multiyear vs. single year, 199
Draftsman plots, 28
Dukes, W. P., 165
Dummy variables, 39
Duplicate investments, 45
Duration, 85–88
  adjusted, 87, 105
  and immunization of portfolio, 104–5

Durbin-Watson statistic, 123
Dybvig, Philip, 207

E

e (mathematical constant), 18 n
Efficient frontier, 182–83
Empirical distribution, 34
  inference from, 35
Employee Retirement Income Security Act (ERISA), 170
Employment forecasts, and vacancy rates, 126
Equities; *see* Stocks
Equity, in real estate, 116
Equivalent time units, 154
Estate taxes, 91–92
Estimation error, 61–62
Estimation risk, 178
European options, 149 n, 156
Excess debt capacity, 55
Exercise price, 134, 148
Expectations hypothesis, 90
Expected return, 173–74
  within asset classes and industries, 180–82
  of a bond, 83
  data quality for calculating, 178–79
  objective for, 187
  vs. standard deviation of portfolio return, 177–78
  transaction price data vs. appraisals for, 179

F

Face amount; *see* Par value
Factor analysis, 45, 48–49
  for stock valuation, 67–70
Factor loadings, 48, 69–70
Factor sensitivity coefficient, 72–76
False probability, 160
Federal Deposit Insurance Corporation, 169
Federal Savings and Loan Insurance Corporation, 169
Fisher, Irving, 103
Fitted values, 38
Flat-fee compensation, 214
Flat price, 80
Flower bonds, 91–92
Fogler, H. Russell, 51

Fong, H. G., 102
Forward rate, 90
Four-factor models, 70, 72
FRC Property Index, 131
Future value, 8
F-value, 38
    for multiple regression analysis, 41 n

G

Galai, Dan, 167
Gambola, M. J., 166
Geometric rate of return, 14–15
GNP sensitivity, 74–76
Gross income multiplier, 111
Growth rates, 12
    estimating for dividend discount
      model, 60–61
    and price/earnings ratio, 67

H

Hedge ratio, 159–60
Hedging strategies, 137
    dynamic, 188–92
    with put options, 138–40
    riskless, 159
Heteroscedasticity, 42 n, 50 n
Highest and best use, 110
Histograms, 22–23
    vs. boxplots, 26
Historical data, 49
Hoag, James W., 114
Holding periods, 8
Horizon premiums, 103
Hudson-Wilson, Susan, 109
Hurdle rate of return, 113
Hypothesis tests, 34–38
    for normal portfolio, 211

I

Ibbotson, Roger G., 79
Idiosyncratic component of returns; see
    Nonsystematic component of returns
Immunization, of bond portfolios, 104–5
Implied variance, 156
Incentive fees, 213–14
    example calculation of, 216–17
    gaming, 219
    valuation of, 215–16
Income approach to property valuation,
    110–11

Index funds, 217
Inflation, and bond returns, 103
Information coefficient, 62
Input/output analysis, 49
Installments, payment in, 7
Interest rates
    and bond duration, 87
    and bond returns, 93, 94
    and bond value, 82
    elasticity of, 105
    forecasting, 53
    and horizon premiums, 103
    long- vs. short-term, 104–5
    term structure of, 88–89, 96; see also
      Yield curve
Internal rate of return, 15–16
    dividend discount model to calculate,
      54
    and dollar-weighted rate of return, 17
    for full funding, 187
    for property valuation, 113
    yield to maturity as, 82–83
Interquartile range, 24–25
Investment horizon, 185–86

J–K

Jarrow, R., 163
Jensen, Michael, 206
Kritzman, Mark P., 173, 195

L

Level of significance; see *t*-statistic
Leverage, 115–16
    and risk, 67, 118
Liquidity preference hypothesis, 90
Logarithmic transformation, 42–43

M

Macauley, Frederick, 87
Macauley's Duration, 87
Malkill, Burton, 66
Margrabe, W., 192
Market analysis, real estate; see Vacancy
    rate
Market data approach to property valua-
    tion, 110
Market factor(s), 46
    multiple, 181
Market model, 46

Mathematics of valuation; *see* Valuation, mathematics of
Maturity date, 80
and correlation of bond returns, 94
and option value, 148–49
Mean; *see* Sample mean
Mean absolute deviation (MAD), 27–28
Median, 21–22
and interquartile range, 25
Merton, Robert, 213
Modal range, 23
Mode, 22–23
problems with, 24
Money managers
Bell System, 203–4
boxplots for, 27
compensation of, 213–17
evaluation of; *see* Performance evaluation
future value for, 8
hypothesis testing for, 37–38
skill of, 207–8
style of, 201, 210–11
time-weighted vs. dollar-weighted rates of return for, 16–18
Moody's, 91
Moral hazards, 170
Mortgages, 115
Multicollinearity, 211 n
Multifactor models for uncertainty measurement, 47–50
Multiple regression analysis, 38–43
and multifactor uncertainty model, 48
for normal portfolio, 211
for stock valuation, 66–67
Municipal bonds, 91

N

Naked options strategies, 136
Net operating income (NOI), 110, 111
Net present value, 6–7
Nonparametric performance measurement, 212–13
Nonsystematic component of return, 46
Normal portfolio, 210–12
Null hypothesis, 36
standard error under, 37

O

Office Network, 119
Oil sensitivity, 75–76

One-sided (or -tailed) tests, 36 n
Optimal portfolio, 182–83
investment horizon of, 185–86
risk-return trade-offs for, 184
standard deviations for, 184–85
Options, 134–35; *see also* Call options *and* Put options
on assets besides stock, 168
and convertible bonds, 93
data for pricing of, 164
on derivative securities, 170
early exercise of, 156–57
margins for, 142–44
optimal exercise date for, 157
and performance measurement, 218–19
pricing; *see* Binomial option pricing model *and* Black-Scholes option pricing model
skewed probability distributions of, 142, 164–65
strategies with, 136–37
value of, 144–47
variables that determine value of, 148–49, 152
Original-issue discount bonds; *see* Zero-coupon bonds
Outliers, 21
and correlation coefficient, 31
facts surrounding, 24
and standard deviation and variance, 28

P

Parkinson, M., 158
Par value, 79
Pension Benefit Guarantee Corporation, 170
Pension fund
ratio of assets to liabilities for, 191–92
return objective for, 187
Percentage error, 42
Percentiles, for universe comparisons, 200
Perfect access, 145
Perfect negative correlation, 174
Perfect positive correlation, 174
Performance measurement, 195–96
benchmarks for, 206–7
consistency in, 200, 201–2
dollar-weighted rate of return for, 197
fees based on, 213–17

Performance measurement—*Cont.*
  gaming, 217–19
  and manager style, 201
  nonparametric, 212–13
  and option pricing theory, 170
  rate of return for, 196–97
  risk-adjusted returns for, 205–6
  and skewed return distributions,
    218–19
  skill vs. chance for, 207–8
  time-weighted rate of return for,
    198–99
  and timing decisions, 212
  and types of decisions, 209–10
  universe comparisons for, 200–204
  value added for, 207–8
Perpetuity formula, 8–10
Personal computers, 1
Phoenix, 127–28
Portfolio
  efficient, 182
  of estimates, 62
  estimating variance for, 178–82
  factor analysis of, 74–75
  normal, 210–12
  objectives for, 76
  optimal; *see* Optimal portfolio
  real estate, analysis of, 131–32
  risk of, 45, 205
  riskless component as insurance for,
    188–89
  risk specific to, 49 n
  standard deviation of returns on,
    175–76
Portfolio insurance, 188–89
  asset to liabilities ratio and, 191–92
  replicating call option hedges without
    options, 190–91
Portfolio weights, 174
Preference curve, 182–83
Preferred habitat theory, 90
Present value, 6
  commonality of, 3
  forecasts for, 52
  of growing perpetuity, 10
  of two-installment plan, 7
Present value formula, 7–8
  for bonds, 81–82
  and dividend discount model, 51–52
  and dollar-weighted rate of return, 197
  in property valuation, 110–11
  short-cut versions of, 8

Price-earnings (P/E) ratio model, 10,
    53–54
  to avoid yield bias, 59
  and capitalization rate, 111
  growth in, 67
Price, forecasting, 52
Principal components analysis, 69
Probability, 56
  of meeting a target, 185–86
  for put options, 139–40
Probability mass, 140
Property valuation
  appraisals for, 114–15, 116–17, 131
  approaches to, 110–11
  vs. equity valuation, 116
  example of, 112–15
  expenses for, 114
  leverage and, 115–16
  market conditions in, 118–29
  regression analysis of resale value for,
    114–15
  vs. sale prices, 118
  subjectivity of, 112
  vacancy rates integrated with, 129–31
Protective put, 138–40
  deposit insurance as, 169
  and performance measurement, 218
  replicating without options, 188, 190
"Pseudo-American" call value, 157
Public utility stocks, 46
Put-call parity, 146–47, 157
  and portfolio insurance, 191
"Put in place" concept, 125
Put options, 134
  Black-Scholes valuation of, 157–58
  maturity dates of, 149 n
  profitability of, 138
  protective; *see* Protective put
  value of, 136, 144–47

Q–R

Quantitative methods
  interest in, 1
  commonality among, 3
  complexity of, 2
Range, 24–25
Rate of return, 12–13
  annualized, 198
  arithmetic, 13–14
  continuously compounded, 18–19
  on discount instruments, 196–97

Rate of return—*Cont.*
  expected vs. actual, 72 n; *see also* Expected return
  factor analysis for, 71; *see also* Factor analysis
  formula for, 13
  geometric, 14–15
  and holding period, 15
  internal, 15–16; *see also* Internal rate of return
  by investment class, 16
  for performance measurement, 196–97
  on real estate investments, 113, 116–18
  risk-adjusted, 205–6
  riskless; *see* Riskless rate of return
  sources of, 210
  time-weighted vs. dollar-weighted, 16–18, 197–99; *see also* Dollar-weighted rate of return *and* Time-weighted rate of return
Rating agencies, for bonds, 91
Real estate
  expected return calculation in, 179
  portfolio analysis for, 131–32
  rate of return on, 116–18, 196
  valuation of; *see* Property valuation
Real Estate Market Index (REMI), 125–29
  for Phoenix, 127–28
Regression analysis, 32–33; *see also* Multiple regression analysis
  analyst's role in, 127–28
  for beta estimates, 46–47
  for bond returns, 94, 96
  and bond yield curves, 99
  of consistency of money managers, 202
  in constant dollar costs, 40–41
  cross-sectional; *see* Cross-sectional regression analysis
  deceptiveness of, 38–39
  and factor uncertainty models, 48
  for property valuation, 114–15
  signs in, 66
  for stock valuation, 62–65
  with time-oriented data, 123–24
  of vacancy rates, 122–23
  weighted least squares, 50 n
Regression line, 32
Reinvestment, 18
Reinvestment risk, 104
Required future value, 114

Residual errors, 33, 63–65
  in multiple regression analysis, 41–42
Reversion, 112
Risks; *see also* Uncertainty
  adjusting to increase incentive fees, 219
  beta for; *see* Beta
  diversification of in portfolio, 45
  factor analysis for adjusting, 71
  and financial leverage, 67
  market vs. company, 205–6
  net, 215
  quantitative methods for measuring, 2
  of real estate investments, 116–18
  systematic vs. security-specific, 49
Riskless rate of return, 45–46, 49, 149
  estimating for option pricing, 153
Risk penalty, 184
Risk premiums, 49
Roenfeldt, R. L., 166
Roll, Richard, 206
Ross, Stephen, 46, 207
Rubinstein, Mark, 144, 157, 158, 163, 164
Rudd, A., 163

S

Sample mean, 20–21
  in hypothesis tests, 36
  sensitivity of, 24
  and variance and standard deviation, 27
San Francisco, vacancy rates in, 119–24
Scatter plot, 28–30
Scenario analysis, 49
Scholes, Myron, 150
Screens, in factor analysis, 75–76
Second generation duration, 87
Security market line (SML), 60–61
Sharpe, William, 46, 184, 205, 210
Significance tests; *see* Hypothesis tests
Signs, 66
Simple average; *see* Sample mean
Single-factor models for uncertainty measurement, 46–47
Skewed probability distribution, 26, 142, 164–65
  and performance measurement, 218–19
Software
  for regression analysis, 32–33
  spreadsheet, 1, 2

Specialization of analysts, 3
Spline smoothing, 99, 102
Spot rate, 90
Spreading strategies, 137
  historical returns from, 166
Standard deviation, 28
  and correlation coefficient, 30
  minimum frontier for, 177
  of optimal portfolio, 184–85
  of portfolio returns, 175–76
  and residual standard error, 33
  and standard error, 36
Standard error, 33, 36
Standard & Poor 500 Index, 72–73
  as performance benchmark, 206
Statistics, 2
  descriptive, 20
Stein estimators, 63–65
Stocks
  beta for, 47
  and convertible bonds, 92
  correlation with bonds, 31
  dividend discount model for valuation
    of; *see* Dividend discount model
    (DDM)
  factor analysis for, 67–70
  multifactor uncertainty models for, 49
  multiple regression analysis for valua-
    tion of, 66–67
  as options on firm's assets, 167
  rate of return formula for, 196
  regression analysis for valuation of,
    62–65
  relationship of small and common, 34
Strike price; *see* Exercise price
Structural reserve, 112
Student-*t* distribution, 37 n
Synthetic call, 145–46
Systematic factors, 71–72

T

Takeovers
  and stock valuation, 56–57
  and time horizon of investments, 59
Taxes, 13 n
  and bonds, 84, 91–92
Theoretical distribution, 34–35
Three-stage model, 60
  dividend growth in, 61
Time-weighted rate of return, 17–18,
  198; *see also* Dollar-weighted rate of
  return

Time-weighted rate of return—*Cont.*
  as present value of dollar-weighted
    rates of return, 199
Timing, 212
  nonparametric, 212–13
Total return measure, 13
Transaction costs, of spreading strategies,
  166
Treasury bills
  discount factors for, 100
  estimating on return for option pricing,
    153
  futures contracts based on, 133
  rate of return on, 196–97
  yield curve for, 101
Treasury securities
  tax status of, 91
  yield curves for, 89, 98, 101
Trennepohl, G. L., 165
Treynor, Jack, 205
Trimmed standard deviations, 28
Truncated distribution, 140
t-statistic (or -value), 37, 62–63
  and value added by money manager,
    208
Two-factor model, for stock valuation,
  68–69
Two-sided (or -tailed) tests, 36 n
Two-state option pricing model; *see* Binomial option pricing model

U

Unbiased estimates, 35
Uncertainty, 43–45; *see also* Risk
  Multifactor models for, 47–50
  probabilities for, 56
  single factor models for, 46–47
Underlying securities, 133
Universe comparisons, 200–204
Unpredictable events, 57
Unsystematic factors, 71
Utility function; *see* Preference curve

V

Vacancy rates, 119–21
  in Atlanta, 121
  correlation matrix for, 122
  data for, 125–26
  integration into property valuation,
    129–31

Vacancy rates—*Cont.*
  modeling, 124–25
  for Phoenix, 127–28
  regression analysis of, 122–23
  for San Francisco, 122–24
Valuation
  mathematics of, 1
  as comparing alternative cash flows,
    5–6
Value added, 207 n
  and nonparametric performance mea-
    surement, 212
Variance, 27–28
  estimation of, 154–56, 178–82
  minimum frontier, 177
  net, 192
  and option value, 149
  of portfolio vs. component securities,
    175
  solving Black-Scholes model for, 156
Vasicek, Oldrich, 102

Vertical spread, 166
Volatility; *see* Variance

W–Z

Warrants, 168
Weights, for option pricing, 150
Whiskers, 25–26
Yield bias, 57–59
Yield curve, 8 n, 88–90
  flat, 8 n, 16
  and internal rate of return, 16
  of Treasury securities, 89, 98, 101
  upward-sloping, 89–90
Yield to maturity, 16
  of bonds, 81, 82–83
  vs. current yield, 84–85
  interpretation of, 88
Yield spread, 88
  and default risk, 91
Zero-coupon bonds, 80–81
  secondary market for, 102